Alexandre Ben

The influence of Alexandre Benois on Russian art this century, and on the Western world's perception of it, has been immense. He founded, with Sergei Diaghilev and Leon Bakst, the epoch-making journal *Mir Iskoustva, The World of Art* and, in 1901, became one of the first artists of distinction to work for the stage, creating the décor for two ballets, *Sylvia* and *Cupid's Revenge*, at the Mariinsky Theatre in St Petersburg.

Benois was born in 1870 to a distinguished St Petersburg family. His father, Nicholas, was an architect and his mother, Camilla, the daughter of Albert Cavos, architect to the Imperial Court. The young Alexandre grew up in a happy, cosmopolitan home frequented by all the notable writers, artists and musicians of the day, and within sight of the Bolshoi Theatre, which his grandfather had built.

At an early age Benois was captivated by his first taste of theatre: the colourful and rumbustious Harlequinades at the Easter Fairs, echoed eventually in *Petrouchka*. In 1884 he saw two works, *Coppelia* and *Giselle*, which would have a profound effect on his own ideas about music, drama and choreography.

In the summer of 1890 Benois met Sergei Diaghilev. Six years later he moved to Paris, one of a talented group of Russian artists, writers and musicians, with Diaghilev at its centre.

Apart from his contributions to *The World of Art*, Benois worked as a journalist and art historian. He also helped Diaghilev to mount exhibitions of Russian art but, even more importantly, he was an essential collaborator in the founding of Diaghilev's Ballets Russes, creating the décor, costumes and libretto for *Le Pavillon d'Armide* (1907), costumes and décor for *Les Sylphides* (1909), for *Giselle* (1900) and *Petrouchka* (1911) for which he also co-wrote the libretto with Stravinsky. In 1914 he created *Le Rossignol* and *Le Coq d'Or*, all works which were seen in London under the patronage of Thomas Beecham.

The unprecedented success of Diaghilev's Paris and London seasons for Russian opera and ballet brought the exhilarating vitality and stimulus of Russian art to wildly enthusiastic audiences. As Benois himself put it: 'We really did stagger the world.'

Despite many years spent away from Russia, Benois' life in St Petersburg was the source of much of his inspiration, and the city plays a major role in this book. Benois' second volume of autobiography will also be published in The Lively Arts series.

The Lively Arts
General Editor: Robert Ottaway

A Mingled Chime · Sir Thomas Beecham
Memoirs · Alexandre Benois
Dance to the Piper · Agnes de Mille
The Movies, Mr Griffith and Me · Lillian Gish
Chaliapin · Maxim Gorky
A Life in the Theatre · Tyrone Guthrie
My Grandfather, His Wives and Loves · Diana Holman-Hunt
Groucho and Me · Groucho Marx
Beerbohm Tree · Hesketh Pearson
Renoir, My Father · Jean Renoir
Liszt · Sir Sacheverell Sitwell
Fun in a Chinese Laundry · Josef von Sternberg

Forthcoming titles include

Ego · James Agate
On Human Finery · Quentin Bell
Unfinished Business · John Houseman
The Baton and the Jackboot · Berta Geissmar
Theatre Street · Tamara Karsavina
Mr Jelly Roll · Alan Lomax

MEMOIRS

*

ALEXANDRE BENOIS

Translated by
Moura Budberg

FOREWORD BY
PETER USTINOV

COLUMBUS BOOKS
LONDON

This trade paperback edition
published in Great Britain in 1988 by
Columbus Books Limited
19-23 Ludgate Hill
London, EC4M 7PD

First published by Chatto & Windus Ltd in 1960

British Library Cataloguing in Publication Data
Benois, Alexandre
Memoirs, Alexandre Benois.—(The Lively
arts.
1. Ballet. Benois, Alexandre. Biographics
I. Title II. Series
792.8'092'2

ISBN 0–86287–397–5

Printed and bound by The Guernsey Press
Guernsey, CI

CONTENTS

TRANSLATOR'S NOTE

I would like to express my gratitude for the help given me throughout by Miss Peggie Matheson, and for the advice of Nadia Benois and Julius Edwardes.

FOREWORD

In the summer of 1957 I visited my Great-uncle Alexandre in Paris. He was asleep when I arrived, and I had time to wander round his studio, which I had remembered with something of the extraordinary clarity he displays in recollecting the days of his extreme youth. The studio had not changed, except that it was infested with cats of widely divergent natures and remarkably similar appearances. The huge window still gave on to a Paris which was almost too good to be true, the mass of slate-grey roofs nesting under the chairmanship of the Eiffel Tower. It all looked like a backcloth Uncle Shoura might himself have painted for Charpentier's *Louise*, although the presence of the Eiffel Tower at such proximity was a concession towards the powers of tourism which he would never have made. Had he been Japanese, he would doubtless have been the one painter never to have rendered Fujiyama.

The ordered chaos of this room was precisely as I had remembered it as a child. A couple of Guardi drawings had been sold, but had been replaced on the wall by copies of such bewildering dexterity that I preferred them to the originals. The copies were, needless to say, by my great-uncle. On the massive easel there was an unfinished stage design, eloquent of the unabated activity of a man who could never think of retirement as a voluntary decision. Piled on the refectory table which runs the entire length of the room were magazines, portfolios, papers of all sorts, ranging from works of erudition in Russian, printed at the beginning of the century, to the latest copies of esoteric French publications concerned with surrealism and other later tendencies.

A rumble from upstairs, a sudden electrification of all the cats and a groan from the floorboards indicated that a post-prandial reveille had sounded and my venerable Uncle Shoura was awake. Step by step he came down the spiral staircase, and I took up my position at the bottom to welcome him. Since I had last seen him I had grown a beard, a fact which I had for some time taken for granted, but when he saw me he sat heavily on a step, and seemed for a moment in a state of shock. 'Mon Dieu,' he muttered, 'mon frère Louis.'

The 'frère Louis' in question was his brother Ludovic, or Leontij, my grandfather, the brother who was nicknamed 'Gros-Gros' because of an inclination towards corpulence. I am no nymph, in fact at birth there was some discussion as to which way up I was, so I can well imagine that heredity had played a fairly unsubtle part in the sudden flash of recollection which caused that alarming moment on the stairs. But heredity is an abiding mystery, with many more uncanny facets than mere corporeal reproduction.

This book is to me utterly extraordinary, since Uncle Shoura writes with a pen which is never cruel but which is nevertheless unsparing, and he reveals his own character as sharply and as honestly as he reveals the characters of those around him. Rarely can prejudices have developed in anyone so young, and even more rarely can memory have been more faithful right back to the very roots of life. It is significant that a book purporting to be a man's memoirs stops when he reaches the age of twenty, and it is all the more valuable for that very reason. After that came maturity, work, negotiations with people as well known as Diaghileff, Bakst, Stravinsky, Nijinsky, Karsavina, all of which is part of the cultural history of our times, and therefore open to controversy and conjecture. There is, however, nothing controversial about this volume. It is the painstaking, tender, humorous, whimsical re-creation of an entire period, seen through the eyes of a child, and even recollected in old age, this vision has miraculously retained its freshness.

From what I know of the Benois family, the importance of childhood was never underestimated, and they invariably posses-sed that Latin capacity for developing the nascent maturity in a child without ever forgetting that they were dealing with a little person still subject to the coltish caprices of immaturity. Uncle Shoura never talked down to me, and listened to my views with respect from an early age, although I myself would today have very much less patience with myself as I was then. Once, in Estonia, I clearly remember pretending to be a motor-car for days on end. It was just after my fourth birthday and I made myself into my favourite make of car. I was an Amilcar, a particularly noisy type of French *voiturette*, which entailed ferocious gear-changes and squealing tyres on every imagined corner. My mother, who had a toothache, understandably lost her temper after the first four or five hundred miles (as far as I was concerned, I was still running the engine in), and shouted at me to stop. Her father, Leontij, was visiting us, however, having been given permission by the Soviet government to travel as far as Estonia, and he held up his hand, imploring a more prudent attitude in his daughter, and saying, 'Be careful . . . his imagination is developing,' in a reverent and cautionary voice.

This attitude of what Uncle Shoura likes to call 'piety' towards those inexplicable capacities we are born with is typical of the entire clan. There were flies everywhere that summer. They drowned in my milk, they settled on my porridge, they threatened to enter my mouth every time I opened it. Estonia was fairly primitive in 1925, and we fought flies with swats, mugs, knives, forks and napkins. Unfortunately what began as a protective measure eventually appealed to some privitive hunting instinct in me, and it developed into a blood sport of undiluted savagery. My grandfather was appalled. 'Sometimes,' he said to me, 'it is necessary to kill a fly in order to protect the food, but why chase flies which have not yet begun to molest you?' To this day I argue with myself about the relative culpability of a fly before I launch my attack, and often the inner debate has given the offender time to escape.

This incident seems to me typical of the atmosphere which pervades the book, the acceptance of natural phenomena as something necessarily mysterious, a feeling of religious gratitude for the privilege of living, an unwillingness to entertain thoughts of a political or sociological nature, believing that existence is all the more wonderful for its transitoriness, and that intolerance, whether it be expressed by some court favourite, by a Soviet magistrate or by a small boy big-game hunting for houseflies is a vile, reprehensible surrender to the powers of darkness.

In an age where art is no longer perpetrated for its own sake, since it would seem self-indulgent and escapist, there may seem to be an element of *laissez faire* in this pure, detached attitude, with its regret at the passing of palaces and uncritical approach towards those who once enjoyed them, but at the same time the devotion to the past has nothing servile about it; it is expressed with the ardour of a lover and with the courage of a pioneer.

Certainly the parades of pre-Sarajevo armies were at least picturesque, and a colonel, however inane, could be relied upon to put up a braver show on the back of a prancing stallion than in the graceless mud of a trench. Today soldiers are dressed for death at the start of hostilities, already the colour of the earth which will soon cover them. Has existence improved because it is now depicted on a vast mural rather than on yesterday's miniatures?

My Great-uncle Shoura will sigh at this point and threaten to fall asleep in self-defence. These are not his problems. He was not born to criticize or to condemn. As the dignified dog who will bark when his own house is broken into, so will he only vent his wit and mordancy on those who invade his zone of interest and nonsense. As to the rest, hard times are to be survived, with honour, with resilience. From earliest youth, he shepherded his natural instincts with extraordinary intuition into the channels of opinion, and he is today very much what he was at the age of seven – a creature remarkable for his spontaneity, unmarked by any affectations of speech or thought, a man who has distilled his vast experience of life into an utterly simple serenity.

He was lucky to be born the youngest of his family. In his penetrating description of his brothers and sisters, the dangers inherent in a family with a reputation for being artistic are made abundantly clear. His oldest brother Albert was trained as an architect, but became a water-colourist and never really faced up to his many talents, dissipating them by facility. My own grandfather likewise never really entertained a doubt in his successful career as an architect, and consequently his work suffered from a certain glibness. Alexandre must have profited greatly by his natural reaction against these tendencies in his elder brothers, since it is natural in a boy of spirit to rebel, and in order to rebel with intelligence instead of mere perversity, it is, of course, helpful to have something to rebel against. The safety of an artistic home is a precarious benison for the individual, especially if the family is an essentially happy one. Standards of criticism are liable to be too formal, and surely the attitude to life will be too sheltered.

I recognize all of my grandfather's temptations in myself, and they have been my enemies throughout my short creative life, but they were brought to my attention long before I read this book, simply because I was the next best thing to a youngest child, and that is an only child. Thought thrives in isolation almost as well as it does in opposition, although it is only now that I have a family of my own that I begin to understand the breadth, power and enigma of a communal existence. My own children have somehow made me understand Uncle Shoura even better, and I always felt I understood him well.

My daughter was a little shy when I took her to see him. He said, rather sadly, 'There's one thing that's depressing about old age . . . it frightens children.' After a moment, however, a contagious smile had done its work, and she cried when it was time to leave.

As generations go, he was closer to his own grandfather than to this little girl, since he was her great-great-uncle, and yet here they were, in the same room, with Shoura reminding me that his grandfather had been born in the reign of Louis XV!

There is nothing I can validly add to this book, except that I feel infinitely grateful to have been born into a family of such diversity of blood and talent, a gratitude I think it only fair to express to my father. When I first appeared on the living stage, Alexandre wrote me a letter which I will always cherish.

'For centuries,' it went, 'our family has been sniffing around the theatre. We have built them, decorated them, written scores for them, conducted in them, directed in them. Now, at last, one of us has had the courage to leap on to the stage himself.'

As Gros-Gros' grandson, my leap was not of the nimblest, but I trust the courage was not misplaced. At all events, I have an unfair advantage with such a dear example before me, a man who not only led an exemplary private life, but inspired all those, like my mother, who had minds of their own and nowhere congenial to express them without inviting the hostility of more reactionary temperaments.

At the age of eighty-nine his enthusiasm and his analytical senses are unimpaired, but what is even more wonderful is his ability to be taken by surprise. No artery of opinion has ever hardened. He is as capable of being enchanted by the most modern of artistic utterances as he ever was by a Verdi aria or a baroque ornament. He has derived some benefit from all the ages of man, respecting them all as he passed through them; he opened his ears, eyes and mind to life very soon after birth, and has paid homage to it ever since with the application of a man in love. In case I make it sound as if he is perfect, he is eloquent about his own faults and very amusing as well. A most human being. I mustn't interrupt him any further.

Peter Ustinov

CHAPTER I

MY TOWN

*

I MUST start my story by confessing that I have somehow failed to become a real patriot. I have never known that passionate devotion to an indefinable and incalculable something, nor have I felt that the interests of that infinite something were my own interests and that my heart should beat in unison with it. I suppose I must have been born with this abnormality. Maybe the reason is that several fatherlands, often at war with each other, have contributed to my heredity: France and the Germanic lands and Italy. The final amalgamation of these elements took place in Russia and yet I have not one drop of Russian blood in me. I was, however, the only one in our family to be such a freak, for my brothers were all ardent Russian patriots with varying degrees of French-ness or Italian-ness in their nature. The fact remains that Russia as it is, Russia in its entirety, I have known only imperfectly and many of her characteristics were unpalatable to me, even at the time when I was only vaguely aware of them.

Petersburg itself I loved. Almost from birth I felt what is called '*le patriotisme du clocher*'. I sensed the beauty of my town, I liked everything in it and later I realised its importance too. For Petersburg I had the feeling that the Romans must have felt for their *urbs*, the real Frenchman for Paris, the Englishman for London, the true Russian for Moscow, a feeling which I do not believe exists among Germans. The Germans are patriots of their country as a whole: *Deutschland über Alles*. I was moved – and still am – by one compelling emotion: *Petersburg über alles*.

I know very well that this is not a feeling which should be at all encouraged or on which one should pride oneself. None the less this feeling of mine has an absolute justification. Of all the errors of the 'old régime' in Russia I consider the most unforgivable to be its betrayal of Petersburg. Nicholas II believed that he was expressing his affinity with the people when he revealed his dislike of Petersburg, but in doing so he also turned against Peter the Great himself, who had been the real creator of his own autocratic majesty. Nicholas's dislike was given open and symbolic expression when he changed the name which the perspicacious leader of Russia had given to his masterpiece. I am inclined to believe that all our miseries came as a punishment for this betrayal, the disregarding of Peter's 'testament' by his inadequate descendants who, with a strange lack of understanding, imagined that there was something humiliating and objectionable in the name given by Peter to the Russian capital. 'Petrograd' stood for something unacceptable to Peter, who saw in his capital something more than a mere monumental allusion to his person. Petrograd, not to mention its flavour of 'slavism', so alien to Peter, indicated something narrow and enclosed, whereas Petersburg, or more correctly Sanct Petersburg, stood for a cosmopolitan city, a city placed under the special protection of the saint who once before had proclaimed the ideal of universal spiritual sovereignty: it meant the 'second' or the 'third' Rome. The very incongruity of the abbreviated Latin *sanctus* combined with the Germanic words *Peter* and *Burg* seemed to stress and symbolise the cosmopolitan nature of Petersburg. I already loved St. Petersburg before I had any idea that one could love streets, stone buildings, canals, a certain air, a certain climate and all the infinite facets of a complex whole, varying according to the season, the hour, the weather. I went on discovering Petersburg for many years, through my own experiences and moods.

How I loved the Petersburg spring with its abrupt change to warmth and its sudden increase of light. What joy, and what gnawing despair too, are to be felt in the Petersburg spring! But then, on the heels of a comparatively short summer, came the theatrically decorative autumn by which I was equally exhilarated: and after it, to quote the poet, 'giving no time to look around, winter unrolled before your eyes'. The frost set in and the snow fell in large flakes, and at the same time something grim, frightening, sinister, lethal, advanced upon you. But it was reassuring to remember that all these horrors would be overcome and people prove more cunning than the elements.

It was especially in these dead months of winter that the people of Petersburg indulged in gaiety and laughter. The season was then at its peak – the theatres open, the ballrooms crowded, the main feasts celebrated; Christmas, Twelfth Night, Carnival week. Winter was stern and awe-inspiring in Petersburg, but it was in Petersburg too that it was transformed into something pleasing and magnificent.

On mild June evenings that coincided with the more ecstatic moments of my personal life, I began to understand my love for the familiar city, for its face, for its personality. Petersburg was beautiful and poetical at different times of the year, but spring seemed to suit it best. In early spring, when the crust of icy snow was scraped from the streets and squares; when streams, appearing from heaven knows where, rushed between the paving stones, glittering in the sun; when blue shadows gave the cubes of houses and the roundness of pillars a special sharpness; when the 'new' air poured into the damp rooms through wide-open windows, freed of their double frames; when the ice on the Neva swelled, turned grey, heaved, cracked and began to swim out to sea – the Petersburg spring was already without peer in this elemental expression of its rebirth. There was now no doubt at all that one season had given place to another, and with the new order came a truly blessed time. Petersburg, which had looked stern for many a month, became soft, tender, captivating. A flimsy foliage covered the trees in the gardens, the pungent-smelling lilac bushes and the sweet and spicy hawthorn burst into blossom, the reflections of the graceful lines of the palaces played in the freely flowing waters. Before the later move to summer dwellings, the people of Petersburg began their pilgrimage to the Islands in quest of nature; the elegant crowd would stroll along the granite pavement of the quay from the Admiralty to the Summer Garden. The Summer Garden filled up not only with nannies and children, old men and women out for their prescribed constitutional, but also with loving couples.

Of many memories of the Petersburg spring the one that lingers most in my mind is that of gliding in silent white nights along our broad and lovely river, either on a small, fussily puffing steam-boat, or in a noiseless rowing-boat scarcely disturbing the slippery surface of the water. Those white nights – how much has been written and said about them! An abomination to some, an inspiration to others! Nowhere did they exercise such a fascination over the mind, nowhere, I would say, did they have such poetical meaning as in Petersburg, on the waters of the Neva. I think that Peter himself, having laid the foundation of his Petersburg in the month of May, must have been struck by the magic of just such a white night, unknown elsewhere in Russia.

I would be returning either from the Islands or from the Zoological Gardens, where it was the custom to watch performances in the two theatres which stood in the middle of the caged animals. Memories of evenings spent in the Zoo are not the most poetical in my past. The crowd was provincial and homely, too much beer was imbibed, and the unfortunate, sickly beasts in their narrow, smelly cages created a very dreary impression. But from the moment I left the gates of the Zoo and got into the brightly coloured ferry-boat these trivial impressions vanished, and when after a few strokes of the oars the boat emerged into the wide space between the pillared buildings of the Stock Exchange, the granite walls of the Fortress and the luxurious palaces, I plunged into a fairyland which has no equal.

Suddenly, in the solemn quiet, in the transparent, slumbering twilight between the darkening sky and the strangely luminous water, plangent crystal sounds could be heard from above, softly descending upon the water. It was the chime of bells from the needle of the Fortress, announcing midnight in two prayer-like songs. The bells played the old Russian hymn 'Kol Slaven' and, directly after, 'God save the Tsar'. The music lasted almost the whole of the journey, for the tempo was slow, but it was hard to distinguish one note from another. The two familiar melodies turned into something new, as the bells were not perfectly attuned and the echo made the sounds catch one another and intermingle to produce a clangour so sad that it brought tears to the eyes. It was said that prisoners in the fortress were driven frantic, insane, by these hourly resonances, by the slow dripping of sounds in the silence of the night.

Alas, the spring and summer weeks rushed past quickly and the white nights came to an end. The change from light to darkness (to be followed by cold and frost) was signalled when the lamp-posts on the Petersburg streets flared up again about the 20th of July. You then realised that summer was really over. Only yesterday I had wandered about a grey, colourless town at an hour close to midnight; today the lamplighter appeared with his ladder and one after the other the tongue-shaped flames of gas exploded in the lanterns. Fairyland vanished, everyday life returned. Yesterday even my own dwelling seemed phantom-like; I entered it a little nervously and would not have been surprised if some apparition had materialised from the dark corners of the front staircase: now the dim gaslight revealed nothing that I did not know already. This gave me a feeling of anticlimax, of boredom.

Even now every picture of Petersburg goes straight to my heart. I tremble in a junk-shop or book-shop when I find the most trite photograph or print, even if it is only of a corner of Petersburg which I did not much care for, as for instance, the Church of the Assumption with its unsuccessful attempt at ancient Russian architecture, its gilt pyramidal cupolas, smooth walls, coloured in the dullest brown. But it hurts me to learn that that church has now been pulled down, for I had been so used to seeing it on my way to school and back again. How many times did I and my fiancée walk round it on our endless evening strolls. My friends, Diaghilev, Filosofov, Nouvel, lived a stone's throw from it and later on my family and I lived for seven years in the same district, on the Admiralty Canal.

Later, when I write of my passion for Tchaikovsky at the beginning of the 1890s and especially for 'La Dame de Pique', I will return to my memories of Petersburg: to the Summer Garden, an early storm, the Winter Canal, to everything that, enhanced by music, brought an even greater pang to the heart. The music of 'La Dame de Pique', with its magical evocation of shadows, I seem already to have sensed in my early childhood, and when the opera was produced I welcomed it as something long awaited. There was in Petersburg a feeling of real dedication to music, which might even be due to the presence of water (Petersburg can compete with Venice and Amsterdam in the number of rivers and canals). Perhaps a sensitivity to music depends on the dampness of the air.

Every one of the marvels of our district gripped my imagination, above all the Church of St Nicholas, sparkling with golden cupolas. It was one of the most splendid and impressive of Petersburg churches. In my early childhood my feelings about it were a mixture of admiration, reverence and fear. I could not get rid of the idea that the group of five domes was a family of legendary giants, their heads crowned with helmets, and that the eldest of them, the one in the middle, was God Himself, with a stern and sorrowful expression on His face. When I felt guilty about something it was this God who seemed to gaze at me with reproach or even wrath. The lower part of the church was infinitely more welcoming. The multi-angular plan of its walls, the curly cornices, the cherubs wallowing in downy clouds over the windows and doors, the intricate golden balconies, the stucco nimbus around the central oval window – all expressed something radiant and invited you not so much to fast and repent, as to glorify God and enjoy His blessings. I never tired of observing all these details and it is probable that my ecstatic admiration of the baroque in general was born from my 'intimate' acquaintance with this wonderful work of the eighteenth century. My father also had a great respect for this masterpiece. Though a devout Catholic, he showed great piety towards the Greek Orthodox creed and therefore I was able to treat this church as my own – all the more so as Father bore the same name as its Patron Saint and his name day came on the Feast of St Nicholas, December 6th.

However, besides things pious, we had also worldly temptations, and two of the most alluring were in our neighbourhood. They were the two largest theatres of the Russian Empire: the Bolshoi and the Mariinsky. And both of them were closely connected with our family. The Bolshoi, originally built by Thomon, was burnt down in 1836 and was rebuilt by the 'Papa of my Mamma', while the second was entirely built by the same grandfather in collaboration with my father.[1] Inside the Mariinsky, by the

---

[1] This theatre was, in fact, built twice by my grandfather, Albert Cavos. In 1840 it was built as an Imperial Circus and, when this burnt down in 1850, the Mariinsky was built on the site.

way, there is a proof of this close relationship. From one of the painted medallions inserted in the arches of the foyer stands out the profile of a gentleman with a large nose and side-whiskers and a very high collar – that was my great-grandfather, the once-famous composer, Catarino Cavos.

Architecturally I preferred the Bolshoi to the Mariinsky, with its magnificent portico, the great Ionic pillars under which carriages drove up, so that people could descend right at the door of the theatre. The rest of the monumental building seemed to me to contain fabulous treasures. Its mysterious character was emphasized by a row of round windows, lining the roof, and even by the fat, ugly, in-congruous iron ventilation chimney with a hood on top, which rose asymmetrically on the side of the building. The Mariinsky theatre had a more modest, less spectacular appearance, but before it was mutilated by additional buildings, it too was a graceful and noble whole. Its system of flat arches and pilasters and the semicircle projecting above them, corresponding to the circle of the auditorium, had, I thought, a somewhat 'Roman' look.

Two other buildings, characteristic of Petersburg, were also near us – the Lithuanian market and the Lithuanian castle, both situated directly behind the Mariinsky. Though serving the most prosaic needs, they were not without architectural beauty. The market, built at the end of the eighteenth century, was vast, with four similar façades jutting out into four streets. The façades were composed of massive archways and niches, with a row of semicircular windows above them. The castle – a prison – was rebuilt in the Empire style from the seven-towered 'Turkish' castle dating back to the days of Catherine the Great. Gloomy in spite of its white paint, this building was one of the best in the classical style that Petersburg could boast, but on me, as a child, it produced a terrifying as well as a fascinating impression. For behind these walls, behind the black windows with their iron bars, I could picture the most formidable bandits, murderers and thieves, and I knew that the Black Marias that I saw slowly driving past our windows, with manacled criminals in them, used to emerge from these gates. The wretches were taken to Semionov Square to hear the death sentence pronounced. I hasten to add that I saw no more than three of these vehicles, and those at the age of four or five. This custom was abolished in later days.

There were other street scenes which I could watch from the windows of our flat. I could observe them at close quarters, for we lived on the first floor. The emotion which I felt when I saw a funeral pass before our windows (which happened almost every day and sometimes several times a day, as it was on the way to the main suburban cemeteries) was quite different from the horror which the Black Marias inspired in me. All funerals had a curious effect on me. Some were eerie, especially when Old Believers carried their dead on their shoulders in an open coffin; others, with their stern ceremony, were uplifting. The more socially important the dead, the more solemn the ceremonial. In those days a man of average distinction, a nobleman, or simply a man of some wealth, could be sure of being accompanied to the grave with great pomp. The Orthodox made their way to their last abode on a dray under a canopy of golden brocade with ostrich feathers on the corners and a golden crown in the middle. A brocade cloth almost completely covered the coffin. The drays of Lutherans and Catholics also had canopies, but they were black and of a more 'European' pattern. Both were drawn by slow-stepping horses, caparisoned in flowing black draperies, boldly embroidered with coats of arms. This custom was gradually losing its traditional character. The heraldic emblems were hired out by the undertaker and did not correspond to the family crest of the deceased. You could choose the most striking and effective ones. Even the rich merchant, though he had no pretence to nobility, would be drawn by horses wearing a coat of arms.

On very important occasions the funeral processions took on the proportions of a feast of lamentation. There were many people of high rank in the capital, generals, admirals, privy councillors, and 'the sovereign's gifts' were bestowed on all of them in the form of decorations, golden weapons and other tokens of distinction. These used to be carried on velvet cushions ornamented with gold braid. My elder brothers were inclined to treat such rituals with scorn, but I was awed by the procession of decorations. One of the grown-ups would now and then identify the medals for us: this is St George, this is Anne, or Vladimir, and here is St Andrew himself.

Flowers, on the other hand, were not in fashion at the time and only two or three small beribboned wreaths lay on the lid of the coffin beside the helmet or three-cornered hat of the dead man. The melancholy solemnity of the procession was emphasized by the fact that the cortège of those carrying the decorations, the clergy and the chariot itself, was hemmed in on both sides by gentlemen in top hats with crêpe waving in the wind, dressed in black from head to foot and carrying burning lanterns in broad daylight. At rich funerals these torch-bearers were finely dressed and marched in order, strictly keeping the distances between them; but if the deceased was not so fortunate (only one pair of horses and a dray without palanquin), then the torch-bearers were dirty tramps, with bits of shabby crêpe on bedraggled hats, who walked at random and staggered about, for they had had time to have a drop too much before the procession.

Officers were accompanied by a detachment of their regiment and in the case of a man of high military rank, several detachments followed the coffin, including mounted men and clattering artillery. How miserable I felt at the sound of the funeral marches played by military bands with their instruments wrapped in black crêpe. I could hear from afar the dull roll of the drums, the squeaking of the flutes and the blast of the trumpets and would rush into the nursery where I hid my head under the pillows to shut out the sounds. But curiosity would overcome me and I would crawl back to the window and stay spellbound in a sort of tragic ecstasy, watching the procession swim past the windows, followed by an endless number of carriages which sometimes stretched out to half a kilometre.

In contrast to the triumphs of death were the triumphs of the military, as the army passed under our windows. The way from the barracks to the centre of the town lay down our street, and we used to see the soldiers every day, either in large or small detachments, and the guard for the Winter Palace from one of the regiments was sure to come our way. Also, the greater part of the Petersburg garrison walked down our street in the spring on its way to the camp. Then I could let my eye rove on many a choice and splendid uniform.

For the May Parade the Gatchina cuirassiers came to Petersburg, and also the Cossacks, and they all rode past our windows on fine horses to the music of their bands. In May I was allowed to go out on the balcony and then I would really feel as though I was taking part in this wonderful ceremony. It seemed as though I had only to stretch out my hand to touch the embroidered regimental flag or stroke the dazzling helmets and armour, whose shiny surfaces reflected the houses and the sky.

There is no doubt about it, the appearance of the soldiers in those days was much more impressive than it was later. This was the reign of the Emperor Alexander II, the son of the famous drill-master Nicholas I, and though some of the equipment was simplified in his time, the uniforms were still resplendent – particularly in the smart Guards regiments.

Some of the infantry regiments had kept the helmets with the drooping, thick white plumes, others had képis, like the French, also with feathers. The red fronts of the uniforms, together with the dark green cloth of the rest of the coat and its gold buttons, and white trousers (in the summer), made a gay combination. The effect was striking of the white and red and gold parade uniform of the Hussars, the golden and silver armour of the Cuirassiers, Chevalier Guards and Horse Guards, the tall fur hats of the Horse Grenadiers, crimson tongues dangling on their backs, the shiny hats of the Uhlans, jauntily stuck on one side.

The bands roused my greatest enthusiasm – those that marched on foot as well as the mounted ones - playing their famous regimental marches (such stimulating marches). The mounted bands made a splendid spectacle: a wealth of gold and silver, kettle-drums embroidered in gold fixed to both sides of the saddle. How majestic was the gigantic drum-major who walked in front of the band! What did that man, all covered in gold braid, not manage to do with his stick ornamented with braid and tassels! He threw it up and caught it in the air and twisted it in all directions.

The apotheosis of military splendour, which I witnessed two or three times during my childhood, was the May Parade of which I spoke a moment ago. This took place on the vast Tsaritsin meadow, surrounded by gardens, palaces and the barracks of the Pavlov regiment, so like a palace too. With the other children I watched the spectacle from the pillared arcades of the barracks. Though the place was called a meadow, there was no grass, but a large square, covered with sand. The beginning of May is rarely warm in Petersburg and so at the age of four or five I was bitterly cold in spite of my velvet coat, cloth hat and woollen scarf. Thousands of my favourite toy soldiers marched past in regular rows in all directions, all in step, but without any apparent effort, with amazing speed, deaf to all but the command of their officers. The clatter of the artillery gave me a feeling of joy tinged with anxiety, but the peak of the spectacle was the trick riding of the Caucasian soldiers, the Tcherkess, the Lesghins. Some of them were still dressed in silver armour, just like medieval knights, and wore silver helmets on their heads. The trick riders dashed past, some standing on their saddles, shooting backwards and forwards; and when they approached the Imperial tent, they slipped under the bellies of their horses and with incredible nimbleness caught the kerchiefs thrown to them by the Empress or the Grand Duchesses.

The march-past of the Pavlov regiment, of which we were the guests, was watched with a specially passionate interest. These tall young men wore high brass helmets backed with red, and their uniforms sparkled with gold. But their most remarkable feature was that they were all snub-nosed – a detail demanded by a tradition going back to the times of the Imperial founder of the regiment, Paul I, who, it is well known, had an almost monstrously snub nose. In ordinary life snub-nosed people just seemed comic to me, but in such multiplicity they were remarkably interesting. When I came back home, I went to the mirror, lifted my nose into the air with my finger and was delighted that it made me look like a soldier of the Pavlov regiment.

The memory of these 'games on the field of Mars' makes it easy to understand the mania for military exercises and uniforms which consumed almost all the Emperors of the past, but which especially imputed to the Prussian sovereigns, Friedrich Wilhelm I and Friedrich II, as well as to our Tsars, Peter III, Paul, Alexander I and Nicholas I. But though it might have seemed ridiculous and caused a lot of misery and torment, how much less cruel and monstrous were the pleasures of the sovereigns of that time compared with the devilish perfection of military power reached by mankind now, even in the most democratic countries.

29

CHAPTER II

FAMILY ANCESTORS

*

WHEN it became a real capital in the eighteenth century, Sanct Petersburg was not viewed with favour by the rest of the Russian Empire. This was at first understandable. It was difficult for the Russian people, for whom Moscow had always been the heart of Russia, to realise that a new town, which they considered a futile and extravagant whim of the Tsar, should acquire an equally great, if not greater, importance in their lives. This feeling of distrust was bound to take deepest root in Moscow, bitterly resentful that an upstart favourite, without rank or tradition, should displace the first metropolis, ancient and holy, rich in historical memories – more especially as Petersburg had a poor climate and was situated in an anaemic landscape. This contempt, even loathing, lasted for a long time. Nothing could stamp out these feelings, neither the grandiose beauty of the new town, nor the glamour of its life (a glamour derived chiefly from the Court), nor the blossoming of culture: the greatest artists, writers, painters, musicians, lived in Petersburg and found inspiration there. The 'real' Russian could find nothing to his taste in Petersburg and continued to regard it as a usurper.

But in spite of the mission conferred upon it by its founder and the direction he gave for its development, and even under the guidance of foreign teachers, Petersburg remained true to its Russian origins. As the window on to Europe, it lit up the abode of the whole Russian people, though of course many varied foreign elements flocked to it owing to the very nature of its mission. It is significant, for example, that of the large number of Christian Churches in Petersburg, many did not belong to the Orthodox creed, and services were conducted in German, Polish, Finnish, English, Dutch and French. The congregations of these churches were exclusively of foreign origin, though to a great extent they were assimilated into Russian life and adopted the Russian language in their common intercourse.

Moscow had known something similar: its famous 'German quarter'. Here foreigners had settled in great numbers at the invitation of Moscow, which had become ossified in its obsolete customs and needed an infusion of progressive elements. However, in Moscow the foreigners lived apart in a separate district, cut off from the rest of the town, a district to which Russians had no entry and where foreigners were able to exist without direct contact with the Moscow population. It was something like the concessions that exist in the East or like the ghettoes of the Middle Ages. There was no such separate district in Petersburg. On the contrary, Peter the Great's rule and that of his descendants, encouraged in every way the fusion of its citizens with the elements from outside who were introducing the desired (and much needed) foreign culture. If foreigners in Petersburg showed any inclination to settle in groups according to their origin, this was done quite freely and entirely from personal motives. For the most part foreigners, to some extent russified, lived dispersed about Petersburg and one could speak of a 'German suburb' in Petersburg only in a metaphorical sense. Such a district existed only as an idea without topographical substance.

Our family belonged to this theoretical German suburb. In spite of having lived for a century in Petersburg, and having become deeply imbued with Russian influences, the Benois family was not wholly Russian, largely due to the fact that we did not belong to the Orthodox Church, and most of the marriages in our family were contracted with immigrants from other countries like ourselves. Pure Russian elements only began to infiltrate into our family towards the end of the nineteenth century; the children of these marriages were baptised in the Orthodox faith and gradually lost the more striking features of their original nationality, only their foreign-sounding names giving rise to the suspicion that French, German or Italian blood might flow in their veins.

The Benois family is of French origin and comes from the small village of St Ouen en Brie in the neighbourhood of Fontainebleau. We cannot boast that we are of noble descent. The most ancient ancestor known to us, Nicholas Denis Benois, is entered in the genealogical table drawn up by my father as a tiller of the soil, in other words, a peasant. He was married to Marie Leroux, obviously also a peasant, but their son, Nicholas (1729–1813), had already risen in the social scale. He had had sufficient education to enable him to start a school in which his own children were educated. My acquaintance with him I feel to be almost personal. The pastel portrait of him, copied by my aunt Jeanette Robert from an original that remained in France, shows a very respectable and charming old man, blind in one eye. The greenish coat buttoned up high at the neck proclaims him a contemporary of the old men that figure in pictures by Greuze. His hand lies on a book with golden edges.

What Nicholas Benois taught, and where and how, I do not know, but he must have been a pedagogue by vocation, for otherwise it is difficult to explain why he broke away from the occupation of his fathers and chose a different way of life. The face in the portrait is kind, gentle and a little sad; his moral lineaments can be drawn from the poem composed by his son (my grandfather) which hung in a frame under the portrait in my father's study, all the walls of which were covered with family souvenirs.

I quote this poem-acrostic, for not only is it characteristic

A, NICOLAS.

Bénois, né le 17. Juillet, l'an = 1729.

Né de parents obscurs, mais honnête a sincere;
Il fut toujours bon Époux et bon Pere:
Content de son état, tranble dans ses Desirs,
On ne le vit Jamais d'une ardeur imprudent
Livrer aux projets vains son âme indépendante:
A rister Vertueux, il bornoit ces plaisirs:
Se rendre utile à tous fils son unique envie;

Bienfaisant sans orqueil, doux, charitable, humain.
Et défendant toujours la Veuve a l'Orphelin:
Ni l'or, ni les besoins ne trontheent sa vie;
On si riche en tout tems lorsque bon fait du bien.
Il agit dans ses bienfaite placer son opulence'
Son bonheur a sensite en sont la recompence.

Par son respectueux Fils.

Louis Benois

of its era, but it still constitutes a kind of summary of ideal qualities for our whole family.

I am sure that the virtues extolled in this poem are no exaggeration, but the simple truth. The same description would have suited, for instance, my father, born in the year my grandfather died, and altogether the Benois family is noted for its inclination to domestic virtues, for a tendency to withdraw modestly into the shadow, and for a dignified contentment in its position.

The numerous Russian Benois came from the youngest son of my great-grandfather. My grandfather, Louis Jules (1772–1822), was born ninety-eight years before my birth, in the days when Louis XV still reigned in France. Louis was educated in France, but when still quite a young man filled with distaste for revolutionary fanaticism, he left his country and in 1794 reached Russia, where one of his brothers had found a temporary refuge.[1] On his way there, grandfather, like all emigrants, had learned various arts and crafts, but apparently his true vocation was the culinary art, for several years after his arrival at the capital we find him at the Court of Paul I, functioning as the Tsar's *maître d'hôtel*. After the death of the Tsar he continued in that position during the lifetime of the Dowager Empress Maria Fedorovna. Grandfather married in Petersburg (in the year of his arrival there) a Fräulein Groppe; she came from one of the many German families who, in spite of the modesty of their social status, formed the cornerstone of the typical Petersburg culture. As a wedding present Louis Jules offered his bride a portrait of himself by the magic brush of Ritt and received in return a magnificent tortoiseshell and gold snuff-box with her portrait, in which she is painted as a pretty young girl in full bloom. Alas, after Grandmother

---

[1] The descendants of my grandfather's brother live in Paris now, but they all belong to the female line and do not bear the name of Benois. The last French Benois died about thirty years ago and was an architect.

had given her husband seventeen children (of whom eleven survived), her beauty and charm vanished without trace, when she was only forty. In the portrait by the Academician Courteil, painted about 1820, we see a heavy matron with sharp features; and twenty years later the daguerrotype and a portrait painting by the Academician Horavsky show us the widow of the *maître d'hôtel*, Ekaterina Andreevna Benois, as an old woman with a sorrowful, bloated face.

To make a pair with his portrait of Grandmother, Courteil also painted a portrait of my grandfather a few years before his death. Here Grandfather looks a stern and rather pompous gentleman. The sheet of paper he holds in his right hand may be meant to suggest his poetical tendencies. In our archives we had a thick notebook containing his attempt at an autobiography: a tale of rather spicy adventures during the French period of his existence, whereas in Petersburg, under the influence of his wife, he settled down and led an exemplary family life. Probably Grandmother's beneficial influence also helped Louis Benois to become a substantial man, the owner of two stone houses. In one, which looked like a country house, he lived with his family, and the other he let.

Grandfather died from the terrible epidemic that mowed down thousands of the inhabitants of Petersburg in 1822 – and as the result of his own imprudence. Having heard that all entrances to the Smolensk cemetery were obstructed by coffins, he could not restrain his curiosity to see this remarkable spectacle and made his way there on horseback together with the husband of his eldest daughter, Auguste Robert. On arriving at the cemetery, they determined to find out whether it was true that the corpses of the victims of this dread disease really went black directly after death (that is why it was called the black death). Whether they saw it or not I do not know, but a day or two later both developed symptoms of the disease and after a few more days they both lay side by side in the ground, not in the Smolensk but in the Volkov cemetery.

Grandfather's entire family appears in a picture painted by a friend of the family whose name, if I am not mistaken, was Olivier. This amateurish piece of work, which it was our custom to joke about and to criticise for its very obvious flaws, was inherited by me. But in later years (when primitive art became a cult and severe academic rules were gradually forgotten), it was precisely this amateur quality that roused the enthusiasm of my friends. Some of them paid no attention to anything else on the walls, except this portrait *à la* Douanier Rousseau. Indeed, it cannot be denied that the picture, like so many spontaneous, childlike works, does have a lot of character.

My father – five-year-old Kolenka Benois – is there among the others. He sits cheerfully smiling behind his brothers and sisters, on the chest of drawers, wearing a Cossack hat and holding in his hand a flag with the double-headed eagle. Apparently he was as much of a militarist as I was myself at that age, but later on neither he nor I showed any signs of belligerence. Also there, to the right of the picture, is one of my father's brothers, Michael, who was preparing to devote himself to a military career and was educated in the Cadet Corps. Having reached the rank of colonel, he ended his life as an instructor in the Corps des Pages. A typical soldier of the era of Nicholas I, Uncle Michael is painted in an aquarelle by Horovsky, sitting astride a chair with a long pipe in his hand.

Suddenly widowed, my grandmother found herself in somewhat difficult financial circumstances and had to alter her whole way of life. The younger children were still at the nursery stage. Luckily, thanks to the Empress Maria Fedorovna's personal graciousness, Grandmother was granted a considerable pension and some of the children were educated by the Crown. My father, the Empress's godson, was the most privileged of all. As he had already shown artistic tendencies in his childhood, he was taken away from the German Petropavlovsk School and placed as a full boarder in the Imperial Academy of Arts, a move that determined his whole future.

To complete the picture of Grandfather and Grandmother, I must add that, according to an agreement which they concluded at their marriage, all the male descendants were baptised Catholics and all the female Lutherans (which was the faith of my grandmother). This religious distinction made no difference whatsoever to the affectionate relations between brothers and sisters; on the contrary, the differences in religion contributed to the unusually broad-minded views, the tolerance and respect for other faiths, which distinguished my father and all the other members of the Benois family.

My maternal ancestors are perhaps more romantic than those on my father's side. They belonged, if not to the Venetian nobility, at least to the wealthy bourgeoisie of Venice. In the seventeenth century a Cavos, who was, if I am not mistaken, a canon of one of the Venetian churches, made a generous donation to the San Marco Library; my great-great-grandfather, Giovanni Cavos, was director of the Venice theatre; his son, Cattarino, was a distinguished musician who wrote at the age of twelve a cantata in honour of the visit of the Emperor Leopold II to Venice and at fourteen composed the ballet *Sylphide* for the theatre in Padua. The concerts he gave in the Scuola di San Marco (which is near the Church of San Giovanni di Paolo) and in the San Marco Cathedral, where he became an organist as the result of a competition, attracted crowds of Venetian music-lovers. After the fall of the Republic, Catarino, like many of his compatriots, preferred to seek happiness in foreign lands, and after a short stay in Germany he went to Petersburg. Here his talents were duly appreciated and he soon started to work for the Imperial theatres. My great-grandfather, who was Director of Music in Petersburg, composed many operas, ballets and symphonic works, some of which can still be found in the archives of the Imperial theatres. Cavos is distinguished in the history of Russian music as the direct predecessor of Glinka. His noble and disinterested nature is proved by the story of how, having seen the score of his younger colleague on the same subject as his own *Ivan Sussanin*, my great-grandfather admitted the superiority of Glinka's *Life for the Tsar* and of his own accord removed his opera from the programme and so cleared the way for his formidable young rival. Unfortunately I can judge his music only by his soft and melodious songs and the solemn stanzas he composed to celebrate the entry of the Allied Armies into Paris in 1814. According to an established tradition they were played at the end of the annual Veterans' Concert given by all the military bands in the Mariinsky Theatre.

Ossokin's aquarelle of Catarino Cavos, which used to hang in my father's room under the poem of Louis Jules Benois, portrays him in middle age. He is an elegantly dressed gentleman, his hair is brushed straight back over the high forehead, his bewhiskered cheeks are propped up by the stiff shirt collar, a broad black stock is tied in a large knot. A long double chain of gold spreads across the waistcoat of the green civil uniform with its gold buttons, a pin with a ruby adorns the jabot of the shirt. The Order of St Vladimir is hung round his neck. The prominent hooked nose (which he passed on to many of his descendants) gives character to his face and his whole demeanour is marked by dignity. At the same time one cannot help feeling that this appearance of unbending sternness is, after all, assumed and that, behind this façade, he is a typical Venetian: conscientious in fulfilling his duties, full of zeal and good will, but rather feckless in his own interests.

Family legend and documents prove him to have been, besides, a man of independent opinion, an enemy of obsequiousness, slander and gossip. Catarino Cavos died at the age of 65, on April 28th, 1840.

His two sons remained to work in their new fatherland, Russia. The younger, Giovanni, had chosen music as his profession and at one time was his father's assistant at the Opera. The elder, Alberto, my maternal grandfather, had graduated in mathematics from Padua University and later occupied one of the most prominent positions as an architect in Russia. Alberto Cavos (1801–64) became widely known as a builder of theatres and his monumental book on the subject was considered a classic. Death carried him away at the very moment when his plan for the Paris Opera, approved by Napoleon III and the Minister Fould, stood a very good chance of being accepted. I doubt whether my grandfather's Opera House would have been as glamorous as Charles Garnier's famous building, but one can at least assume that it would have better conformed to standards of comfort and acoustics and that the stage spectacle would not have been so overshadowed by the surrounding splendour. This supposition is prompted by a comparison of the Mariinsky Theatre with the Grand Opera House in Paris.

I doubt whether in the whole world there exists a more welcoming theatrical building than the vast airy auditorium of the Mariinsky Theatre. It was so constructed that from every seat, whether the back chair in a box or the side seat in the gallery, the stage should be clearly visible. The decoration is also in its way perfection. True, the decorations, in the rococo style of Louis-Philippe, are not in fashion now, but nevertheless the style is extremely graceful and unobtrusive; the combination of blue hangings in the boxes, and the stalls and barriers upholstered in gold on a white background, create a harmony of remarkable gaiety and at the same time cosiness. It is noteworthy that even in the worst periods of Petersburg life, during the years 1919, 1920, 1921, and in spite of the distinctly proletarian appearance of the audience, the Mariinsky Theatre retained its aristocratic atmosphere and even lent a touch of elegance to the Bolshevik comrades.

Quite different was the Bolshoi Theatre, demolished at the beginning of the 1890s, and its close counterpart, the present Bolshoi Theatre in Moscow – both the work of my grandfather. The aim of these theatres was to amaze with splendour and luxury and this aim became excessive, particularly in the Moscow Opera, probably because the rebuilding of the entire theatre was rushed through by a special date – the Coronation celebrations in 1856. In both theatres the decorations were red and gold, the gold covering most of the architectural part. Both auditoriums were considered to be models of elegance and the acoustics satisfied the most exacting requirements.

Grandfather Cavos was overwhelmed with huge orders which permitted him to achieve a certain wealth and he was thus able to live luxuriously and to satisfy his passion for collecting. His house in Venice (on the Grand Canal) was a real museum. He pulled down a blank wall that protected a small garden which led on to the canal, and built a passage with marble pillars which exists to this day. What was there not in that Venetian house! Beautiful pictures, antique furniture, mirrors, china, bronze, crystal. All these treasures were hung and arranged harmoniously so that the house should never appear to be an antiquary's storeroom. Later on many of the things were taken to Petersburg and after Grandfather's death divided between his widow and his other heirs. The elder son, Alberto Cesare, got the major part, but many of the pictures and other *objets d'art* from his collection adorned our flat in 1880.

I did not have the happiness of knowing this grandfather

either. He died six years before I arrived in this world, but I felt nearer to him in a way than to Grandfather Benois. I was attracted to him by his passion for collecting, which I inherited from him. While still very young, I felt real gratitude to him for the possession of so many beautiful things which we owed to this passion (about which my mother spoke with far less enthusiasm). Through these family souvenirs the magic of Venice was always familiar and close to me. When I spent hours gazing at a long, narrow, coloured panorama of Venice that hung in Father's study (with the inevitable moon), when I dreamt of gliding one day, myself, past these palaces, when I examined two little pictures representing views of Grandfather's house – it seemed to me that I knew it all personally and that my grandfather's impressions of life, his joys and artistic curiosity, were living again in me.

Grandfather Cavos's widow continued to play a prominent part in our family circle even after his death. Everybody adored her, not only the Cavos progeny, but also the Benois. She was not a grandmother in the direct line, since she was my grandfather's second wife, but that made no difference.[1]

Xenia Ivanovna Cavos was a striking figure. In her youth she had been a real beauty and the love affair between her and my grandfather was exactly in the style of romances by Eugene Sue or Murger. As he was passing along one of the streets of the Vassili Island in Petersburg, Albert Cavos saw through a ground-floor window a fascinating fair-haired girl bent over her needlework. Without further ado, Grandfather entered the shop and ordered a dozen shirts, paying a large sum in advance. He came to fetch them in a week's time and on this occasion addressed a few words to the blonde beauty. He followed up this manoeuvre by

[1] We had but a vague notion about our real maternal grandmother. This poor 'forgotten' grandmother died as early as 1830. She also was a Venetian and her maiden name was Carobio. My grandfather married her in 1820 and my mother was only three when she died.

getting an introduction to her mother and, a month later, asked her for Xenia Ivanovna's hand in marriage.

After the wedding, the couple left for Italy, which, during a perfect honeymoon, in the company of a brilliant and handsome young man, became for this simple Russian girl almost a Paradise on earth. Madame Cavos remained faithful all her life to this passion for Italy and everything Italian, of which no criticism was ever allowed in her presence. Everything about Italy was indisputably beautiful; but most wonderful of all was Venice, the birthplace of her husband, where she suddenly found herself the owner of a charming house furnished with valuable antique furniture and hung with old masters.

Unfortunately the Venetian idyll could not go on for ever. Grandfather was expected back in Petersburg to undertake some architectural work (among other things, the building of the Imperial circus), and after a few months' absence the happy pair returned to Petersburg and were installed in an apartment granted to my grandfather in one of the wings of the Corps des Pages.

But this romantic start did not bring Xenia lasting happiness. Albert, whose fickleness was proverbial, soon tired of his lovely wife, transferred his attentions to other women and then fell under the spell of a clever adventuress. Her husband's unfaithfulness threw a shadow over Xenia's life, and after he died her financial situation was difficult, for Grandfather had left both his Petersburg houses to his new passion, besides, no doubt, a considerable sum of money. But in a few years, Grandmamma succeeded, with the help of her sons, in putting her affairs in order. She forgot the humiliations and sorrows and remembered her husband with true piety. In her apartment, smaller than the former one but still elegant, his portraits hung together with hers; in the sitting-room, on a special stand, stood a Sèvres vase sent by the Emperor Napoleon III with a personal letter to Grandfather, and a whole wall of her bedroom was occupied by pictures of the interior of the Cavos house in Venice. In the dining-room, sitting-room and even in the passage hung aquarelles and sepias by Zichy, Sadovnikov, Charlemagne, pictures of the façades and interiors of the theatres built by Grandfather as well as the fantastic illumination which celebrated the opening of the Bolshoi in Moscow at the time of the coronation of Alexander II.

I must often have visited Grandmother Cavos as a child and I have never forgotten a day in early autumn in 1884, when Grandmother gave a banquet in honour of my brother Misha, who had just married his cousin Olga Cavos. The dinner consisted of Venetian national dishes and, as the *pièce de résistance*, directly after the minestrone, a *timbale de maccheroni* was served, specially made by the famous Pivato in Great Morskaia Street. It was not all this delicious food, however, nor the glasses of champagne, that filled my heart with a singular ecstasy, but the purely visual delight that I experienced. The candles in their crystal chandeliers were resplendently reflected in mirrors set in intricate golden frames painted by Domenico Tiepolo; graceful porcelain figures crowded the *étagères* and the shelves; the table service, the crystal of the glasses and carafes, even the embroidery on the tablecloths and napkins, were unlike anything I had seen in other houses. Grandmother must have pulled out of the depths of her trunks all that was most striking and valuable, and perhaps she had borrowed a few things, too, from her Italian friends. The servants, however, bore no likeness to their Venetian counterparts. Grandmother had a typical Russian butler with long side-whiskers, who was really a servant in the house of one of our relatives but who was always 'hired' out to those who relied on his vast knowledge of table etiquette; and Lydia, a Russian cook, who had learnt to

43

prepare the most exquisite Italian dishes and appeared, according to tradition, in order to receive compliments from the guests for every new masterpiece created by her hands.

Grandmother had dressed with particular care for this occasion, but no trace of her past beauty was left in this sixty-five-year-old, slightly spread-out woman, although she had any amount of regal dignity and affectionate gaiety. On her shoulders, over the dark violet taffeta dress, she wore the famous white mantle bordered with ermine. The fur was a little worn and the velvet had begun to show signs of long service, but it was still a very elegant and romantic garment that spoke of past glory and splendour. A fan lay beside her on the table according to an old custom; when Grandmother used it from time to time, you got the illusion of seeing a picture of the past, not of Grandmother's past, but a much more distant past, of the Venice of Goldoni and Gozzi. It was just about this time that I had begun to take a serious and not merely a boyish delight in the charm of olden times and that no doubt was why I was struck by this occasion and remembered it so well.

In the last years of her life Grandmother underwent a great change. A disease affected her legs, she lost the lovely elasticity of her stride and had to use a crutch. Her face, however, though it grew old and withered, still remained attractive in its way and remarkably noble. Her bearing resembled more and more the mellow majesty of Catherine the Great as we imagine it from her portrait. Her whims and eccentricities, which increased with the years, contrasted all the more sharply with her appearance. Her frankness of speech, which once upon a time had been merely charming, now became almost brusque in its roughness. Grandmother never properly learnt to control her fits of temper, which were sometimes quite unbearable. Some of her whims had a more innocent character. For instance, she would exclaim often and without any particular reason:

'Oh, Sant' Antonio di Padova!' Later she russified this ejaculation into a plainly familiar: 'St Anton' and an even plainer: 'Antoshka'. Because of this, her small great-grandchildren, the children of Genia Cavos, called her 'Babushka Antoshka' and she became known under this nickname in wider circles.

Dear 'Babushka Antoshka'! I feel the need here to express to her my special and personal gratitude. Remembering perhaps how hard it had been for her at the beginning to overcome the frictions and obstacles she met in the society to which she had come to belong, she regarded with great tolerance and sometimes with open protectiveness the love affairs that excited our family. In the same kind way she treated the love of my life at a time when both our families were as shocked by our behaviour as the parents of Romeo and Juliet had been. 'Can you imagine it! Shoura seems to be in love with Atia Kind, the sister of Maria Karlovna from whom his brother Albert has just separated.' Grandmother Cavos, on the contrary, having taken my beloved to her heart, kept repeating: 'Let them do as they like and you'll see that they'll find happiness together'. Grandmother, generally speaking, showed great wisdom of the heart as well as penetration. In the jocular way characteristic of her, mixing Russian, French and Italian expressions, she made very shrewd appreciations of people or threw the right light on complicated situations. It is natural that she should have been attracted by people of a congenial nature. She liked my Atia precisely because she found in her the same straightforwardness, natural gaiety and complete lack of affectation or pose.

Her particular favourite was her granddaughter, my sister Camilla, with whom she used to stay for long periods. Her favourite spot in the house was a large covered terrace, with a view over a pond covered with water lilies. She would sit for hours at the end of the terrace where the pergola permitted the sun to shine through and warm her (Grandmother suffered greatly from the cold and would wrap herself up even in the summer), her bad leg resting on a stool, watching the boisterous games of Camilla's children in the garden. Maybe she was remembering the time when her own children played in the same way in the narrow garden of the Venetian Casa Cavos. Grandmother survived all her three children and had it not been for her daughter's son Sereja Zarudni (who from a baby orphan turned into a student of law and from that into a Public Prosecutor), she would have lived alone and there would have been no one to inherit all the memories and all the souvenirs which continued to fill her apartment in spite of many moves and sales. Grandmother died among these treasures, a very old woman, in 1903.

CHAPTER III

MY PARENTS

*

I REMEMBER my father only as a rather elderly man with grey hair and side-whiskers, beginning to grow bald and wearing spectacles. Papa was about fifty-seven when I was born; my earliest recollections of him go back to when he was sixty. Mamma did not seem young either, though she was fifteen years younger than her husband. She had probably aged prematurely because of her numerous pregnancies. She looked altogether frail. I remember her with a pronounced stoop, a tendency to plumpness and faint wrinkles in her forehead. But she did not look like that in the portrait by Kapkoff, painted at the beginning of 1850, which used to hang in our sitting-room. There she appears as she was when Papa 'got' her – very young, slim, straight as an arrow. I could hardly believe it when I was told that this was Mamma, and only one entirely external symbol persuaded me that it was the same beloved mother whom I never left for a moment: the familiar lorgnette which she holds in her pale, transparent hands in the portrait. The slightly sad expression on her face was also very familiar, an expression well caught by the artist. For there was a certain fundamental sadness in Mamma's nature; she did not trust life, and she believed that disasters loomed in front of her and of all those dear to her. At times this mistrust became pathological – for instance, when she was out driving, particularly in a sleigh. Her expression would become distraught, miserable and she would keep looking for help.

She was constantly preoccupied about our well-being.

This anxiety about insufficient security for her husband and children was all the more distressing because, unlike Papa, Mamma was not religious, though she did practise a religion of her own with a tinge of materialism in it. Possibly at the bottom of her heart she did not believe in anything supernatural (and least of all in life after death), but she preferred to keep silent on this subject and her true, secret convictions were only rarely revealed by accident. Was her Venetian origin responsible for this? She was not the child of that Venice which fought heroically for supremacy on the seas, built churches and palaces of magic beauty, but of the Venice whose grandeur was now beginning to expire, the disappointed, decimated town.

Father, on the other hand, was filled with an energy that knew no moment of gloom, and he had an unshatterable belief in God. I remember him always gay and brimming over with vitality, never troubling about what would happen next. He had the haziest ideas about economising and it was frail little Mamma who regulated our budget. With the help of her two brothers she even attempted (sometimes quite profitably) to launch into financial operations, about which she in fact knew nothing. Papa was completely blank about everything that had to do with money and banks and, alas, I inherited this trait from him. He thought only about his art, his family, how to make his children happy and above all how to express his adoration for their mother. The morrow simply did not exist for him.

He went to Mass every Sunday, whatever the weather, and knelt throughout the service, following it carefully with the prayer book. Once a year, at Easter (and sometimes more often than that), he confessed and took communion, and his religious adviser, a quiet, cosy little Dominican priest, Father Lukashevicz, was a friend of the family and took part in all our family events and celebrations. But there was no trace of bigotry or fanaticism in my father. Believing as he did implicitly in the teachings of the Catholic Church, he would make the sign of the Cross in front of Orthodox churches and when he happened to be present at an Orthodox service he joined in the singing in an undertone, as he knew all the ritual and hymns from his Academy days. He had a deep respect, too, for the Lutheran and Protestant clergy as well as for the representatives of the Jewish religion.

Papa's great religious tolerance (almost a type of pantheism) was one day expressed in a reply which vastly surprised me. At the age of ten I asked him whether Jupiter, Apollo, Venus and Minerva had really existed. I was going through a phase of great admiration for the Greek and Roman gods and never tired of looking at their images in books or at sculptures of them as I wandered through Petersburg or the Summer Gardens. I was distressed by the thought that these divine beings had never really existed and were only figments of human imagination. When I expressed these views to Papa, not only did he not deny definitely the existence of pagan gods but even admitted the possibility that they might have lived once upon a time, which caused me great happiness, as I accepted implicitly his verdict in such questions.

I doubt whether I was much more than two when my father carried me about in his arms, wrapped in my bedclothes, trying to soothe me and lull me to sleep during the spells of insomnia from which I then suffered. It was no easy task, for I was overcome with indescribable terror by night and haunted by the most horrible visions. He walked with me round the whole apartment, through each of the big, dark rooms, the only faint glimmer of light coming from under the door of my parents' bedroom. Now and then the dim reflection of a passing carriage would spread fan-wise over the ceiling.

The atmosphere of eeriness was enhanced by the ticking

of the grandfather clock that stood in the corner of the dining-room. It was a beautiful, tall, English mahogany clock of the eighteenth century. I thought of this clock as a live being, with a sad, round face on a long body. Later I learnt to love it, and regarded it as a sort of family palladium. Was it not strange that at the moment of my mother's last breath (she was dying in the next room) this clock that stood guard on time should suddenly stop?

But of course a child of two trembling with fear in the arms of his father knew nothing about time or death, and the clock filled me with infinite awe. What terrified me most was the preliminary stammering and coughing that announced the striking of the hour or the half hour. I shivered and hid my face in my little pillow and in Papa's dressing-gown. And then, simultaneously with the distinct, loud striking of our clock, there arose from below a strange nocturnal music – the chimes of the many clocks hanging and standing in Sirach the watchmaker's shop, which was situated in the ground floor of our house. When all these strange and frightening noises had quieted down all I could hear was Papa's soft humming, in which I could distinguish the lullaby gently urging me to go to sleep.

The portraits on the walls – there were many of them in Papa's study – conjured up other horrors. I could not distinguish them by night, but I knew they were there and that one of them particularly was following me watchfully with its eyes.

I always awoke from my nightmares covered in sweat and after that could never go to sleep again. The nightmares were either of escapes that ended or threatened to end badly, or of various monsters, sometimes quite improbable ones, sometimes of the horned and hairy devils that torture sinners in the inferior woodcuts of the Last Judgement. But my most tormenting and persistent dreams were about the railway. There were two versions. In the first I am standing on the grass by the railway track, not in the least afraid for I know that the train runs along the lines and cannot touch me. But smoke appears above the trees, the engine springs out of the forest and instead of passing me by it turns and with a strange ferocity dashes straight at me. It is the end! The second is rather like Anna Karenina's dream. There is the railway track again, but this time I am not on the grass, I am on the platform. There is no train in sight, though I expect it to arrive. A strange, beardless, toothless, crooked little old man, who looks like a beggar and carries a stick in his hand, keeps murmuring into my ear: 'Coming and going, coming and going'. I always knew beforehand when I would have this dream; it was inevitable and somehow particularly ominous, since it always came as a warning of illness. I was perhaps already half delirious when I was dreaming it.

One of the nightmares which pursued me in my childhood I have remembered all my life and as a child I believed it to be prophetic. I must have been five or six when it first occured. I dreamed that a strange boy to whom I took an immediate liking came to visit me. I played with him as though we had always been friends. He was older than I, not good-looking but somehow fascinating, and was dressed in a red suit edged with white braid. We played all sorts of games, till suddenly he disappeared and I knew that a great disaster had taken place. I ran through the rooms looking for him, calling him, but there was no reply. All at once I saw a machine standing in the corridor, and in it the little boy was struggling to free himself from knives and screws that were tearing his body to pieces.

I can still see Papa carrying me in his arms, trying to soothe me after those terrifying nightmares. Or there he is, holding me on his lap and watching me seize a pencil and cover one sheet of paper after the other with my drawings; presenting me to admiring aunts, when I was in my nightdress or totally naked, by holding me up above the alcove screen like a Punch and Judy show. And there are even earlier recollections of me sitting on Papa's lap in a state of ecstasy while his pencil produces soldiers, trumpeters by the sentry box, barking dogs and sleeping cats, a knight in armour, a sleigh harnessed to a trotter, and all sorts of jokes and caricatures, at which I laugh until I cry, hiding my head in his dressing-gown, while he tickles me and pummels me and kisses me, repeating 'Papa's boy'.

Every time I recall these things I see my god as I used to see him then. I see his sweet smile, his dear grey-green eyes, half concealed by the shiny spectacles. I can smell the dressing-gown, imbued with the aroma of cigars, I can distinguish the veins on the ageing hands, I can hear his voice, his jokes and ditties and the nicknames which he showered upon us in an unknown language – a whole series of them were devoted to me, the last child. Now Papa sits down at the piano in the sitting-room to play (by ear) a regimental tune, to which I march with a rifle in my hand and a helmet on my head, trying to turn about in true military fashion. I can see Papa working on the days when I was forbidden to disturb him. Puffing at his cigar, he is drawing something at the drawing board in the studio, while round him his assistants watch what he explains to them, without interrupting his drawing. Or he is sitting in his study on a chair with an intricate back[1] and leather cushion, and writing, writing something by the light of his special oil-lamp kept from the days of his youth.

When I evoke a picture of my father in those early days of my life, I see him as a very close, but at the same time remote deity. On the other hand, I can hardly visualise my mother at all in these years. She was so near to me with her warm and tender love and care that I was unable to see her. Having come into this world shortly after the death of my

[1] We had two genuine Chippendales, not of mahogany but carved out of oak.

little sister Luisa, a grief which left my parents inconsolable, I naturally became the object of their special affection, what German nannies used to call *Schosskindchen*. Finding my mother unable to resist my despotism, I naturally tormented and exploited her without being in the least aware of what I was doing and therefore unable to feel at all guilty about it. Mamma never complained and defended me even when I did not in the least deserve it.

Later the relationship between my parents and myself underwent some changes. As I grew from a child with a dim personality into a boy with an independent and rather capricious nature, my contact with my father became less strong. And when the boy became an adolescent, this contact was sometimes interrupted altogether. Thank God there was never a real break, but there is no doubt that Father and I ceased to understand one another and this is all the more natural because the difference in age between father and son was not a normal one but a whole half century; though now it often occurs to me that, because of this great disparity, we were perhaps not as far from one another as might have been expected. The ideals of my father's youth became mine. Like my father I was imbued with romanticism, whereas the positivist ideas that took possession of so many minds about the 1870s were alien to me and even repulsive. Only during a very short period, under the influence of more 'progressive' people and casting aside all prejudices, did I acquire, at the age of fourteen, some of the attributes of the cynic. This short period was precisely the one that saw a deterioration in my relations with Papa. A man of seventy did not have the patience to probe into what was going on in my mind and to discover how superficial and unimportant my childish rebelliousness was. He was too upset and indignant about it. Whereas I, with the absurdity characteristic of this ungrateful age, started almost to despise my father for his 'obsolete' ideas.

A few sharp altercations with him at that period exacerbated these misunderstandings and I became convinced that our natures were diametrically opposed and incapable of mutual understanding, and of course I considered that my nature was incomparably superior and more refined than that of my single-minded and old-fashioned parent.

The process of 'separation' from my mother led to something entirely different. Only from that moment did I begin fully to appreciate what she was really worth, only then did I realise the deep link that continued to bind us indissolubly together. Gradually, from a part of myself, she began to be transformed into my friend. The initial unison turned into harmony. And this metamorphosis of feeling took place with all the unobtrusiveness of an organic process. As I reached my tenth year I began to be conscious of the fact that I adored my mother, that she was dearer to me than anyone in the world and that she understood me better than anybody else. This does not mean that there were no disagreements between us or that I did not often upset her or resent her authority. I was too self-willed and erratic for relations *de tout repos* to exist between me and anybody else.

Papa was a natural artist and poet, Mamma a prosaic person who reacted against the aesthetic. In pictures she liked precision, neatness, realism, and in literature a true replica of real life. This daughter of a collector felt a real revulsion against all collections of works of art. Perhaps the fact that everything her father had collected had gone the way of all flesh and was dispersed without bringing any real profit, contributed to this reaction. Pictures on the walls, and particularly all kinds of bric-a-brac, she called '*attrapes poussière*', and she had no taste for them. Sometimes she distributed among her friends very valuable articles simply to get rid of useless and cumbersome objects. Of the history of art she knew what every educated person should know; the names of great masters were familiar to her, but she was unable to admire their works. The pictures of painters like Rembrandt or Delacroix must have been distasteful to her for the simple reason that they painted so 'untidily'.

Neither had this granddaughter of a remarkable composer any artistic appreciation of music. She did not have a good ear, she knew only one piece by heart (which she had learnt to play for her last examination in the Smolni Institute), she had difficulty in following a score and she had no sense of rhythm. She went to the opera almost every week but preferred the coloratura and fioritura to real musical quality; in piano performances she mainly admired dexterity and did not try to penetrate into the intricacies of a composition. Yet my mother was the true inspiration of my father and of all our household. Her manner of thinking and expressing her thoughts, her absolute truthfulness, her deep understanding of others (*tout comprendre – c'est tout pardonner* was one of her favourite sayings), her tolerance, the limitless kindness that caused her always to sacrifice herself and made her incapable of self-indulgence – all this glowed from within her. She was a rare, integral and accomplished human being. Insensitive to poetry or phantasy, unreligious as she was, at the same time she was permeated with the grace of God. She had no talent for the arts, but she had a genius for love.

My own memoirs are not the place to talk of my father's artistic career. It deserves a whole book, and at one time my brother Leontij intended to publish a monograph on his work, for which he had prepared the index and illustrations, but the revolution prevented him from fulfilling this expensive task. But I must say in a few words what my father was as an artist and what was his social position. This is easy for me for, though I knew my father only in his declining years, through the stories he told me and the many drawings he made for me I felt I had known him in the days when he went to the Peterschule and when, later, at the command of his godmother the Empress Maria Fedorovna, he entered the Academy of Arts, where in 1836 he graduated brilliantly in architecture with a gold medal. After that he spent four years in Moscow, participating in the building of the grandiose Church of the Saviour under the guidance of the famous Constantine Ton, and then went to Germany and Italy, where he spent most of his grant money in Rome and Orvieto. In 1846, on his way back home, he visited Switzerland, France and England. On his return he very soon won the admiration of Emperor Nicholas I, for whom he planned a series of remarkable buildings. But Nicholas died, Alexander II came to the throne and after the defeat in the Crimean War an era of intensive economy was established in Russia and brought my father's career, so brilliantly begun, to a standstill. His creative activities were limited to projects of a utilitarian rather than an artistic character. The expenses of keeping a large family made him turn to local government. He was a member of the City Council of Petersburg for a quarter of a century and for many years head of its technical department.

Of all Papa's stories about his past I was most fascinated by those about Italy and especially Orvieto, where he spent two years with his closest friends, Riasanov and Krakau, devoting himself to the study of the Cathedral, that splendid architectural monument, the pride of this small town of the Papal domain, picturesquely situated on a rock. From morning till night the three of them worked, measuring and drawing every detail of the construction on special scaffoldings erected for them by permission of the Holy Father. Wishing to make a return for such favours, the Russian architects washed the whole Cathedral with sponges with their own hands and at their own expense, including the mosaics in the tympanums and the fine bas relief in the front, which had been obscured by dirt. To commemorate this feat a medal was coined, presenting the Cathedral on one side and, on the other, the names of the three voluntary restorers. Each of them also received a large, beautifully bound volume of Piranesi's prints from the Papal chalcographical department. Several years later the results of their studies were published in France and this work is still the standard reference book on Orvieto Cathedral.

All three had been educated in the strictly classical style, but during their stay in Rome they all, and especially my father, fell under the influence of the Eternal City at the time when the pious Overbeck was preaching the return to medieval purity, when young painters paid more heed to Beato Angelico, Pinturicchio and Perugino than to Raphael, when Romanesque and Gothic architecture was held in particular reverence and baroque art with Bernini at its head was considered beneath contempt. My father's choice had fallen on Orvieto because it was the home of one of the most remarkable monuments of Italian Gothic art. Although he would have liked then and there to turn to the more perfect examples of the ogive style in France, Germany or England, the rules of the Academy required a stay of several years in Italy so that *faute de mieux* he and his friends began to study Orvieto Cathedral. They found consolation in the belief that Italian medieval architecture had much in common with Old Russian architecture and they aimed to bring about the renaissance of this architecture on their return home.

Papa's entire stay in Italy was spent in a Romantic atmosphere, in the spirit of Christian Rome which permeated the work of the best painters and poets of that time. They came to Rome from all the ends of Europe and led a separated cosmopolitan life of their own within its walls. My father was personally acquainted with most of these artists and writers, such as Overbeck, Möller, Alexander

Ivanov and Gogol. Sometimes he would meet them in the haunts of the foreign colony, like the Café Greco, and sometimes he would visit them at their homes. Father remembered vividly the sulky gloom of the great 'creator of laughter' (as we imagine Gogol from his works) and the sickly sadness of the author of *The Appearance of Christ*, whose own appearance was a true caricature – dark spectacles under a tall straw hat, a shabby cloak, an eternal umbrella and galoshes. Ivanov's figure and his eccentric manners did not prevent my father and the painter Vassia Sternberg from revering the saintly painter, and Ivanov in his turn often made an exception in their favour and opened the doors of his studio which were closed to nearly everybody else.

Sternberg, a young and highly gifted painter, was my father's best friend, but to his great grief this friendship came to an early end when Sternberg developed consumption which brought him to an early grave in the cemetery at the pyramid of Cestius, where "heretics and schismatics" were usually buried. Among Father's friends were also the Russian painters Fricke and Scotti, the sculptors Ramasanov and Loganovski, the architects Rossi the younger and Eppinger. Only little old Fricke was alive when I came on to the scene, but I seemed to have known them all, so familiar were their looks, immortalised by my father in sharp, fine drawings and water colours (sometimes gently caricatured).

Papa's friendships with German painters led to his being elected a 'knight' of the famous club that met and caroused in the '*caves*' of Cervara. His knight's diploma and the programmes of some of the boisterous gatherings of this *Ritterschaft* were kept with Papa's Family Chronicles. I was fond of the masterly vignettes (the etchings of Neureuter) that adorned them and cannot forgive myself for leaving them unprotected in my Petersburg flat. Even more upsetting is the thought that when I left my native land for ever, I did not take with me all my father's works left me in his will. What would I not give to be able to study them now, and especially to relish the drawing which describes in nine episodes the journey of N. Benois and his friends on a ship from Ancona to Venice?

How delightful were my father's albums illustrating his journeys! What a keen sense of nature in every drawing of a landscape, how much understanding in every portrait of a building! What taste, masterliness and precision! Views of places alternated in these albums with architectural sketches and genre and costume drawings. During his trip to Venice he was particularly struck by the types seen in the streets and the market places – graceful women carrying water, fishermen and gondoliers, monks of various orders, mysterious silhouettes wrapped up in wide *almavivas* and finally the dashing, elegant Austrian officers in their white and blue uniforms. Papa's albums (we each inherited two of them) were a real feast. One could sense that he had left part of his heart in Rome and Orvieto and that this young man full of vigour and vitality had had sentimental adventures there, even some quite serious ones.

The happiest period seems to have been the years in Orvieto, when he settled down in a place of his own. The cold in winter was acute and there was only one lamp – a *lucerna* with three wicks without glass or shade – but Papa managed to create an atmosphere of cosiness wherever he happened to be. He worked by night as well as by day. By the light of his primitive lamp he made his finest aquarelle drawings, in which, for example, you can see every stone of the Cosmati mosaic outlined with absolute precision. What is remarkable is that in spite of the strain, Papa preserved perfect eyesight up to a great age and until a year before his death he could draw and paint as though he were twenty-four instead of eighty-four.

In his later years Papa put down on paper all that impressed him, amused him or gladdened his heart. The most remarkable albums are those that he produced in 1885, when our whole family stayed in my sister Katia's country house, and one in which he immortalised the summer of 1891 which he spent in Finland. Where are they now, this wonderful series left in Petersburg, worthy of comparison with D. Chodowiecki's *Journey to Danzig*?

My father had so strong an urge to capture everything in pictorial form that I wonder sometimes if his real calling was not painting. Although very busy with tedious office work, he never let a day pass without making a drawing and then colouring it. His technique might seem old-fashioned (it was that of the masters of the beginning of the nineteenth century), but he had so much knowledge, such precision and assurance. Masses of water colours illustrated his letters to his children and relatives. Unfortunately their charm probably provoked vandalism in the recipients. Instead of preserving them as documents, my brothers, in their admiration of the pictures, cut them out and stuck them in special albums, discarding the text as unworthy of survival.

Papa was a 'cosy' person, a trait that is unusual in the French and must be attributed to his half-German origin. He was the essence itself of *Gemütlichkeit*. If I too feel something of it and delight more than most people in the warm, simple pleasures of the home; if, when I read Hoffmann or Stifter and look at the pictures of Ludwig Richter or Schwind, I experience an unusual pleasure, it is because I was surrounded by this *Gemütlichkeit* in my father's home and in his company. At the time I took it for granted; it seemed that it could not be otherwise. When I reached the ungrateful age, I even began to criticise the special atmosphere of our home and introduced a jarring note that spoilt its harmony. But towards the age of twenty my rebellion abated and when I entered into my independence the creation of this cosiness became an ideal, which my wife later helped me to achieve.

Papa's capacity for working in public was astonishing. Not only could he go on working to the hushed whispers of the people around him, but he stood with angelic patience the noise made by the children, who often became quite boisterous. More than that, it was he who fixed a swing in the wide doorway leading to the hall and on it, until the age of thirteen, I and my nephews executed dangerous flights accompanied by cries and shrieks right behind Papa's back. He stood it all, and only when someone was expected on business or the ladies began to protest was the swing taken off its hinges and the door into the hall closed.

Another torment for Papa was the music that came from the hall where there was a piano and a harmonium. There my friend V. Nouvel and I played *fortissimo* on both these instruments the *Ride of the Walküre*, the overture from *Tannhäuser*, the march from *Nero*, etc. Papa bore it all without a murmur, only sometimes turning to us with a meek request to restrain the deafening violence of our performance.

In summer Papa's clothes emphasised his cosiness. In winter and '*mi-saison*' he was always dressed (if not in his dressing-gown) in a black coat with a white shirt and black tie. To go out into the frost he wore an old fashioned fur cap with a leather peak and a heavy bearskin overcoat; on less chilly days a bowler of an old-fashioned oval shape and a cloak with a pelerine. In the summer, however, he liked to wear white linen suits or yellowish Chinese silk suits and on his head an absurdly large panama hat. A grey cloak served as an overcoat. In this light attire I remember him either returning from town to Peterhof or Pavlovsk, or sometimes working in the garden in our summer residence. He was at work every minute of the day and if weather permitted he would sweep the garden, weed the paths, water the flowers, nail something here, saw something there. And all with wonderful skill.

The middle of the summer was marked by a series of family celebrations. They began on the 1st (13th) of July, Papa's birthday; then came Cousin Olga's nameday (11th July); then Mamma's and my sister Camilla's (15th); my sister Katia's birthday (19th); the nameday of my brother Albert's wife, Marie (22nd); and when my Atia became a member of the family two other days were added: her nameday (July 26th) and her birthday (August 9th). But the most splendid occasion of all was July 1st. Papa's many colleagues would be there for luncheon, and the entire tribe would assemble for dinner. The weather itself, our capricious northern weather, looked benevolently upon this gathering of good men, because I clearly remember that it never rained on July 1st; the table or tables were set out in the garden. We children were especially excited by the occasion, which had an exceptional quality: something exotic and bohemian, tremendously bustling and gay. Our own maids, helped by temporary servants in light-coloured cotton dresses and white aprons, flitted about, their starched skirts rustling, carrying dishes from the kitchen to the tables and serving them round; we were exhilarated by the sound of the corks popping out of bottles of mead, beer and champagne; it was strange and gay to feel the sand under your feet instead of the parquet floor; to throw, carelessly, dainty titbits of food on the ground which were instantly eaten up by dogs and cats.

The *pièce de résistance* at these luncheon banquets was always a colossal fish pie, and for supper the Cavos family soup, the Venetian *risi bisi*, so delicious that no guest ever refused a second helping. We greedy children would eat three helpings. If the day happened to be very hot, an iced Russian soup was served as well as this hot soup. I was a particularly greedy boy, and managed to eat not only three plates of the first but also two of the second. And I was not the only one. How did our stomachs stand it? How was it that no one fell ill? Mamma was ever abstemious, even on these great occasions, but she always urged others to eat their fill: *'N'ayez aucune crainte; au grand air on peut se permettre certains excès'.*

After dinner the tables were carried away and tea would be set on the veranda, where again you could indulge yourself with yoghourt and sour milk or pile strawberries on your plate. Between luncheon and tea it was customary to play *'bocci'*. Papa and many of his friends were passionately addicted to this game. In our family it was not played as it is abroad on specially rolled green lawns, but simply on rough garden paths. When bowling his first 'small' ball Papa would take liberties; sometimes he would throw the ball so far that no one could see it, and sometimes he would throw it almost under his feet. 'The Italians', Uncle Kostia and Uncle Cesare, would protest in the name of the rules, but those of us children who were allowed to take part in these games were delighted by Papa's mischievous tricks. We were much amused by the heated discussions that arose when two or three balls were found at the same distance from the 'small' ball. These distances had to be measured with handkerchiefs, or sticks, or by pacing them out, and then our dignified and respectable uncles would let loose their Italian temperaments and sometimes the cries of indignation were loud and long. This was greatly appreciated by the gleeful young. They were delighted to see the uncles, cited as examples of good behaviour and held in some awe, behaving just as we did ourselves. Usually Papa remained blissfully undisturbed by these discussions.

During June or early July lights would not be put on in the evenings in the homes and the streets of Petersburg, and that again was mysteriously exciting. But darkness came about 9 p.m. at the end of July, and progressively earlier every day, and by then the lamps and candles had to be lit. I was excited when the candles were lit in special candlesticks made for the open air. The flame was protected by a glass bulb and the candle, propelled by a spring from beneath, rose automatically. Midges and moths collected around the lights and lots of large night butterflies. The picture round the summer tea-table was no less cosy and delightful than the gatherings in the winter under a hanging lamp.

It must have been to a certain extent this inclination for *Gemütlichkeit*, together with a lack of rancour and a non-resistance to evil, that prevented my father, with all his talent, from making the triumphant way through life that opened before him from the time he returned home from his Roman tour. Father had not a trace of the intriguer; he had no guile in his nature; he disliked pushing himself forward and was incapable either of sucking up to his colleagues or of by-passing them. That is why he remained in the background, although he was without doubt the most gifted and erudite architect of his day in Russia.

During his lifetime, the Emperor Nicholas I (who was very much attached to my father) entrusted him with various important projects. One of the most remarkable buildings he planned was the Court stables in Peterhof, superior, I believe, in splendour even to the famous Condé stables at Chantilly. It was a little town in itself, built in the medieval English style beloved of my father and his august protector. It is the fashion at present to despise all such 'pseudo-Gothic' styles; few people are willing to revise their opinions and admit that not all the architecture inspired by Louis Philippe, Nicholas I and Queen Victoria was ornate and in bad taste. In fact some of the buildings of that time, such as the Houses of Parliament in London, are incomparably more impressive and simply more beautiful than what followed them. The general plan and exquisite detail of Papa's Peterhof stables can stand comparison with the best that was done in that manner in the West. As a whole they are remarkably regal, harmonious, beautiful. But, alas, that majestic building and a few others started in the reign of Nicholas I were the flower of my father's architectural work. His later work, up to his death, is to be respected, but it is rather characterless and not worthy of a place in the history of art. During that time his less talented colleagues managed to erect a number of important buildings: for example, Riasanov built the palace of the Grand Duke Vladimir, and finished the grandiose building of the Church of the Saviour in Moscow; Krakau built the Palace of Baron Stiglitz which afterwards came into the possession of the Grand Duke Paul. Other architects who devoted themselves to the development of the Russian style, such as Godike, Grimm, Kusmin and others, achieved special success owing to the increase of nationalistic (more precisely pseudo-nationalistic) tendencies. Papa had to content himself with private houses and villas or with such dreary tasks as the almshouse in Peterhof.

Nevertheless my father's jubilee celebration in the autumn of 1886 was a genuine triumph. It took place in the central round conference hall of the Academy of Arts, with a huge audience under the chairmanship of Alexander III's brother, Vladimir, the former President of this, our most distinguished artistic establishment. As the family of the guest of honour we had a box over the entrance and a magnificent view of the entire ceremony. Papa, always so modest in appearance, was transformed as he sat between the Grand Duke and the Princess of Oldenburg. He wore a new Court uniform, embroidered with gold, and white trousers with golden braid. His breast was covered with orders and decorations and the scarlet ribbon of Saint Anne. In the amphitheatre sat all the important personalities, and the gold of Court uniforms, the sparkle of decorations and ribbons, was dazzling. Deputations from various institutions and societies came up to the table and made flattering speeches, and after each greeting a volley of trumpets from the Academy orchestra rang out from the 'Raphael' room next door. The most solemn moment arrived when the Grand Duke, after speaking a few words in his loud, raucous voice, handed my father a medal cast in his honour, with his portrait in profile.

What Mamma meant to my father, what kind of wife she was to him, I cannot judge. I think that the fragrance of our home atmosphere came from their love. That love started with a real *coup de foudre*, during a ball in the house of the principal of the Academy of Art, a famous painter F. Bruni. Young Camilla Cavos, just out of school, was being brought out by her stepmother Xenia, who was only a few years older than her daughter and attracted much attention by her majestic beauty and beautiful clothes. Mamma was a modest, timid girl, quite unaccustomed to dazzling receptions. None the less, this 'violet' was noticed and chosen at the ball (as noted in our chronicles) by N. Benois, aged 34, just returned from foreign lands and already distinguished by the benevolence of a formidable and magnificent Emperor. The schoolgirl, too, after the first quadrille, realised that this man, not so very young, was her fate. Papa proposed a few weeks later and a few months afterwards, on September 15th, 1848, their marriage took place in the beautiful church of the Corps des Pages, situated in the same group of buildings as my grandfather's flat; and on that same day the young people settled in the flat in which my grandmother had lived before and in which they were to live peacefully all their lives.

The only way my mother ever betrayed my father was by being the first to leave her husband for the other world, the existence of which had never seemed credible to her. But it did to Papa, and it was a great consolation to him that during the seven and a half years of life without her he never stopped hoping to be reunited with his beloved 'Camilunsa'.

Mamma's lack of faith had a very special character. It was her own intimate affair, she did not burden anyone else with it nor was anyone blamed for her lack of religious consciousness. She did not believe because she did not find in her soul the essential something which could convince her. Coupled with the absence of what is called the state of grace was her distaste for any kind of self-deception. My belief is that her relinquishing of faith came about gradually and not without a struggle; that in spite of an ardent desire to remain in a state of grace (of the existence of which she was perfectly aware) she even lost her faith and was unable to recapture it. In later years, however, the struggle was no longer apparent in her; all that remained was sadness and resignation. Her disbelief had an absolutely honest foundation, and Mamma never had any trace of the materialistic convictions fashionable at the time. She was simply incapable of lying to herself.

Mamma was the head of the house, and it was in this sphere that her talents were properly realised; it was her calling. She performed her household duties with a model smoothness which greatly contributed to the family's wellbeing and the contentment that reigned in it. At home she held the reins of power indisputably; but outside her own house she acted with consummate tact only in an advisory capacity. In other words, she was the ideal mother-in-law, and I do not remember a single instance of friction between her and anyone who married into our family.

CHAPTER IV

MY TOYS

*

M Y favourite childhood plaything until I was about
eight was soldiers. My love for them was like that of
some military-mad German princeling. A close friend of
ours nicknamed me 'Boom-boom', which was what I
myself called the soldiers, and he continued to call me
Boom-boom until he died, though by then I had almost
reached the age of forty and had long ceased to be a rabid
militarist and had become an uncompromising pacifist.

I had several hundreds of soldiers, of all shapes and
sizes. Some were of tin; others of paper made by Papa, who
in order to satisfy my apparently insatiable appetite even
made soldiers for me out of playing cards. He bent them in
two and cut the edges in a way that made them fairly stable,
though it was not when they stood up but when they fell
down that I experienced the greater pleasure. If, for instance,
you blew on the first, it subsided upon its neighbour which
then fell upon the third and so on until the whole row was
brought down. I was not conscious of cruelty during this
process, any more than the modern pilot who drops a
bomb on a town feels specifically cruel as he does so. He
may even get the same 'innocent pleasure' out of it as I did
when I slaughtered my cardboard legions.

The tin soldiers I liked best were those that might be called
the aristocracy among the inhabitants of my boxes. They
were the most expensive and best made, round, chubby
little soldiers, the cavalrymen astride horses to which they
were attached for greater security by little screws that fitted
into a hole in the horse's saddle. When they were dis-

mounted these riders looked comical. Their legs remained bowed as though they had just wet their trousers (the unpleasant feeling of wet trousers was familiar to me at that time), yet it gave them a strong resemblance to real cavalrymen who became permanently bandy-legged from riding. My brother Kolia was a living example of this in his later years. These soldiers were sold in boxes together with other military equipment – canvas tents that could be set up, guns on wheels, etc. I was thrilled by them, but as they were imported they were rather expensive.

The local toys on the other hand cost next to nothing, and you could buy wooden soldiers at any market. Unfortunately they did not resemble the tin ones in size, the smallest being three times as big. This, however, did not prevent me from being equally fond of my wooden regiments. I liked them for two reasons, because they had very bright colours (sky blue uniforms with yellow buttons and white trousers), and also because they had a wonderful toy smell, the delicious smell that permeates all toy shops.

There were other simple, home-made toys which I liked as well as soldiers, toys with which I became acquainted in my early childhood and also enjoyed in later years. There was, for instance, the bowing gentleman dressed in the morning coat of 1830 and his lady, who was dressed in a voluminous pink dress and waved her hand. What a quantity of these couples I must have used up over the years! These remarkable mechanical toys were first made in the time of Gogol and were later reproduced by the craftsmen of the Troitsky monastery. In the 1890s, when I started to collect toys systematically,[1] I was delighted to be able to acquire a few surviving models. Another joy of my childhood was toy landscapes, with ducks swimming in a pond to the accompaniment of tinkling string music, bright-coloured

[1] My large collection of toys was bought by the Russian museum in Petersburg in 1920 and is probably there still.

birds and animals cut out of papier-mâché (the sheep bleated, the birds sang).

I must mention two other kinds of toys to which I was addicted. One I will call the 'dwarf-world', and the other could be described as 'optical' toys. Both elicited a response from the depths of my nature, since both had a link with the theatre and with all art that represents life.

My fondness for the 'dwarf-world' must have been stimulated by my father, who also had a passion for miniature objects, and who constructed models for his children as well as for his patrons. In his bookcase, together with a whole village of tiny houses brought from Switzerland in the 1840s, he kept a model of a railway station which he had assembled as a presentation to the Emperor Nicholas I. My brothers told me that he made such models as a preliminary to almost every arge building he constructed, spending a great deal of time on meticulous work that was more for his own pleasure than anything else.

In 1875, for my birthday, Papa decided to make for me a whole apartment to replace the rather clumsy and bulky carpenter-made wooden doll's-house which I had inherited from my brothers. The preparations for this present were kept secret, but I soon began to suspect that there was a treat in store for me. As I passed Papa's studio, where he disappeared with my elder brothers Albert or Leontij after his day's work was over, I could catch a glimpse of tiny window-frames, something that looked like an oven, something else that resembled a piano. At last the great day came, April 21st, 1875, and when I walked, shy but radiant, into the dining-room, my hair carefully brushed, wearing a velvet suit with a lace collar and new striped socks, I saw, standing between two pots of hyacinths, a real miracle that filled my heart with ecstasy. Like most children I lacked all sense of gratitude (those eternal naggings of '*Dis-donc merci*, Shourenka' were both useless and irritating); but on this occasion I was fairly brimming over with gratitude and even burst into tears. Mamma and the servants who were standing ready to offer me their greetings imagined that once again Shourenka was being ungrateful, and they were about to scold me when I overcame my confusion and muttered between heartrending sobs: 'I'm crying because I'm afraid I'll spoil it'. Then I hid my head in Papa's dressing-gown and bestowed a frenzy of kisses between its folds.

It is true the house was only of cardboard and the rooms were no higher than eight inches, but nevertheless it was a remarkable reproduction of a real and rather smart apartment. There were three rooms; the largest was the ballroom, and there were a dining-room-cum-bedroom and a kitchen. The ballroom had white wallpaper, and contained a fireplace lit with a cold flame of red tinfoil; above the chimney-piece hung a mirror and upon it were placed chandeliers and a clock; lace curtains adorned the window (made with mica instead of glass); a piano with a lid which opened stood in the corner; framed pictures hung on the walls. In the red-papered dining-room, besides the dinner-table and the chairs, there were a comfortable sofa, a rocking chair and a large sideboard with microscopic pieces of real porcelain and glass. The adjoining kitchen was filled with pots and pans and had a bell hanging on the wall that gave a shrill ring when the front door was opened. Plumbing at that time was only just being introduced into Petersburg houses, but it was already installed in my house, judging by the taps and the sink.

The nominal inhabitants of my apartment were two prettily dressed dolls: a gentleman and a lady. An iron bed and a mattress and pillows had to be bought for the lady, while the gentleman had to content himself with the sofa, on which I laid him down without taking off his clothes. But the real inhabitant was, of course, myself. I did not need these 'extras', which I very soon removed into a box with all sorts of miscellaneous objects, and I would sit for hours in front of my apartment, moving the furniture, laying the table, kindling the fire in the fireplace, in which, behind an iron fender, lay a poker and a broom. I would imagine that guests were expected, then that they actually arrived, and wonderful dishes would be brought for them out of the kitchen. It never occurred to me that a hostess might be required, and I held endless conversations with two imaginary friends, Petia and Sasha, who visited me in the apartment. I would go on talking to them even after my governess had taken me to bed.

My attachment to the 'dwarf-world' reached a peak when I became acquainted with *Gulliver's Travels* in a Russian translation. How I wished I could go to the capital of the Lilliputians, and peer into the windows of their houses and see how they lived in their tiny homes! So vividly did I imagine these little men, their horses, their clothes, their weapons, that at times it seemed to me that I, like Gulliver, had really held them in my hands, felt how they wriggled in fear, brought them right up to my nose to be able to see them more clearly – and perhaps I did see it all in my always very realistic dreams. In the evenings, after I was tucked into bed and the lamp was extinguished, I would gaze into the twilit room with its lonely candle in the hope that there would be a rustle on top of the cupboard or on the shelf and that it would turn out to be a Lilliputian. Had one really appeared I would certainly not have been afraid, though I would have died of fright at the sight of anything shaggy or horny. I was eager to know the exact size of Gulliver's Lilliputians. When the book said that they were *seven* inches tall I was greatly upset that they were not as tiny as the people I had created in my imagination and with whom I so wanted to become friends.

I must also mention the castles and little towns made of

cork which were sold at the fairs before Easter, in which the cardboard attire of the knights symbolised the death of romanticism. A five-year-old boy, however, had no idea of romanticism as a literary movement. All I knew was that the characters of my favourite fairy tales lived in these castles – Blue Beard, and the Ogre who was changed into a mouse and gobbled up by Puss-in-Boots, and so on. My brother Isha had told me a lot about castles and I had seen some in Papa's albums, so I knew about drawbridges and the machicolated walls with towers at the corners; I even had an idea of the lay-out inside, of the staircases, the halls, the passages.

Who were the creators of these wonderfully poetical objects ? Who was the artist who probably long before Palm Sunday Fair collected the corks, cut them up, glued them together in such a varying combination of material ? It was this anonymous magician who covered the cork rocks beneath the many-towered castles with bright green moss; who planted the tiny groves of feathers; who set little mirrors into the cork beaches to represent pools of water; it was he whose tapering fingers moulded the tiny wax swans that swam past the harbour wall. Did this architect, I wonder, survive to know in old age the perfidious transitoriness of taste ? Did he, poor and wretched, create all this magic in order to earn enough money during the seven days of the Palm Week Fair to keep himself alive ? Soon the fashion for these castles began to wane and few were sold, though they cost little. People failed to realise their genuine poetry: they were considered to be old-fashioned. Now, though never a year went by without my buying one, even I have none left in my possession.

I was equally enthralled by an exhibition of models in one of the halls of the Academy of Arts. It was a large but not very bright room. At one end, where there was most light, rose the stupendous cupola of San Pietro; on the floor in front of it were casually laid out the Isaak Cathedral, Mikhailovski Castle, the Petersburg Stock Exchange, Smolni Monastery and a dozen antique ruins. Each miniature building was complete in every detail, the roofs, chimneys, pillars, façades, towers and spires. Here, indeed, was Gulliver's town! I was allowed to walk among these buildings, of which few were taller than I was, so that I could easily peer through the windows. Some of the models were cut in half, which allowed one to see the interior, sometimes a very luxurious one. But to me the most splendid of all was the Cathedral of St Peter. In fact when I found myself in front of the real Papal Cathedral many years later, my admiration was not as great as when I had stood, a spellbound child, before that majestic mass of stone no more than three yards high. I knew nothing then of the aesthetic value of this monument, by whom it was built or when. I had only a vague notion that it was the biggest church in the world, that it was in Rome where lived the Pope, the Tsar of all the priests. But my admiration for this Cathedral, a truly genuine and spontaneous emotion, and my other admiration for Raphael, were the guiding stars of my life.

Optical toys also played a large and special part in my childhood. There were several of them: the kaleidoscope, the microscope, the praxinoscope, the magic lantern, the peepshow '*Guckkasten*' and the stereoscope. Of these the kaleidoscope was then the most ordinary. At any tobacconist trading in cheap toys as well as in cigars and cigarettes you could buy for almost nothing this cardboard tube with a hole at one end and a dull glass at the other. All you had to do was look into the hole and in the tube turned to the light you saw a remarkable spectacle produced by multi-coloured bits of glass reflected in the walls of the mirrored prism. Permeated with light, these bits, transformed into precious stones, joined together at every turn of the tube, fell apart and then formed new designs. There were expensive kaleidoscopes with a metal tube covered with coloured leather and a lens which could be adjusted like a microscope; but the patterns inside were no more wonderful and one had to take good care of the instrument. On no account was one allowed to open up such a tube and examine its inside, whereas the life of a cheap kaleidoscope usually ended in such an operation. How amusing it was to spill the bits of glass into the palm of one's hand, those bits that a moment before had been rubies and sapphires!

A microscope was not a toy. Brother Isha inherited one from Albert, who had got a superior model, but in Isha's hands the old one served a more useful purpose than in the hands of its previous owner. Isha was so curious, he knew so much, he learnt such a lot outside his school lessons. But for the small boy that I then was a microscope was of course a toy and all the more magical because it was never given to me to hold. I can remember Isha carefully placing a speck of dust, taken from a cheese rind, on the glass, and myself waiting breathlessly while it was prepared. Then, shutting one eye and sticking the other to the cold metal, I would see a very frightening world of shaggy monsters, something like the nauseating creatures that peopled my nightmares. It made me wonder where these beasts lived and why God should have ever created them, and why He put them on something as delicious as gruyère cheese!

Probably few people now know what a praxinoscope means, but half a century ago it was the predecessor of the cinema. In fact the principle of the praxinoscope was the foundation of moving pictures. In its simplest form it is a cardboard drum with narrow, vertical slits, containing a ribbon on which is depicted a series of successive moments of action, a child with a skipping-rope or two men boxing. Only the part of the ribbon immediately opposite the viewer's eye is seen, so that as the drum is rotated the pictures flash by, melting into one another, and create the illusion of continuous movement. Some of the subjects on the ribbon were most ingenious, some were even terrifying, such as devils jumping out of a box and seizing a clown by the nose and a lamplighter climbing on the moon.

The zootrope is a variation of the praxinoscope.[1] The principle is the same, but what you see is not the ribbon itself but its reflection in the little mirrors that are placed criss-cross in the middle of the circle. Of the pictures of this kind, usually drawn as silhouettes, the one I remember best was a waltzing couple. The illusion that they were turning was complete, and they appeared to be almost three-dimensional. I liked this instrument particularly because it belonged in a way to the 'dwarf-world'. These Lilliputians danced to entertain me and I could remain for hours watching their performance.

But none of the optical toys enchanted me so much as the Magic Lantern. These two words evoke in me even now a special emotion, though in our house, in which Russian and French intermingled and we called many things by their foreign names, the expression 'Magic Lantern' was less in use than *Lanterne Magique* or *Lanterna Magica*.

The instrument we had was not of good quality, but it could project remarkable images on a blank white sheet in a dark room; and in days when the cinema had not been invented this was enough to provoke the wildest enthusiasm in the audience – and one composed not only of children. One had only to light a lamp which stood in a tin box, push a coloured slide in the passage between the lamp and the front tube, and pictures of immense size, beautifully coloured, appeared on the wall.

The fact that these performances took place in the dark added to the mysterious and magic character of this toy:

[1] I did not know any of these scientific terms when I was a child. All these instruments were 'turning wheels' to me.

darkness plunged one into the right mood. A dark room is a terrifying room. When I had to go alone through our dark ballroom in the evening I preferred to shut my eyes very tight and grope towards the door, for fear of seeing something that might make me die of fear. But round the Magic Lantern the terrifying, hostile darkness became desirable and alluring, no longer frightening to the children assembled in it. Encouraged by the sound of familiar voices, laughter, the outburst of a quarrel or suppressed giggling, one even dared to try and frighten someone else, to crawl up and suddenly seize a leg or pull a girl's plait of hair.

The preparations alone for a performance of the Magic Lantern were exciting. My elder brothers would set up the machine on a stool. A sheet was fixed to the wall and we, the audience, took our seats on chairs brought out of every corner, with some of us squatting on the floor in front. The tradition of the home demanded that the servants should also be present, especially the two maids, Stepanida and Olga Ivanovna. Had I then known anything about Greek tragedy I would have compared the part they played to that of a Greek chorus. They competed in expressions of admiration, astonishment or compassion at the pictures on the sheet, and even if they had seen them many times and knew them by heart their 'Ohs' and 'Ahs' increased our own excitement.

Finally the audience settled down, the small ones in front, the older ones behind. The lamp on the table in front of the sofa was taken into the next room and the doors were closely shut, so that the room seemed to sink into impenetrable darkness. Even before anything appeared on the sheet the air began to smell of soot, for the lamp in the lantern had an incorrigible habit of smoking, and the hot lacquer paint that covered the tin box also produced a strange smell; but these different aromas only added to the mysteriousness of the moment. Unfailingly the same scene was repeated before the performance began. Mamma pushed her head through the door and called out in an anxious voice: '*Mon Dieu, que cela sent mauvais!*' 'Take care, children, don't set the house on fire!' At this sober and sensible interference everybody protested, but at the same time we felt slightly elated: our sacrament was apparently connected with some danger! We were even able to set the house on fire; our black magic could end in a real, horrible catastrophe! This possibility was for some reason highly exhilarating.

Then a large circle of light appeared on the sheet and into it the first picture crept sideways, growing to enormous proportions. Shouts broke out. The usual mistake with the slide had occurred, and the image appeared upside down. The operators exchanged reproaches in an undertone; but thereafter all went smoothly and the illusion was maintained.

Our Magic Lantern performances usually began with the *Sleeping Beauty*. By the throne stands the Princess's cradle, surrounded by the King and Queen and several fairies. 'Those are good fairies,' brother Misha explains, though we have known this all along. But why do the fairies turn away from the baby and glare in horror in the opposite direction? The explanation is soon forthcoming, because as the fairies disappear into the corner on the left Fairy Carabosse appears from the right with a wart on her long hooked nose and her finger raised in a threatening gesture. Why, oh why has she been invited? Then comes the next episode. A hunchbacked witch, surrounded with flames, has raised her wand in a sinister way to work her cursed magic, while the other fairies and the royal parents implore her mercy in vain. The Princess at the first prick of her finger will fall asleep for a hundred years. But, alas, the story is interrupted by the most annoying gaps. For instance the Princess, grown into a striking beauty, enters the old woman's room while she is sitting at her spinning-wheel – but of the ensuing fatal scene all that remains is half the hand and the wheel, the rest having been destroyed when, on some other occasion, the slide fell on the floor. Again, the Prince ties up his horse at the gate of a castle overgrown with wild roses – but of the scene when he kisses the sleeping Princess all that is left is the top of the luxurious bed and her crowned head.

The fairy-tale part of the programme did not end there. After the *Sleeping Beauty*, stories of *Tom Thumb*, *Cinderella* and *Puss-in-Boots* glided across the bright circle. These slides had been bought recently; they were in good condition and shone with all their vivid colours. At the end of the fairy-tale series, a single picture was invariably shown: it was a slide that had survived from the days of my brothers' childhood. No one could remember to what story it belonged but this fragment produced a shattering impression. It was a funeral procession. Noble gentlemen and ladies in medieval costume walked in a dense crowd and behind them a coffin was borne shoulder-high. Who was lying in it nobody knew, but there was no doubt that it was a person of Royal blood, for crowned heads followed in its wake and a crown lay on the coffin. If Albert happened to be with us (in spite of his twenty years and his beard he enjoyed these performances as much as we did) he made his way on tiptoe to the piano, opened it noiselessly and softly played Chopin's 'Funeral March'. How much that music did to emphasize the solemn atmosphere!

The performance ended with a series of comic numbers and these slides showed all sorts of grotesque faces or else complete little scenes, some of them not only laughable but also terrifying. If you pulled the handle in the wooden frame of the slide the cook's head appeared on the dish he was carrying, while the pig's head moved from the dish to the top of the cook's fat body. Another slide depicted a boy skating happily on the ice, but when the handle was pulled he had disappeared into an icehole with only his legs sticking out of it. The most effective picture was the one showing a large fat merchant guzzling pancakes; one pancake after the other disappeared into his huge mouth and his belly swelled before our eyes. What laughter this primitive humour provoked among us! The children roared and our respectable Olga Ivanovna laughed almost more than anybody.

CHAPTER V

FAVOURITE BOOKS

*

THE first book in my life was certainly *Der Struwwelpeter* in the German edition. By an incredible piece of luck the original copy, which belonged to my brothers before me, has been preserved and I have it now in Paris. Once upon a time, more than eighty years ago, my *Struwwelpeter* lost its original cardboard cover, which was replaced by Papa's own creation in green marbled paper. The inside of the book is also not in mint condition; some pages are frayed, a whole page of one of the stories – the one about Johnny Head-in-Air – is missing. But as a child I had been so used to not knowing the beginning of that story, my imagination had adequately filled in with what led up to the moment when the absent-minded boy falls into the water of the canal, that I was a little disappointed when I read the full version of the story in a complete copy of the book.

What a wonderful book it is, though it is now discredited by specialists who consider it to be harmful to children. Its author was a children's doctor called Hoffmann (not to be confused with the famous romantic writer), who in order to amuse his little patients told them stories, embellishing them on the spot with primitive illustrations. The stories were collected and published and the success of the book has been astounding. Mothers, nannies and children themselves seized upon it, and the book since then has gone through innumerable reprints and been translated into many languages. There was a Russian version, but it was more of an adaptation into which specifically Russian characteristics were introduced. From the artistic point of view the illustrations in the Russian edition by Aghin, a well-known illustrator of the 1840s, are superior to those of the original.

The virtue of *Struwwelpeter* is that it is completely convincing. Many stories have been printed and illustrated to amuse and instruct the young, but none so stimulating to the child's imagination as the absurd and naïve legends which are contained in Dr Hoffmann's *Struwwelpeter*. The author of this book of genius never again succeeded in reaching the same superlative height of artistic creation. He wrote several other books, in which the illustrations are drawn with greater care, but none of them, though they are enchanting in their way (*Bastian der Faulpelz, Im Himmel und auf Erden*), can compare with the first creative effort of the good-natured Aesculapius.

Each character in *Struwwelpeter* has a real existence for me even now. In my childhood I believed that the street along which the good boy allowed himself to be led by his mother was our Big Morskaia Street, and that the canal into which the absent-minded boy tumbled was the Kriukov Canal beside our house. The front stairs where the lady appeared who forbade her son to suck his thumb were *our* stairs, and the door through which the terrifying tailor emerged was that of our neighbours, the Svetchinskys. It is the simple and universal character of these drawings that encourages the childish mind to supplement them from imagination. I would not have remembered *Struwwelpeter* as well as I do if the pictures had been more detailed. Besides, children have a flair for artistic truth although they have no idea what it means. In *Struwwelpeter* there is just that quality that appeals to the love of fantasy in a child, who can remain unaware of inaccuracies and absurdities while unconsciously correcting and adapting them according to his interpretation of life.

The subject matter of *Struwwelpeter* corresponds to a child's interests and in fact contains a kind of summary of real-life drama. The fact that it is presented in burlesque form does not make it less convincing and indeed softens the impact upon the imagination of impressions which might otherwise upset the child. The experts missed that when they discredited *Struwwelpeter*. A child is surrounded by plenty of cruelty and terror, even a child who leads a sheltered life – but there is a specific childish defence that protects him. sees everything differently, in his own modified way, and the most horrible sight can thereby become acceptable. It is this acceptable standard of horror to which the *Struwwelpeter* stories conform. Everything is terrifying, merciless, but the manner in which the story is presented, the childishness that exists in the author and pervades his picture, transform the terrifying and the cruel into something amusing without infringing on reality.

I have remained true all my life to my admiration for *Struwwelpeter*. If the impressions of some classical paintings – of Raphael in particular – helped to form my permanent aesthetic attitudes, *Struwwelpeter* inculcated in me the capacity of feeling and sensing truth, particularly artistic truth. It was upon the basis of *Struwwelpeter* that I came to admire Ludwig Richter, G. Doré, W. Busch, Oberländer, and, later, Chodowiecki, Menzel and Breughel, the Dutch and French primitives, the Italian painters of the Quattrocento, Rembrandt, etc. Any falsehood in art is deeply repugnant to me, though given an inner truth I am ready to forgive any discrepancies and mistakes.

Three other books were equally faithful companions of my childhood. The first brought me into touch with my friend Harlequin, the second introduced me into the realm of music, while the third transported me into the divine clarity and harmony of the ancient classical world. I cannot recall the name of the first. It disappeared from our household when I was still a child and although I tried to find it later in second-hand bookshops I did not succeed. It must be a bibliographic rarity. But I remember distinctly each separate picture and, so far as one can trust childish memories, I believe the pictures had something in common with Daumier. There is no doubt that they were coloured lithographs.[1] Of the many pranks of Harlequin (the book is devoted to them), I particularly remember one. In the first picture Harlequin is busy preparing a malicious joke which involves a rope stretched across a street, while from afar one can see the figure of Cassandra slowly approaching the fatal spot; in the second picture Harlequin, hiding round the corner, pulls the string and the venerable old man, caught unawares, falls headlong over it. Other pranks, like stealing food, have a more criminal character and the story ends disastrously. Harlequin is tried and sentenced to be hanged, but fortunately the hangman in a moment of compassion frees him from the noose. In the last picture we see Harlequin, wearing a black mask on his face so that no one shall recognise him, running as fast as he can across a field; in the distance is the gallows with a bundle of rags hanging down from it.

I would like to expatiate a little here on my adoration of the strange character of Harlequin. I used to dream of him; indeed, I longed to become Harlequin myself. I worshipped the little Harlequin which was among the puppets my grandmother brought me from Venice. Even now I remain faithful to Harlequin, in spite of the vulgarity to which he has been reduced in modern times, because of the deep impression made upon me by that book: the impression of a young and adorable creature like a good fairy. Later, when I understood the rôle he played in Italian comedy, I was upset and even affronted on behalf of my hero.

---

[1] These lines had been written before by a real miracle I found the book at a book pedlar's at Fontainebleau. It is called *Fourberies d'Arlequin* and the charming illustrations are by Baric.

Harlequin – with a beard! Harlequin – a beggar! Harlequin in the guise of an ugly negro! Still, it is not unreasonable to assume that under the ugly black mask, the black chin or the beard is concealed the same poetical figure of my mischievous charmer, that indeed the rascal is not devoid of noble feelings. When I saw the fairies showering favours on him at funfairs and even giving him a magic wand, I was not surprised in the least and considered that Harlequin was getting only his due.

There were many illustrated books in Papa's library, but in the days of my early childhood most of them inspired me only with respect not far removed from distaste. I was particularly hostile to the huge architectural folders containing plans and designs. But there were several books that I liked and repeatedly asked to be shown. Among my first favourites were *The Adventures of Violedamour* and *Dushenka*, two Russian books that consisted of pictures with separately printed text on pages of a different size. But I did not really need the text. I never took the trouble to read the story about Violedamour by 'Cossack Lugansky', and although I later read the text of Bogdanovich's *Dushenka*, I was certainly not so impressed by it as by Count Feodor Tolstoy's illustrations. After seeing them the story seemed to me rather silly and vulgar.

The illustrations of *Violedamour* were by the clever and observant amateur artist, Sapojhnikoff, who published these original lithographs in the 1830s. It was through this series of illustrations that I became deeply impressed by Gogol's Petersburg even before I connected it with any particular period. This is the story. Violedamour, whose parents considered him a musical genius, learned to play a variety of musical instruments; but in spite of this he was pursued by the most cruel misfortune to the end of his life. He did not even get a proper grave, for he died a pauper in the streets and there was only a hillock to mark the place of his eternal rest. His faithful dog – oh, how I loved that Archet – whom Violedamour had once saved from drowning as a puppy, did not wish to survive its unfortunate master and died on the spot where he was buried.

In my childhood I disliked all sad stories and I especially loathed those with which the Russian teachers of the time instructed the young with the purpose of developing in them compassion and other noble sentiments. Instinctively I sensed the falsehood and hypocrisy of these writings and protested when one of the grown-ups tried to read them aloud to me. But *Violedamour* was different. In the first place it was a book for grown-ups; and secondly it was a funny story, with laughter through the tears, or rather tears through laughter. I was very sorry for Violedamour, but the story had not been invented to inspire pity and that was not the intention of the illustrator either. He wanted to portray reality, and he did so by taking all his subjects straight from life and selecting those that were commonplace and ordinary. I was particularly amused by the scenes which depicted Violedamour playing one instrument after another, each time provoking a noisy reaction from his vociferous dog. The episode of Violedamour's concert was also a memorable one. His friends tried to get the passers-by to take tickets, even using persuasion at the point of a gun. But when the unfortunate virtuoso finally appeared on the platform before a distinguished audience in an elegant tailcoat, his hair waved in the latest fashion, his appearance provoked indignation instead of enthusiasm, for the poor fellow had caught a violent cold before the concert and instead of a melody all the audience could hear was coughing and sneezing.

The love story was equally breathtaking. It described poor Violedamour's efforts to see through the keyhole into the apartment of his beloved, and how he was suddenly struck on the nose by the door opening to let out his lucky rival. But the picture before which I trembled most was of Violedamour's preparations for suicide. In order to invest his end with a poetical atmosphere, the unrecognised genius hung his room with crêpe draperies and, putting on a large-brimmed hat with a mourning band like a funeral torchbearer, he sat down in the coffin and prepared to write his own Requiem with an expression of tragic exaltation.

This shows how the aesthetic idea of death both attracted and frightened me as a child to a remarkable extent. Even in the lighthearted series of the Tolstoy illustrations to Bogdanovich's *Dushenka*, in which this poetic Russian artist through his wonderful creations permeated with the Hellenic spirit rises high above his literary inspirer, I was most drawn to the scene when Dushenka meets Death. I was captivated by everything in this symphony of Paradise – the women, the sweetness of love, the images of the realm of Venus, Olympus, the abode of Cupid. But the moment of genius is contained in the terrible threat of the inevitable end that everyone has to face, when Dushenka, in despair at having lost her husband Cupid by her own fault, implores upon her knees the bald-headed, bony scarecrow to cut off her head with his scythe – the scythe with which he mows down the grass and flowers of the fields that incarnate everything alive in this world.

It might seem that such books were hardly suitable to give to a boy of four or five – though when I say give I do not use the right word, because my small hands were unable to pick up or hold such a huge volume as *Dushenka* which was more than a yard wide. It was not given to me to hold; Papa would place the volume on the table and sit me down on a chair before it on top of a pile of cushions. This manoeuvre was generally accompanied by a short argument between my parents. Mamma did not think it right that I should look at such pictures '*qui pourraient lui donner des idées*'. And she was right; I was not impervious to the sight of Dushenka entering the water naked at the bathing house, or lying without any clothes in the arms of her husband under a canopy held by winged cherubs. Though knowing nothing about the pleasures of love and having a very limited idea of sex, I must have absorbed a certain amount of their poison. But if one looks at the matter from another point of view, Papa, though hardly aware of the danger, was also right in his way. In his heart he must have realised that by looking at these pictures I was preparing a foundation upon which to build my artistic development.

A few of my other favourite books were *Les Contes de Perrault*, Emile Souvestre, Madame d'Aulnoy, Hans Andersen, Baron Münchhausen, and the novels of the Comtesse de Ségur. When I reached the age of ten I turned to the novels of Fenimore Cooper, Daniel Defoe's *Robinson Crusoe* and Jules Verne's *Twenty Thousand Leagues under the Sea*, which was the first book I read without any outside assistance.

I loved most of the Hans Andersen tales, but not those with a moral. Some of them I did not like at all, though Mamma, out of educational and moral considerations, tried to explain to me the beautiful thoughts they contained. But his less well-meaning stories, like *The Brave Tin Soldier* and particularly *The Mermaid*, were among and still are among my very favourite stories. Their strange mixture of sad drama and of something radiant and magical made them particularly touching.

In the *Tin Soldier* (as in *Gulliver* or in Hoffmann's *Nutcracker*) I loved the charm of the miniature toy world. In *The Mermaid* it was the combination of sweet and bitter that enchanted me, and that blending of all worlds which is particularly agreeable to the young. The underwater world was the one that attracted me most; often when bathing in the Finnish Gulf I would risk swallowing water by remaining too long below the surface, as I imagined myself in the realm of Neptune and his lovely daughters. I was not at all perturbed by the thought that they had fishes' tails instead of feet: on the contrary, these appendages added considerably to the charm of creatures in whose existence I believed implicitly.

Altogether I was avid for anything exotic or eerie and terrifying in my childhood, and even in later years. My fondness for E. Th. A. Hoffmann, whom I came across when I was fifteen, was due to this inclination, as well as my liking for *Le Foyer Breton* by E. Souvestre, in which his Breton legends typify the *Juste Milieu* period. I do not know whether I preferred Souvestre's stories or the adorable illustrations by Penguilly, one of the finest draughtsmen of the Romantic period, now unjustly forgotten. Some of the illustrations have left an indelible impression on me, particularly one of a beautiful lady tied to the skeleton of her husband; and another of a Breton peasant pursued by a whirl of tiny sprites; and yet another of a coffin by the bed in the room where a traveller had settled down for the night. These scenes came back to me when I was sleepless; I would bury my head deep in my pillow to shut out the sight of those fierce bogies and the coffin surrounded by candles.

I derived a quite different kind of pleasure from the comic and humorous, though this is such a large field that I am unable to list all that please me most. I will simply give four names: Baron Münchhausen, a literary liar of genius; and three humorous artists, Bertall, Busch and Oberländer.

The combination of the last three names is permissible only from the child's angle, because the three had the same effect on me at that time; but from the artistic point of view of course their quality is not comparable. Bertall is a pleasant and amusing French draughtsman who produced a few charming books like *Misha, the Absent-minded Boy*, and *Gosha of the Long Arms*. I do not know the French titles; as a child I had the Russian translations, produced in Paris. Both are very funny stories and the illustrations done with a quick pencil are rich and full of life; but they are nevertheless mere illustrations for children. Busch and Oberländer are quite a different matter. What can I say about these two colossi of humour? I could compare them, perhaps, to Dicky Doyle, a contributor to *Punch*, and Gustave Doré; yet Busch rises high above them all. Busch was undoubtedly a man of genius, equal in stature as a designer to Daumier, and as a writer to Swift and Rabelais. His work is permeated with laughter, but under the laughter lurks the element of tragedy – a wonderful combination, all the more so because it can be perceived naturally, without effort.

Many modern educationists dislike Busch even more than *Struwwelpeter*, but it seems to me that there is no better book of life than the one portrayed by Busch. It was not without good reason that the Germans published his complete works as a code to behaviour and called it the *Home Treasure*. But I do not wish to launch into a discussion of Busch's flaws or qualities, and will content myself with expressing my deep-felt gratitude to this friend of my childhood who has remained a friend until my old age. I wonder what I would have become, what my conception of life would have been and how I would have dealt with it, had I not been influenced by this buffoon, this wise jester with his remarkable gift of creating in a few strokes of his pencil the most magical images and likenesses that ever took possession of one's imagination.

My first acquaintance with Busch was through the *Münchener Bilderbogen*, and in its picture pages I also got to know Oberländer and many new and valuable things, including the history of costume which was to be so useful to me in the future. My father used to give me these separate folios of the Munich publication, beautifully coloured, on every possible occasion, either at Christmas or on my birthday or when I was ill. He would take great care that I should not damage them in any way. As soon as I had had a look at them he stuck them on a piece of cardboard, one folio to each side, and these cardboards were preserved in a special folder. One side might display a story illustrated by Busch or Oberländer, or a charming story by Steub about the trained poodle, Caro; and on the other side there might be something instructive, like scenes from ancient history or the life of the Red Indians. The funny side usually had the greater success, but the other was not overlooked and in this way I gradually assimilated valuable knowledge presented in a painless form. These useful pictures were well composed and coloured, and were accurately documented without being pedantic. An imitation of the Munich folios was published, I believe, in Stuttgart, in a slightly more academic version.

This list of my favourite books and pictures might lead the reader to believe that German culture dominated our home. This would not be surprising when one remembers that my grandmother on my father's side was a German, a Petersburg German, and that a large part of Petersburg society at that time had a preference for everything German. Moreover, the aristocracy and bourgeoisie entrusted the education of their children to German governesses, recruited mainly from the Baltic provinces. Nevertheless, it would be wrong to deduce that German culture was predominant in our home. Though Papa loved the purely German atmosphere of *Gemütlichkeit*, though we did have German governesses, though Mamma in spite of her Italian origin *faisait grand cas* of German educational methods, the general direction of our cosmopolitan family veered more to the French side. Our parents constantly sprinkled their conversation with French sentences, they wrote letters more easily in French, and we were taught to say our prayers in French. Two of my brothers were enthusiasts about France and the French; they even considered it their duty (probably under the influence of the Franco-Prussian war which broke out soon after they had reached the age of reason) to hate the Germans and all things German. As for me, before I became a convinced and inveterate cosmopolitan who despised ugly and absurd national prejudices, in my childhood and youth I used to be in turn a Francophile, a Germanophile, an Italophile and a Russophile. The last was probably predominant, but I was unaware of it and at times even regarded my Russian nationality as a little shaming. I could not bear Russian children's books except *Violedamour* and *Dushenka* (which were not really children's books). I was irritated by the poor quality of their illustrations and by the sloppy sentimental style mainly favoured by Russian writers for the young.

I learnt about English children's books (not counting the translations and adaptations of *Gulliver* and *Robinson Crusoe*) when I began to learn English, particularly from my second English governess – an odd little old woman looking exactly like the bad fairies painted by Bertall and Doré but whom I remember with great tenderness. It was Miss Evans who enriched my library with English books like Caldecott, Kate Greenaway, Dickens, Marryat. I liked particularly the delightful illustrations by Caldecott to the classic story, *The House That Jack Built*, and *Pictures of English History*, which I still possess. Almost all the pictures in this last book (there are four on each page) represent a murder, a war scene or an execution. That was what I liked about them, as well as the bright colours of the costumes and the atmosphere of the landscapes. Some of them are so vivid in my memory that it is an effort for me to visualise King Alfred, or Shakespeare standing in front of Queen Elizabeth, other than the way they are, rather naïvely, represented in these pictures. I also became acquainted with the delightful style of English designers when I bought, for a mere song at the Palm Sunday market, a book with the story of *The Yellow Dwarf*. It was a Russian edition, but the full-page coloured illustrations were printed in London. Now I know that these pictures (among which I thought the most beautiful was a double-page featuring an incident between fairies and turkey-cocks) came from the pen and brush of Walter Crane, and though my liking for him did not last, I am still grateful to him for the joy he gave me as a boy in Russia. If I am not mistaken, buying that book was my first independent gesture as a bibliophile, and I must say in justice that it was a credit to my taste.

CHAPTER VI

MUSIC AND PICTORIAL ART

*

THOUGH all the plastic and visual arts, even architecture, gave me immense delight in my childhood, music, perhaps, aroused my deepest emotions. My most vivid early impressions were not of pictures but of music. Very early in life I began to feel the urge for personal expression in this way. The piano was irresistible to me and what my fingers drew from it was spontaneous, whereas my drawing was often premeditated and self-conscious.

During my life I have had many opportunities to observe the effect of music on children; but I have never seen a child react to it with such sensitiveness and exaltation as I myself did in my early childhood. As soon as someone started playing the piano three-year-old Shourenka, whatever he might be doing at the time, would drop it and make a mad dash towards the sound. And in our house not only the piano, but the violin, the viola, the harmonium and other instruments were constantly in use. We often had evening concerts at home and then nothing would induce me to go to sleep. All the family played some sort of instrument, my parents, my brothers, my sisters, and cousins and friends of both sexes. Nothing produced in me so overwhelming an emotion as my brother Albert's improvisations at the piano. His own original style of playing went through me like an electric shock: I was entranced, transported to a different plane and floated in a different sphere. Sometimes Albert, who was very gentle with me, would use his gift to illustrate the stories that he himself invented, and under its spell I sometimes felt almost faint as I listened to the melody and harmony of my brother's musical illustrations. My mental images of the story grew in vividness through the music; I wallowed in bliss as it conjured up for me magic castles and gardens; a shiver would run down my spine when loud and dramatic music prepared me for horrors and devilry. I knew that any movement, any action, walking, running, pursuit, flight, swimming, a storm, could be represented by sounds in the same way that music could convey the emotions of evil, fear, joy, laughter, grief, prayer, damnation. And here was I, a favourite of fortune indeed, presented with this gift in all its freshness while the images were actually being born. Albert hardly ever repeated himself, and never completely; his musical ideas, if not always aspiring to higher things, were always new.

But besides Albert's will-o'-the-wisp music, I knew and loved pieces of a more stable and established kind. I cannot say that I then showed very exclusive taste: on the contrary, as well as famous pieces I also liked the most ordinary Russian and foreign tunes. Papa had to play military marches and Russian folk songs for me, play by ear with his own variations. Mamma had her own programme, which included a piece remembered from her schooldays in the Smolni Institute. My sisters played the overtures of Mozart and Bellini as duets, and I forced my godmother, Masha Andersen, to play *Russlan* to me; and my brother Leontij, who adored Italian music, imitated in a masterly way the style of various Nicolinis, Cotonis and other singers in the masterpieces of Rossini, Donizetti and Verdi.

As a child my two favourite pieces were *Le Reveil du Lion* by Kontsky, a modern composition for four hands, and the Bach-Gounod *Ave Maria*, which cousin Sasha played on the harmonium and Albert on the violin.

My family were amused by my musical memory, and by my attitude to music. Knowing that I was busy in one of the back rooms my sisters would start playing *Le Reveil du Lion*, and however faint the distant sound of their playing, I would relinquish my drawing, my tin soldiers or my favourite picture book and rush along the passage to the ballroom so as to arrive at the moment when, after the overture, the bright, exhilarating music indicated the advance of the lion in the desert. Since then I have heard many finer pieces of music, some of which have induced in me an urge for plastic expression (the desire to dance when I hear music is alive in me even now); but nothing ever moved me so irresistibly to heroic ecstasy as did *Le Reveil du Lion*, that flimsy little piece which now seems so banal and commonplace!

On the other hand, when I was five, *Ave Maria* awakened in me an infinitely sweet emotion. In my imagination I saw angels floating in the sky, then the sky opening up and a soft light pouring from the clouds, on which, as in Raphael's pictures, God sat with His company of saints. These mental images filled me with sweet languor, a heavenly sense of joy. Fortunately none of my family ever broke this spell by criticising *Ave Maria*; no one accused Gounod of sacrilege for daring to superimpose his melody on to the work of the great Bach. The voice of carping criticism was never raised in our simple household where works of art were appreciated for whatever way they appealed to one's soul. What, indeed, is music for if it is not for such emotional experience?

I must mention my music teachers, though it would take too much room to refer to all of them. I will name only three: my sister-in-law Masha (Albert's wife), the pianist Mazurkievicz and my cousin, Nettinka Khrabro-Vassilevsky. It was natural, when such a wonderful professional musician as my sister-in-law, Maria Benois, came to live with us, that she should suggest to Mamma that she teach me music. Mamma gladly agreed, and I too was very eager to learn. I sat down for my first lesson convinced that I would soon be able to play like Masha.

But the very first lesson ended with a minor tragedy and I went away disappointed and disgruntled. Masha was too impatient, too exacting in the matter of details, and I could not bear to be spoken to in such a tone of voice. The second lesson ended with shouting on her part, tears and fury on mine, and Mamma's rather inefficient intervention. The whole arrangement was dropped after the third lesson. For quite a time afterwards I even hated Masha and considered her to be an enemy and a traitor. Now, looking back (and how far back!), I still believe that she was in the wrong. She tried to teach me as she had been taught by her stern father, Carl Kind, who would allow no joking about music; whereas with me she should have tried first to inspire confidence, awaken my interest and make the lesson amusing.

It was the same story all over again with the unfortunate Mazurkiewicz – I say unfortunate because he was a handsome Pole who had lost a leg in a railway accident. He was a skilled pianist and at first his playing used to enchant me. I was also desperately sorry for him and I swore to myself that I would never upset the poor cripple and would obey him in everything. Oh, that poor, lonely leg; those crutches which he handled so dexterously, first leaning them against the piano and afterwards gathering them up and inserting them under his arms; that limp of his, and the sound of the rubber tips of the crutches on the floor: it was all so pathetic that it touched my heart with pity. All went well at first, but at the fifth lesson the same disaster occurred. Mazurkiewicz, convinced that I was unable to grasp the principle of rhythm, lost his temper and reprimanded me severely. All my good intentions vanished. I grew stubborn, I hated him, and after ten lessons he had to give up for I declared that I would not have him as a teacher. I admit that I wept as I was making my announcement – but only out of pity for my unfortunate teacher.

Then my cousin Nettinka took over the part of teacher.

97

She was really my cousin, though the difference in our ages was over forty years. But because she was my cousin and not my aunt I had no respect for her, although I loved her dearly. Nettinka, who was no beauty, was nevertheless a very pleasant woman, good-natured, radiant and gay. She had little reason to be: she had had a hard life, for her husband turned out to be a bad lot and had left her without any means to provide for a large family. It was her remarkable gift for music that rescued her from this difficult situation. She earned her living by giving music lessons and by playing dance music at balls. In the 1880s she was quite a celebrity in Petersburg; she had more engagements than she could fulfil, and there was always a queue waiting to engage her as a pianist at their dances, for she played dance music divinely. The dates of dances would be changed if Nettinka was otherwise engaged.

This musical gift was the reason for my adoration of her, but as a music teacher she proved inadequate. I was always glad to see her, but my playing did not progress at all. This time it was not a matter of incompatibility, but because both she and I approached the matter of lessons with a certain cynicism. By a tacit understanding we made a game of my lessons during the five years that they lasted. We sat for the appointed time at the piano; I did my exercises and played a few pieces; the lesson even ended in our playing a duet. But during this performance I cheated, and she covered up my cheating. She did this by playing my own part in every duet as well as hers, so that I could memorise it. Then, instead of making sure that I had grasped the essentials, she was quite content if I appeared to be making progress, although in fact I had no idea of musical notation, or tempo, or how to read a score. I succeeded in playing at speed the pieces I learnt by ear, enriching them with improvisations, but I remained as I was, a musical ignoramus, unaware of the meaning of musical language. I believe, however, that Nettinka herself was not far from being that. With her, too, everything depended on memory and ear, on instinct and inspiration, more than on knowledge. But how beautifully she used her gifts; how wonderfully she played valses, mazurkas, polonaises, quadrilles, often in her own somewhat fantastic but always effective variations. She had composed two complete pieces: one a dashing gallop on the theme of Ponchielli's *Gioconda*, and a ravishing variation of a valse from *Eugene Onegin*.

Who were the favourite composers of my adolescence? I did not have any in particular, I think, though there were many pieces that I adored, chiefly arias from operas and especially from *Faust*, which was considered the king of operas in those days. Even Albert, who was indifferent to music other than his own (and even that he had no respect for), loved *Faust* and knew it by heart from beginning to end. After *Faust* came *Aida*, *Rigoletto* (which I did not like half as much as *La Traviata* and *Il Trovatore*), *Wilhelm Tell*, the *Barbier de Seville*, a little later *Le Roi de Lahore* and later still Rubinstein's *Nero*. But the first musical compositions that drove me quite crazy were *Carmen* when it reached Petersburg in 1882 or 1883 and the ballet *Coppelia* in 1884. Thanks to my memory I could play most of that music by heart. I also learnt the overture of *Tannhäuser* (I heard the whole opera much later), the valses of Liszt on Schubert's themes and his rhapsodies, the mazurkas, *études* and ballades of Chopin, and finally Schumann's *Carneval*. I worshipped all these. On the other hand, although I got to know a lot of Beethoven, his music was always alien to me. I felt no enthusiasm for serious classical music and I knew nothing of Russian music, apart from the polonaise and mazurka out of *Life for the Tsar* by Glinka and his 'Chernomor' from *Russlan*. So I experienced a real revolution in taste when I heard Wagner's *Ring* in 1889 and the works of Tchaikovsky, Rimsky-Korsakov and Borodin in 1890.

Among the many singers whom I heard in childhood and adolescence were the Italians, Masini (the most wonderful tenor I ever heard), Cotogni, Uetam, and Devoyod, and Nielsen, Repetto, M. Durand, Sembrich and Ferni-Germano, the last, in spite of her physical unattractiveness, was the ideal Carmen. Two of the famous pianists I heard were the great virtuoso Essipova, and Anton Rubinstein, whose playing is in my view still unsurpassed. I regret that I heard him only three times, but these three performances are unforgettable. It was truly inspired playing. He often 'fluffed', played wrong notes, added passages of his own, but even the most familiar and hackneyed pieces took on a new and exultant life under his fat, apparently clumsy fingers. I liked his whole appearance, his half-closed eyes, the mop of hair, and his curious combination of the athletic and the feminine. What a strange figure he was! What a charmer! How ably he portrayed a sweet simplicity when making up to ladies – I often watched him at that game when he came to visit my sister-in-law. He was the sun of the musical world: there is no other way of describing him. Nevertheless I cannot forgive him for the part he played in the destruction of the splendid Bolshoi Theatre building, which had been assigned as a gift to the Conservatoire of which he was the founder.

There is a family legend that when I was eighteen months old I was offered a pencil which I seized and held at once with the fingers folded around it in the correct way.[1] Everybody saw in this an augury that I would be an artist. I believe I have indeed inherited an artistic gift; and in any case the artistic atmosphere of our house, the artistic inclinations of almost all those around me, and the fact that Papa made me draw when I was not yet one year old, must

[1] No doubt only relatively correct.

have combined to direct me towards art from my very
cradle. Unfortunately my early artistic efforts were to a
certain extent nullified by my precocious ambition. As
soon as I became at all aware of what I was doing, I stopped
drawing for the love of it and instead consciously aimed at
success. I had to surprise people, to provoke admiration, to
satisfy my hunger for approval. I looked about for striking
and unusual subjects and thus lost even in my very early
drawings that spontaneity and quality of freshness which
gives most pleasure in children's works.

This does not mean, however, that I worked only to show
off. I still drew mostly for my own pleasure, but often,
especially in the presence of strangers or guests who wanted
to please my parents by admiring my cleverness, I did put
on an act and flaunted my gift, which left a mark upon my
later artistic development. Many years were to pass before
I realised the absurdity of an ambition that prevented me
from doing anything really worthy of my talent and gave
me no personal satisfaction, even though I had a living
example before my eyes of the proper approach to art in my
father. But in spite of my delight in Papa's drawings and in
my brothers' water-colours, I could not help treating them
with a certain superciliousness: it was the attitude of a
five-year-old nonentity who, ever since the age of three, had
been declared another Raphael who was to startle the world
with his work.

I mention the name of Raphael Santi not rhetorically but
deliberately, because it was the first name among all the
names of artists that I remembered, his Vatican compositions in the reproductions at the Academy of Arts having
made such an impression on me. They were all copies in
the original size made by the best Russian artists – Bryullov,
Bruni, Bassin, Borispoltz and others.

The first time I went into the Raphael room in the
Academy I was overwhelmed by the huge pictures I saw;

the 'Bolsen Mass', the 'Athenian School', the 'Expulsion of Heliodorus', 'St Peter Freed from Prison'. Papa explained the subjects to me very clearly, but I was not interested: to me it was their beauty that mattered. Indeed, even at three or four years old I was completely overwhelmed by my admiration of these works, and a feeling of sacred indignation was aroused in me whenever I became aware of the indifference of others to what seemed to me so disturbing, so supernaturally beautiful.

I was especially fascinated by the kneeling figures in Raphael's *Messa di Bolsena*. I could not imagine anything more noble than the side view of the Swiss officer in the lower right-hand corner of the picture: the beauty of that figure did not lie in the features nor in the splendour of the clothes, but in something indefinable which is the essence of beauty.

I did not need to wander in the rooms of the Academy to satisfy my passion for Raphael. I could indulge it at home. At that time a publication appeared in Italy of large-sized prints of all Raphael's paintings in the Stanze in the Vatican and tapestries woven from them. Papa used to receive this publication regularly, from a funny little bald old man, who worked on a commission basis. He also supplied us with real Italian macaroni, Chianti wine in straw bottles and excellent oranges. I loved him for all this, but to my shame I do not remember the name of this modest and gentle Signore, whom Papa always welcomed with warm expressions of friendships (Mamma was more restrained, as she did not very much encourage Papa's artistic follies). I am particularly ashamed, because the old man used to bring me the most exotic presents. There were, for instance, walnuts fashioned out of papier-mâché, each half containing a little chapel with altar, candles, flowers and cherubs made of finely carved ivory – a perennial delight. You closed it and it looked like any other walnut;

you opened it to find an intricate miniature world inside. These wonders, made in an Italian monastery, were unfortunately soon destroyed after getting into my hands, for I was unable to resist the temptation of poking my fingers into their frail insides to find what was behind the altar and why the windows, lined with red, seemed to be ablaze. Obviously after such an application of brute force nothing remained but fragments.

Every new issue of Raphael prints (they appeared twice or three times a year and the publication stopped, I think, in 1880) was greedily perused by the whole family. Everything superfluous was removed from Papa's writing desk, the black oilcloth that covered it was carefully wiped and the new folios were displayed on it with suitable solemnity, each covered with transparent paper. When all the pictures of the latest issue had been examined, Papa put them away in a huge folder he had made himself especially for them, and there they remained in safety. Nobody was allowed to touch that folder without Papa's permission.

In the end Raphael became such a by-word with us and I myself was so convinced that I was Raphael reincarnated that I decided one day to prove it indisputably. We all did a lot of copying in the family, including my sisters: indeed Katia was such an expert that she took orders for copies in the Kushelev Gallery of pictures of sweetish painters of the middle of the nineteenth century. So why should I not copy a Raphael ? I never doubted that I could do so with absolute precision.

At my request Papa extracted from the lilac folder the reproduction of the *Messa di Bolsena*, pinned it on to a large board, settled it on an easel and sat me down on a stool in front of it.

I was then five years old, and it was a long time since I had drawn little circles with two sticks underneath and a bayonet at the side and imagined that I was drawing soldiers:

it was even some time since the circles had become animated with eyes and noses, with legs attached to bodies instead of straight on to the heads, and with buttons on those bodies, and since bayonets had been thrust into hands that nevertheless looked more like rakes. There had been rapid development since that stage; my drawings had become elaborate and coherent: horses had put in an appearance – or what I thought were horses; there were explosions of bombs, guns that fired showers of bullets, battle scenes. Under my brother Isha's influence knights began to appear in my pictures, in helmets and visors with lances and spears in their hands, riding caparisoned steeds which were both easier to draw than uncovered horses and more effective. One day I even tried to draw a portrait of Papa (sister Katia had just done one), but I was upset when it did not quite come off. I achieved some likeness, it is true, because both Papa and the portrait had side-whiskers and eyes concealed behind spectacles, so the family as usual was in raptures. In short, I had already made some headway and, drunk with praise, could really imagine that I was another Raphael. That is when I suffered my first great disappointment.

I began by copying reasonably well the semicircle that enclosed the composition from above, and the square outline of the window below, but failure came when I started on the first figure. After a few minutes of drawing I grew quite limp and terribly tired, sweat stood out on my forehead and a flush appeared on my cheeks. I felt ashamed, resenting the fact that nothing came of my efforts, and angry with Raphael for being such a hard nut to crack. Still, I believe that this failure actually did me a lot of good. For the first time I realised that art was difficult; for the first time I looked at a picture not only with admiration but also with reverence.

Unfortunately, so it seems to me now, this failure of mine

was not put to good enough use at the time. After inspecting my efforts, my brothers Albert and Leontij merely said to me: 'You should draw from nature, Shoura.' They themselves set me a practical example: Albert painted realistic pictures from nature while Leontij created fantasies from natural themes. But this advice only irritated me, for I saw nothing special in nature at the time and was much more inclined to paint soldiers and knights. Although I took great delight in nature as only the young can, I felt no urge to reproduce it.

Unconsciously my mind registered many subjects that deserved to be reproduced on paper or represented in colour, but I was not consciously aware of their value. *Night in the Ukraine* by Kuindji, which found shelter with us for a time, first revealed to me the poetical value of landscape. Looking at the fathomless dark sky, the flicker of light in the small hut whose white walls shone with a phosphorescent glow, I became aware of the poetry of the picture as well as of its exquisite skill. But at that time I would not have dared to try anything of the same kind, and having understood, after a number of failures, how difficult all this was, I preferred, with increasing doubt in final success, to paint anything that came into my head, either inventing comic stories (the repercussions of my enthusiasm for Busch and Dicky Doyle) or trying out more impressive compositions of a historical character.

The colossal impression made on me by Schnorr's Bible inspired me to depict stories from the Gospels, and one of my copybooks devoted to the Creation was carefully kept by the headmistress of my kindergarten until she died. The text and illustrations of a *Histoire de France* for children made me familiar with the appearance of Francis I, Henry IV and Louis XIV; conventional portraits, it is true, but all the more enchanting to a child's imagination. As a result I tried to reproduce on a large scale imaginary portraits of them which I gave my father either for Christmas or for his birthday. My visits to the opera also added their effects: my heroes invariably had a little goatee beard – *de rigueur* with the tenors of the time – and wore lace at the bottom of their trousers. As for the drawing lessons which I endured at the kindergarten under the supervision of the nice, dim, soft-hearted artist, Lemoch, they were of course a dull and futile waste of time.

No doubt my passion for the theatre was largely responsible for my later artistic development. I remember among these early theatrical experiments a décor painted with a generous brush, in brownish colours, representing *a learned study* with a crocodile hanging from the ceiling, and also *a dark forest* in which I liked the scale of greens and browns. Another theatrical experiment in which I took much pride at that time was a sort of theatrical *maquette* representing Europeans in a battle with Zulus. (The Prince Imperial had just lost his life in Africa.) It consisted of a row of figures surrounded by palms and shrubs, drawn with ink, coloured and carefully cut out, stuck to a cardboard representing the earth with grass growing on it. It seemed to me that I had not only succeeded in expressing the movement of the figures and the cruelty and fear on the faces of the warriors, but that I had achieved a most harmonious effect with the colours by laying them on transparently within the outlines of ink.

From the beginning of the 1880s I drew and painted progressively less (I had been painting only with water-colours; oil paints were not used in our house after Sister Katia left it). These years, however, were not wasted. Raphael continued to be a dominant worship, but as something exceptional, to be glorified in his entirety and never to be analysed. I approved of other artists for definite aspects of their work – clever brushwork, effects of light and shade, composition (as, for instance, the illustrations by Neville in Jules Verne's *Twenty Thousand Leagues Under the Sea* or the Doré illustrations to La Fontaine's *Fables*). Colour began to impress me in a positive as well as a negative sense, independently of what the picture represented. At an exhibition in the Academy I was charmed by *The Fun-Fair* and the *Removal of the Carpet* of K. Makovski. In the Kushelev Gallery I admired pictures by German, French and Flemish painters of the middle of the nineteenth century.[1] Other pictures moved me, sometimes deeply, by their subjects. I was entranced by Delaroche's picture, *Cromwell in front of Charles's grave*; I could gaze for hours at *Night in the Ukraine* by Kuindji, which I have already described. What enchanted me most (in reproduction, for I did not go to the Hermitage till 1883) was Bryullov's *Last Days of Pompeii*, and it seemed incredible to me that Papa could have known personally such a divine genius! To me, Bryullov was almost a Raphael. Then, in 1881, brother Leontij brought back a lot of photographs from a journey abroad, and for the first time I was moved to the bottom of my heart by the sad eyes, the frail bodies and the shy, chaste movements of Sandro Botticelli's Madonnas, and by the frescoes of Michelangelo in the Sixtine Chapel.

I began to refer more often to the books on the lower shelf of Papa's yellow book-case, examining them carefully and assiduously. From them I learnt the significance of architectural monuments, the history of costume and other matters of cultural and historical interest, and also what various famous people looked like – musicians, writers, philosophers. I gazed avidly at the quite tolerable reproductions of splendid works of painting and sculpture. In 1883 my brother Leontij gave me a popular *History of Art*, by René Ménard, which I studied very thoroughly.

As well as the *Magasin Pittoresque* and the *History of Art*, I gathered my impressions and my knowledge from various

[1] All these pictures have been in the Hermitage since 1920.

other sources: from the review *The Bee*; from several copies of *Illustration*, in which I admired most the caricatures of Bertal, Cham, Marcelin and Dicky Doyle; and from the *Musée Français et Anglais*, published during the Crimean War, which contained some reproductions of work by Doré. I was also indebted to a series of books which Papa inherited from his father and which were called *Les Annales du Musée*. This collection of more than forty volumes bound in pink boards occupied three-quarters of the top shelf of Papa's red book-case, and in order to reach them when I was ten I had not only to climb upon a chair, but also to stretch up my arm as far as it could go. I studied these *Annales du Musée* with growing interest. They consisted of illustrations with only very short explanatory notes. The illustrations were of paintings and sculptures in the Louvre, and included not only the permanent collection but also all the artistic trophies acquired by Napoleon, as well as the best works from the Paris 'salons' of the beginning of the nineteenth century. The arrangement of the illustrations was quite arbitrary, with mythological subjects opposite biblical, and allegorical next to realistic. The illustrations in the *Annales du Musée* were merely line reproductions, but this did not detract from my enjoyment of them. I was familiar with line reproductions and liked them, since knowing *Dushenka*. It now seems to me that the clarity of this method of reproducing works of art taught me, without my realising it, what is in fact the foundation of all visual art: drawing, in all its aspects of composition and rhythm and technique. I studied the explanatory notes, and found that they included reasoned criticism as well as details of colour and tone and also facts about the lives of the painters and sculptors. The *Annales du Musée* and the *Magasin Pittoresque* were my first artistic textbooks, and chiefly from the *Annales* I acquired at least a summary knowledge of the history of art. Many of the illustrations in the *Annales* were of pictures of the Napoleonic era, which inspired in me an enthusiasm for the classical school of the end of the eighteenth century.

Almost all the works of art that I admired in the days of my childhood were foreign or unfashionable or out of date. However, I had also seen many examples of modern art, among other places at the large exhibitions in the Academy of Art, to which I was taken yearly either by Papa or Mamma or one of my brothers, with whom I could afterwards discuss my views. I was particularly impressed by the 1882 exhibition at the Academy of Arts, which included many famous pictures by contemporary Russian artists afterwards to be exhibited in Moscow. I saw those masterpieces by Repin, *The Burlaks* and *The Departure of the Recruit*; the historical pictures of Jacoby and Wenig; the forest landscapes of Shishkin; and seascapes by Aivasovsky, which I then admired like everybody else. About this time I was also greatly taken with the vast painting *Lights of Nero* by Semiradsky, and by some of Vereshchagin's paintings shown at both private and public exhibitions organised by this famous artist.

The crowds that gathered at Vereshchagin's exhibitions were so great that people had to queue in the street to get in; but these ordeals were rewarded by the sight of *The Arrival of the Prince of Wales in India* and the *Funeral Mass* (a priest officiating on a battlefield littered with naked corpses) which acquired a remarkable effect of truth when illuminated by the dazzling, recently discovered electric light. I used to go to these exhibitions with Mamma who, although rather indifferent to art in general, could not resist the temptation of seeing something that was the talk of the town.

It may seem odd that in the process of my initiation to art I have not mentioned the Hermitage nor the most progressive exhibition of that time – the Peredvijniki. The reason is that the Hermitage did not make any conscious impression on me until I was thirteen; and as for the Peredvijniki, it was not the custom in our family to go to these exhibitions, as my father and brothers were convinced that art could only prosper in the Academy of Arts. To them the Peredvijniki were 'nihilists', destroying the very foundations of art. But my Uncle Misha had more progressive views than the rest of the family, and whenever one of these exhibitions opened there was an uproar at the next family dinner, provoked by his appreciation of a new picture by Repin, or Surikoff, or V. Makovski or Savitski. Then other members of the family would take up the cudgels, and a verbal duel would follow between those who had not been to the exhibition and had no intention of going and those who had been and were ready to label as masterpieces the pictures Uncle Misha had approved of.

One of these violent discussions finally compelled me to go and see for myself who was right and who was wrong. I had by this time learnt to form my opinions independently; and when I went to the exhibition, which was held on the Nevski that year (1884), I ran no risk of falling under some undesirable influence. I left the show quite overcome by the impression made on me by Repin's picture *The Unexpected Guest*. The freedom of the style and the freshness of the painting surprised me. I found it daringly simple and genuine, although utterly unlike everything that had hitherto been considered worthy of attention at home. The next year I waited for the opening of that exhibition as the most important event of the year; and this time, though the effect upon me of Repin's *Ivan the Terrible* was less overwhelming than with the previous picture, it was still staggering. It was Repin's pictures which awakened in me a more serious interest in modern art, Russian as well as foreign. True, the originals in Germany and France were beyond my reach, but I made the most of foreign publications, books and reviews in trying to satisfy my curiosity and urge for new artistic impressions. There was no system in my browsings, but now and then I would find a genuine pearl, and when I did my enthusiasm knew no bounds.

In 1885 I came to know Repin personally, and even had the opportunity of watching him at work day after day and listening to what he had to say about art when he started to paint the portrait of Albert's wife in my brother's apartment on the floor above us. Repin painted my remarkably beautiful *belle-soeur* playing the piano and caught very cleverly her expression, that of a 'cold' bacchante. But the work was somehow interrupted and the portrait which promised so well remained unfinished. For me those five or six sittings were highly rewarding. I watched him stealthily, afraid to make the slightest movement, in a sort of silent rapture; I observed how the master peered closely at the model, how he mixed the paints on his palette with great assurance and without hesitation transferred them to the canvas. Nothing looks more like magic than the birth of an image under the brush of a great artist. I tried to make use of these lessons in my own work, though at that time I had almost given up drawing altogether and very seldom used my watercolours. But the true value of this experience lay in having seen how it was done, in learning how real art is created.

CHAPTER VII

INTRODUCTION TO THE THEATRE

*

IT cannot be said that my introduction to the theatre began in a spectacular or dignified manner. The first performance I ever saw was a dog's theatre, held, not at a circus, but in an ordinary flat on the Admiralty Square hired for the purpose by a travelling dog impresario. I was not more than four years old, and Mamma had to stand me on her lap throughout the performance so that I could see over the heads of those who sat in front. I remember most clearly a remarkably intelligent, beautiful black Labrador, who barked the necessary number of times when someone in the audience pulled the right card out of the pack. He also executed the well-known dog's valse on the piano with his master in a duet for two hands and two paws. I learnt afterwards to play that simple little piece.

Perhaps I am not quite accurate in calling this my first theatrical experience. I had very early been enchanted by the Petrushka shows (Punch and Judy), though I cannot remember when I saw the very first one, for I had the good fortune as a small child to see so many and in such different places. I certainly remember seeing Petrushka when we lived in our summer residence at Peterhof. From the house I could hear in the distance the sharp squeal, the laughter and the occasional words uttered by the producer through a special machine which he pushed into his cheek (you can reproduce the same sound by pressing both nostrils with your fingers). After getting our parents' permission, my brothers invited the producer to come into our courtyard.

The coloured print screens go up, the musician places his instrument on a folding sack, his nasal, plaintive notes create the right atmosphere to stimulate your curiosity – and suddenly above the screens appears a tiny, hideous manikin. He has a huge nose, a broad smile that never leaves his lips, and on his head is a red-crowned hat shaped like a comet. He is astonishingly nimble and quick in his movements, with tiny hands which he uses effectively to express his feelings and thin little legs hanging over the top of the screen. Petrushka immediately assails the musician with silly, impudent questions to which the latter replies gloomily. That is the prologue to the tragedy which is then unrolled before our eyes. Petrushka is in love with the hideous Akulina. He asks her to marry him, she agrees and they perform a sort of honeymoon stroll, hand in hand. Then in comes Petrushka's rival – a sturdy, moustachioed policeman, whom Akulina obviously prefers to Petrushka. The latter in a fury strikes the guardian of law and order, and as a punishment is forced to become a soldier. But training and discipline do not suit him, he continues to riot and then – oh, heavens! – he kills his N.C.O. This is followed by an unexpected interlude. Suddenly, for no particular reason, two negroes appear dressed in brightly coloured clothes. They both carry sticks, which they throw skilfully up into the air and from one to another, and then use to hit each other over the head with resounding blows. The incident is over. Petrushka again appears on the screen. He continues to gesticulate, entering into a rude conversation with the musician; he insults him, squeals and giggles. Suddenly a shaggy little figure appears by his side. Petrushka is intrigued. He asks in his nasal voice what it is, and receives the reply from the musician at the barrel-organ that it is a lamb. Petrushka is delighted, strokes the little animal and jumps astride him. The lamb meekly walks backwards and forwards two or three times along the screen and then

suddenly rears up and throws his rider and – oh, calamity! –
it is not a lamb at all, but the devil himself – a devil covered
with black hair, with horns and a crooked nose and a long,
red tongue protruding from a toothy mouth. The devil
gores Petrushka and shakes him mercilessly, his little legs
and arms dangling on every side, and then drags him into
the underworld. Petrushka's wretched body is thrown up
into the air a few more times, then his death-rattle is heard
and an eerie silence follows. The musician plays a gay
gallop and the performance is over.

In Petersburg, too, in spring, when the first warm days
allowed one to take out the winter double window-panes
and open the windows, I remember how we watched other
Petrushka shows that took place in our courtyard. On such
occasions the performance had a more democratic character.
We sat, as in a box, on the window sill, while below the
caretakers, handymen and shopkeepers arrived at the
double, and numerous heads of maids and cooks adorned
the windows. Probably the text was also adapted to lower
tastes. Sometimes the crowd around the screen roared with
the kind of laughter provoked by dirty jokes, and on such
occasions my brothers threw conspiratorial glances at each
other and Mamma looked anxious, hoping that Shourenka
would not hear 'ces choses indécentes'. But Shourenka, even
had he heard, would not have understood. In any case he
was not interested in the text; he was merely excited by
the actions and squeals of Petrushka.

Certain aristocratic impersonations of Petrushka stand
out in my memory beside the democratic ones. He was a
constant 'number' at all Christmas parties and children's
dances. I hated these parties, and would always make a
scene when I was dragged to them, but if I was promised
that there would be a Petrushka, I meekly surrendered to
the hands of Mamma or Nanny, allowed myself to be dressed
in a new suit and complicated operations to be performed on

my hair, and when we arrived at our destination permitted myself to be hugged and mauled by strangers, enduring all this so that I might enjoy Petrushka. But as soon as Petrushka was over I insisted on being taken home, and would be sent home with my nurse while the other members of the family remained at the party.

These 'social' presentations of Petrushka took place at Uncle Cesare's, at the Zarudnis, the Olives and many other houses. I saw them dozens of times but I never got bored. In smart apartments the show would be set up in the doorway of the drawing-room behind the thick, luxurious draperies, and this added a festive and theatrical appearance to the performance. The producer who put on these shows was not the simple, grimy one who appeared in the street, but a drawing-room gentleman wearing evening clothes. He had silver screens with velvet edges and golden tassels, and the player was freshly shaved and properly turned out. His instrument was new and its tones were soft, unlike the squeaky hiccupings produced by the street musician. The dolls wore satin dresses and bright spangles. The negroes were particularly effective, not chipped and faded but freshly painted and black as night, with ostrich feathers on their heads and sticks covered in silver braid. The audience laughed till the tears came, and the faces of the pretty little girls dressed in pink with coloured ribbons in their flowing hair shone with delight.

It was unavoidable that we should have amateur theatricals in such a theatre-minded house as ours, but in my early childhood I was not in the least interested in participating in grown-up plays and charades. On the other hand, I loved toy theatres and was particularly fascinated by décor and costumes. The theatre that had once belonged to my brothers was still there, but at the age of six I was given one of my own and I gradually collected several of them, for my relations, knowing my passion for them, often brought me presents of sets containing a stage, décors and a troupe of actors cut out of cardboard.

There is no longer a fashion for these toy theatres, and separate parts can be found only among collections of antiques. But at the time of which I write they were at the height of their success, and every toyshop displayed a variety of types. The performers were of two kinds: either they stood on little cardboard bases that gave them the necessary stability (but also immobility) or they dangled on wires by which you could move them about the stage. My box with the play *The Hunchbacked Horse* had such mobile characters, among them the mare and her colt, the colt carrying the Prince, the whale and other underwater inhabitants.

Some of the theatres you had to build yourself. You could buy all the necessary materials, from the drop curtain to the last stage-hand, printed on sheets of paper and coloured; these were stuck on cardboard and carefully cut out. For three or four roubles you could buy a large packet of forty sheets made in Germany, which contained all that was necessary for *Wilhelm Tell*, *Don Juan*, *The Maid of Orleans*, *Faust*, *L'Africaine*, *The Night Watch* and even the once-popular *Die Hosen des Herrn von Bredow*. The style of these decorations and costumes was very operatic and troubadourish. But it was impossible to imagine any performance at that time without such exaggerated theatrical effects, the ridiculousness of which I realised only much later when I learnt something about the history of costume.

Besides the flat paper dolls, I also had marionettes on wires which Grandmother Cavos brought me from Venice. These included lifelike little cavaliers in felt hats with gold braid, a gendarme in a tricorne hat with a sabre in his hand, Harlequin with his *batte* and Pulchinello with a tiny lantern and Columbine with a fan. They had tiny wooden or tin hands and feet that dangled at every movement. Some of these Venetians lived with me for many years and some were even used by my children.

My best toy theatre was a Doinikoff (the name of the maker), a construction which took up a lot of space. It did not cost much – about ten roubles, perhaps even less. It was of wood, with a proscenium adorned by a flowery portal with golden ornamental and allegoric figures, and a deep stage built on several planes. Over it there was a clever contraption which withdrew the scenery and dropped it down behind, which facilitated a rapid change of décor. All that was necessary was to pull the string attached at the side. It was most efficient and with careful handling could last for years. The flaw in these theatres was that the actors had to be moved from the stage on small horizontal sticks to which they were glued, and this was not easy.

All these toy theatres were at my disposal, and when one of them was damaged I used to be given a new one. But in 1878 Papa ordered the carpenter Adamson, who lived in one wing of our house and gave me lessons in carpentry, to make specially for me a stage which looked like one of those *maquettes* used by professional scene-designers. This realistic theatre gradually put all the others in the shade, especially as Papa started it off with some very beautiful sets, among which I remember a luxurious room with real tulle curtains and a sea that gave the complete illusion of space and distance. I gradually added other sets to these which I invented and built myself; and this is how my career as a theatrical artist first began.

The performances of Thomas Olden's marionettes were, I think, the most striking among the theatrical impressions of my childhood. He appeared with his toy theatre for the first time in Petersburg at the Shrove Fun-fair, with a reputation for being without a rival in his sphere. The Petersburg audience was justifiably enthusiastic. Later I saw many marionette theatres, including the Venetian theatre Minerva, the Roman Piccoli, the Munich Kasperle, as well as the remarkable toy theatre of the well-known caricaturist Albert Guillaume, who performed during the exhibition of 1900. I have wonderful memories of them all, but none of them equalled those of Thomas Olden, and I am certain that this view was due not only to the rose-coloured spectacles of childhood but also to the genuine quality of his work.

The performance started with a circus number, with clowns, a balancing act and acrobats. The next item was a skeleton which was dismembered and put together again, after which the skull expressed its joy by noisily clicking its jaws. At the end there was a pantomime, *Beauty and the Beast*. I did not like this décor, which was too brightly coloured and ornamented with spangles; but the Beast was so terrifying that it caused panic among the children. Eighty years have gone by since then, but I can still see this performance clearly in my imagination: I can even hum two or three melodies of the funny American music that accompanied the various numbers.

Olden first appeared with his dolls at the fun-fair of 1877 or 1878. I was already familiar with fun-fairs, and what I saw at the fun-fair theatres might be considered my first proper theatrical experience. The performances, which were given in hastily constructed sheds, were one of the greatest attractions on these occasions. These fairs have been popular entertainments in Russia from the eighteenth century. Though modelled on the fairs in Western Europe, they were imbued with a specifically Russian spirit; the gaiety was more violent, more elemental. They were full of local colour, often picturesque and comical, and there were more drunks roaming about these fairs than anywhere in Europe. Towards evening, tipsiness of a boisterous, noisy, sometimes frightening kind would spread among the simple folk who dominated the fairground in the square, giving an almost demoniacal character to the entertainment. This atmosphere is admirably reproduced in the fourth scene of Stravinsky's *Petrushka*.

That my first memories of fairs belong to the spring of 1874 when I was not yet four is confirmed by the fact that my brother Isha – who died the following autumn – was among those who took me to the fair. I remember as though it were only a month ago how Isha took care of me on that faraway enchanting first day at the fair, how he arranged my felt bonnet, saw that my coat was properly buttoned and sat me on his lap in the theatre when he saw that the people in front were obscuring my view.

The year 1874 saw the last (or the one before the last) of the fun-fairs in Admiralty Square adjoining the Square of the Winter Palace. From the beginning of the reign of Nicholas I, considered such an oppressor of popular culture, these wild fairs had taken place in front of the very windows of the Tsar's residence – a striking confirmation of his true patriarchal attitude towards the people. In 1875 the fairs were moved to the 'Tsar's Meadow' (afterwards known as the Champ de Mars) where they took place until 1896.

Here is the story of the 1874 fair as I remember it. I see myself in our large nursery with three windows that looked out on the street. It is lit up with the reflection of the snow that fell overnight and is bathed in the oblique rays of the morning sun. Birch logs crackle gaily in the stove. Nanny walks to and fro softly in her slippers preparing to get me up. It is curiously still in the street: no footsteps, no trample of horses or clatter of wheels – all is hushed by the thick carpet of snow. Then a new silvery sound can be heard – it is the tinkling of bells on the harness of the Finnish sleighs. 'If you're a good boy', says Nanny, 'you'll be taken for a drive on the Finnish sleigh to the fair.'

Does anyone now remember these sleighs, I wonder?

They were an important feature of the Petersburg streets during the short week of the fair. It was their custom, encouraged by the police, to arrive in Petersburg on the Sunday before Lent and drive the inhabitants about for the whole week. The sound of their bells, the sight of the little yellow, well-fed, sprightly horses with their white manes and white tails, were an incitement to gaiety in our otherwise gloomy streets. Children loved them. To drive in them was a *sine qua non* of the feast, although these low-seated sleighs were not without their dangers. With a sinister sense of humour the Finn would try to glide right under the wheels of the huge four-seater carriages of that time, and it often happened that the sleigh turned upside down on the sharp slope as they turned. But children took a special pleasure in these adventures, without realising the danger. However, the sleigh was so low that you were unlikely to hurt yourself in falling, for you could touch the ground easily with your hand as you sat in it.

A contrast to this simple amusement were the drives of the pupils of the Smolni Institute, another example of the patriarchal charm of the existing Russian way of life. The girls, in Court carriages drawn by four splendid white horses and attended by coachmen and footmen in red livery and three-cornered hats, drove in a procession of about twenty carriages around the square allotted to the fair, the gay young faces of the noble girls peeping out under the severe supervision of their mistresses. These aristocratic prisoners could never enjoy the popular feasts with their big swings and switchbacks and brightly coloured theatres – but this occasion was real entertainment after the grey, dull everyday life behind the convent walls.

We arrived on our sleigh in the square, facing the main street. On the right stood a row of big buildings made out of freshly cut, sweet-smelling pinewood, glistening in the sun. On the other was a haphazard group of smaller miscellaneous buildings. The large buildings were the theatres managed by owners whose names stood in huge letters on the walls. There were a few poor little theatres also among the small buildings, but their side of the square was chiefly occupied with roundabouts, switchbacks and inumerable booths where you could buy sweetmeats of every description: gingerbreads, nuts, caramels, mints, sunflower seeds, as well as buns and cakes. On a large shed at one side with a big smoking chimney protruding from it, under a huge, broadly smiling face borrowed from the satirical review *Der Kladderadatsch*, hung a poster inviting people to eat 'Berlin doughnuts'. There, in the open air, stood rows of tables with hundreds of glasses, from which you could drink hot tea poured from fat teapots painted with bright flowers and made from boiling water in the huge samovars. And how thirsty we were! We had eaten too many blinis at luncheon, and nothing gives one such a thirst as blinis.

But not all the strollers drank tea and ate the hot rolls carefully wrapped in a thick cloth which were carried round by the pedlars. A great many of them turned into pubs or wine-houses and returned to the feast rather tipsy, singing songs at the top of their voices, some with a bottle in their pocket from which now and then they took another swig, becoming even more arrogant and noisy than before. Drunks on weekdays, in the centre of the town, were an unpleasant sight, but at the fair there is no doubt that these staggering men added drama to the festive and colourful crowd.

The roundabouts, owing to the cold climate, had to be erected in a hut, the outside walls of which were decorated with pictures of various beauties, together with landscapes and comic pictures and portraits of famous generals. From the inside, along with the vapours of steam and wine, came the deafening noise of the band and of the machine that worked the roundabout. Standing on the balcony outside the hut was the *'Dyed'* ('Grandpa'), whose chief job was to call out to passers-by and invite them in. Two dancers with heavily made-up faces skipped around 'Grandpa', and two strange figures that frightened the children, the Goat and the Crane, emerged at intervals from the inside. They were dressed in long white shirts, and from their necks, about three yards long, dangled a bearded snout with horns and a bird's head with a long beak.

It should not be assumed that 'Grandpa' was an old man, of an age suitable for a grandparent. His pink neck and the smooth back of his head revealed his youth. But in front he did look old because stuck to his chin he had a straw beard, falling to the ground. He was busy with his beard all the time. He twirled it, stroked it, swept the snow with it or dropped it from the balcony, trying to reach the heads of the crowd. 'Grandpa' was in constant movement. He fidgeted astride the balcony rail, waved his hands, kicked his legs higher than his head and sometimes, exhilarated by the frosty air, he jumped on top of the narrow rail and began to run up and down it and turn somersaults, in constant danger of falling on to the listeners. I wanted to listen to his chatter and to hear what he was singing. It must have been very funny, for broad smiles never left the faces of his audience and sometimes they rolled about with laughter, wiping their eyes. But I was not allowed to stop long enough and was dragged away under the pretext that I would catch cold. This, however, was not the real reason. 'Grandpa's' talk was seasoned with rude remarks and obscene words, and the little grimaces with which he punctuated them hinted at their ugly meaning even more eloquently than the words themselves.

Another popular figure was the peep showman. He was just as constant a feature of these occasions as 'Grandpa', but his method was more delicately insinuating. His session did not last long, but in these few minutes you could make a journey round the world or even enter the depths of hell. His recitations were very comical, and his chatter helped to fill in the gaps in the story.

The small theatre sheds were not worth visiting, unless it were to laugh at a naïve bit of nonsense. The next building was the zoo, painted outside in bright colours with a tropical forest of palms and lianas and bamboos. From it resounded the cries of wild animals – the roar of lions and tigers, the trumpeting of an elephant, the jabbering of monkeys and the screeching of parrots. But alas, it was disappointing inside: the left-overs from more famous zoos were ending their days there, cold and probably hungry. There was a lifeless camel, no longer able to stand on his feet; sleepy, mangy lions who looked more like poodles; consumptive monkeys pressing close to one another. Only the elephant was still rather impressive, but I had seen a more regal-looking elephant in the zoo book. What struck me most in this zoo when I first visited it was the graceful dancing on the stage of a ballerina dressed in a bright blouse and a short spangled tulle skirt, and – oh, horror! – with a face covered with a thick black beard!

The next spectacle I saw fully came up to my expectations of magnificence and beauty. Here, in one of the big wooden theatres, were the traditional performances of the Harlequinades. Isha loved Harlequinades and had already told me a lot about them; but what I saw with my own eyes surpassed all my hopes. I was almost dazed by this first experience of 'theatre', and the memory has never to this day lost its freshness and power. I was already acquainted with the story of Harlequin, and felt an admiring tenderness for this rogue in disguise. But now I saw him alive, victorious, cheeky, ridiculing everyone who stepped in his path. I fell in love with him; I wanted to become Harlequin myself, and seriously dreamed of having a magic wand like the one given to him by a kind and beautiful fairy. I kept this a secret from Mamma, but I prayed silently that the fairy would appear and present me with this wand.

How cold it was waiting in the wooden entrance to get into the auditorium! I was wrapped up from head to foot, my felt *bashlik* covering my ears over the collar of a thick winter coat, and I wore felt boots – but I was miserably cold in spite of it. The prickly feeling in my toes and the tips of my ears was insupportable and I was terrified of getting a frozen nose; I kept asking Isha whether my nose had gone white, and to prevent it from doing so I rubbed it as hard as I could with my woollen mittens. Everybody waiting there in that unheated entrance danced on one spot to keep warm, sneezing and coughing and blowing their noses. But nobody weakened, nobody abandoned the place of torture; they had reached the gates of the magic realm and would wait for them to open.

The magic moment at last arrives. Three minutes pass, during which the auditorium is abandoned by those who have already enjoyed the spectacle, and I have to cling to my guardian for fear of being trampled on or squeezed between the doors. Then we find ourselves sitting in our seats, before a curtain of bright scarlet and gold. Isha seats me on his lap. The auditorium is a huge wooden shed, lit by a row of dim kerosene lamps hanging on the walls and exuding a strong smell. The dim light and the smell only strengthen the mysterious spell. Suddenly a kind of cataclysm takes place behind us: it is the audience who have seats in the second and third rows and have been waiting their turn on the outside stairs. They rush in, shouting, squealing, making a terrific noise, yelling: 'Help, they're killing me!' The crowd moves with the force of an attacking army. The front detachments, with great agility, leap across the benches stretched across the entire hall and try to reach the first rows; we are terrified lest this wild herd will burst the walls and stampede us to death.

Gradually calm is restored, and the crowd is hushed in expectation. The orchestra, who have managed to get a hot drink between the performances, return and resume their seats; the conductor (he is the first violin as well) raises his baton, the overture starts and the curtain slowly rises. We see a village landscape, not at all Russian; on the left in the shade of a large tree stands a little house with red brick walls and a high slate roof; on the right is a hillock and in the distance is blue space. Everything is just as it is in real life. Immediately we are plunged into a situation which is at once unusual, disturbing, comical and frightening.

Old Cassandra is going to town and is giving instructions to his servants. One of them, dressed in white with his face covered in white flour, has a silly, bewildered look: he must be the lazy sluggard. The uneducated call him the miller, but I know that he is Pierrot. I even know the song about him *'Au clair de la lune, mon ami Pierrot'*, though I am not yet very familiar with the language of my ancestors. But why is Harlequin wearing such a shabby, dirty costume? I turn to Isha anxiously for an explanation and he gives it to me: 'Those are his working clothes. Wait a moment, you'll see what will happen next.' Something terrible happens. Having started their work, Pierrot and Harlequin begin to quarrel; they come to blows and, oh, horror! that clumsy lout of a Pierrot kills Harlequin. Worse still, he cuts up his old friend into small pieces and starts to juggle with the head, arms and legs (I cannot understand why there is no blood). In the end he is terrified by his crime and tries to bring his victim back to life. He pieces together the separate parts of the body and leans it against the door, after which he takes to his heels. It is then that the first miracle takes place. A fairy, brilliant with gold and precious stones, emerges from the hillock which has become transparent. She approaches the folded corpse of Harlequin, touches it, and in one moment all the members grow together again. Harlequin is alive once more; better still, after a second touch of the magic wand Harlequin's shabby attire falls off and he appears to my extreme joy in the guise of a handsome youth shining with spangles. He kneels down in gratitude before the kind fairy, while Cassandra's daughter, the adorable Columbine, comes running out of the house. The two are united by the fairy, who, by giving Harlequin her wand as a wedding gift, makes him richer and more powerful than any king.

The second act is chaos. The scene is the kitchen in Cassandra's house, where the revived Harlequin plays revengeful practical jokes on Pierrot and upon his former master. He turns up in the most unexpected places – in a pot of boiling water (which produces real steam), or in the box of the grandfather clock, or in the tub containing flour. He is chased by the servants who are led by the chef, but he escapes, vanishing in the middle of the floor. He flies first through the open window, and then jumps inside the mirror, but no sooner is the sound of broken glass heard than he is seen dashing astride a dragon across the stage. His pursuers of course are covered with humiliation. They rush out of one door after another, stumble against each other, fall in a heap and in their vexation come to blows. They try in vain to move a large cupboard behind which the rascal has hidden, until the cupboard moves of its own accord and begins to pursue them.

The scene of the third act is my native Venice, with Cassandra and his friends falling down together with the balcony, from which Harlequin has just leapt down. After that the magic returns. Harlequin and Columbine lead their pursuers out of a dark forest, in which the fairy reappears, into a Hell lit up with the red light of Bengal lanterns and with clouds of smoke swirling out from the wings. It seems as though both pursuers and fugitives are threatened with death, but it was merely the fairy's sense of humour:

Harlequin and Columbine come to a happy end. The scene of Hell is transformed into Paradise, garlands of roses supported by cherubs fall from Heaven, and again the fairy unites Harlequin and Columbine. But disaster is in store for Harlequin's enemies. They grow horrible snouts, and the end comes with their gestures expressing infinite confusion. This climax is so clear in my memory that I could draw a picture of it now. I even remembered the music for a long time, but it has now got lost in the store-room of my memory.

I saw this pantomime three or four times in later years, adorned with a few new tricks. Then this theatre disappeared from the fair, leaving only one other in which, although Harlequin again appeared on the scene, the actors to my disgust spoke extremely stupid lines, evidently meant to be witty. Harlequin had a beard peeping out from under his mask, and there was nothing in common with the former characterisation that had so enchanted me. Pierrot never stopped yawning, and this was meant to be comical; Columbine was old and ugly and seemed to be freezing in spite of the woollen pants that showed under her shabby tulle skirt. The only effective décor were the sparkling wheels on which the fairies came driving, and the dolls that danced in a comical way and showed their empty insides when they fell down, which produced general laughter. I also liked the décor of Hell, in which squatting devils were painted upon the huge wings with heads that reached the top of the stage and paws that seized Harlequin's enemies and swung them about to the sound of hellish music. But this theatre was in process of disintegration; it was already half empty, and there was not the same rush for the cheap seats as in the other theatres where the stairs were on the verge of breaking under the weight of avid spectators and where there was a regular battle before every performance.

From 1880, the onset of nationalism penetrated even into these theatres, and lighthearted Harlequinades and other pantomimes of foreign origin disappeared in favour of heavy Russian folk dramas. Frightful melodramas of national (pre-Peter the Great) history became popular; Pushkin and Lermontov came into fashion; the trend of entertainment was all towards morality and sobriety. But the general atmosphere of the fair remained the same: the bands still roared, the Turkish drums still clattered, the great square hummed so loudly with excitement that the noise could be heard in the centre of the town. The carriages with the young ladies continued to process, the peep-showman and 'Grandpa' still clamoured for attention, and here and there was the echo of Petrushka's laughter.

Then it all vanished. The Temperance Society (the palace of its chairman, Prince Oldenburg, looked out on the square) arranged that these saturnalias should be removed from the centre of the town. For a few years the fairs continued to carry on in a miserable way in the suburbs, and after that they went the way of all flesh. This genuinely popular entertainment died and with it vanished its own peculiar culture, its customs and traditions. To the next generation the words that had given me a thrill of excitement had already become a dead sound, an old wives' tale.

I could not have been more than three when I first went to the circus, in a wooden building situated quite close to our house. But I remember better the performances of a travelling circus, and afterwards those in the famous Circus Ciniselli, built about 1875. The latter, decorated on the outside by paintings of antique hippodromes and medieval tournaments, was not very impressive from an architectural point of view. Inside I was always fascinated by the huge portraits of famous horsewomen, beginning with Queen

Tomiris, on the ceiling of the cupola. But I must indeed have been predestined for the theatre, for I was upset by the fact that the performance took place in an arena and not upon a stage, which I much preferred. What I liked least in the circus were the complicated pantomimes featuring horses and other animals which came at the end of the programme.

I ought to have been transported by the story of Red Indians, or the Eastern pantomime which ended with the killing of the fierce Eastern potentate by his rival, a beautiful prince out of *A Thousand and One Nights*. I can remember the terrible gleam in the villain's eye while he was dying under the spotlight, how heavily he slumped from his horse, how delirious the joy of the young slaves liberated by the knight. But it all took place too close to my person, almost on top of me. The sight of the audience sitting around us in their fur coats and the orchestra playing right in front of us on a brightly lit platform; the pursuits and escapes which took place across the arena; the setting up of hills and rocks during the intervals before our eyes and not behind the curtain which in the theatre preserved the mystery: all this together spoiled my pleasure and, strangely enough, embarrassed me. And I did not like the vulgar noisiness of circus music.

There were, however, several joys that I experienced in the circus: the performances of the trained horses – a speciality of the members of the Ciniselli family (Scipione, Gaetano and their sister, adorable, in my view, in her riding kit); the ballerinas who danced on the flat drums that served as saddles to the beautiful snow-white horses, and who jumped through the rings; several remarkable turns, like the acrobat who was fired from a gun and seized a trapeze in his flight, or the Red Indian girl who held a rope in her teeth and flew from one side of the circus hall to the other. She had long, black, flowing hair and when she reached her destination she nimbly jumped on a velvet pedestal and gave a piercing shriek that rang through the building, adding poignancy to her wild act. I loved the musical clowns, the trained dogs and monkeys, though what I enjoyed most was the performance of a ventriloquist who manipulated a whole group of large comical dolls. But the circus was not my true domain, and I prefer to pass on to the real theatre, which was closer to my heart and my taste in every way.

CHAPTER VIII

REAL THEATRE

*

I WAS first taken to the theatre when I was five. It happened quite by accident – the theatre management sent the family a box for a matinee, and I was taken with the others, though the performance was not meant for a child. It was held in the Mariinsky Theatre, only a stone's throw from our house, where Russian operas and plays were usually produced. This was a concert by a travelling ladies' orchestra, and I had to sit through a long series of overtures, pot-pourris, valses and almost a whole symphony. Though it was rather boring, I was so interested by the novelty of my surroundings, from the liveried attendant who let us into the box to the marvellous curtain, that I stood the ordeal valiantly and did not drop off to sleep or even ask to be taken home. When the curtain rose it disclosed a mountain of white dresses, ample in the fashion of the time, picked out with instruments of which my curiosity was specially attracted both by the terrifying trumpets that looked like large beetles and the elegant golden harps. During the interval, in front of a décor representing a garden with tall cypresses, two clowns entertained the audience.

What was most important to me in all this was that I was at last in a real theatre, with the opportunity of becoming acquainted with its atmosphere and with its general appearance. Avidly I examined all the details of this odd splendid space sparkling with light and gold that stretched above and below me. I was awestruck by the semi-circular auditorium built up in five tiers, each outlined with a row of little boxes. Over the blue curtains of the Tsar's boxes fat white cherubs supported golden crowns and crests of eagles, and from the domed ceiling, painted with dancing maidens, hung a huge chandelier, burning with a multitude of candles. The black hole from which it emerged, and through which Papa said it was removed for cleaning and lighting, was a mystery in itself. I was also struck by the smell of the theatre. Theatres at that time were illuminated by gas, and they smelt of the gas as much as they did of the audience. For a long time after electricity was introduced this smell still lingered in the corridors and auditoriums of the State theatres, and even now the smell of gas always reminds me of the theatres of my childhood and youth.

The curtain was down when we entered the box at the Mariinsky and only barely lit by the footlights; but bright lights were switched on before it rose and it then appeared to us in all its splendour. I never lost my admiration for this remarkable curtain of the Mariinsky, which was later replaced by another very tasteless one. I learnt later that Bakst and Somov and my father also shared my feeling for it. A magnificent frame, entwined by roses and supported by cherubs, surrounded the picture of a semi-oval temple with the statue of Apollo of Belvedere in the middle, done in soft shades of blue, while from above and on the sides hung raspberry-red velvet draperies. The designer of this master-piece was, if I am not mistaken, Aubé, a Parisian artist.

Having concentrated on my impressions of the audi-torium and my experience of delight in the chandelier and the curtain on my first visit to the theatre, I could turn my attention on my next visit to what took place on the stage. This was a spectacle in the wooden theatre a few steps away from the Alexandrinsky, and it concerned an English-man, Phineas Fogg, who, accompanied by his valet, was making a journey round the world in eighty days. I under-stood little French at that time, but the grown-ups told me the general outline of the story and I could easily follow the incidents. I was not so much interested in the fat, round, bewhiskered little Phineas Fogg, who had accepted a wager that he could not go round the earth in eighty days, as in the clever, cheerful, agile valet, Passepartout, who pulled his master out of the difficulties into which Phineas fell at every step. The play is divided into twelve or fifteen scenes, each of them containing at least one dreadful incident. No sooner have Fogg and Passepartout sobered down after a visit to an opium den in Bombay than at the risk of their lives they save a beautiful Hindoo girl, Aouda, the widow of a Rajah, from being burned to death on his funeral pyre. Aouda next escapes the snakes that have surrounded her; the travellers escape the Red Indians who attacked their train in a snowbound landscape; and they all narrowly escape drowning in mid-Atlantic. However, all ends well for the hero, and Phineas Fogg finds his reward not only in an enormous sum but also in the humiliation of those who had dared to doubt his ultimate success.

The mechanics of this play excited general approval and pleased my own childish imagination. Everybody particularly admired the scene with the snakes crawling from a palm tree and the walls of a cave; and the scenes where the engine, emitting sparks, emerges into a snow-covered landscape, and another in which a huge ship glides over the waves, were also considered very effective. I liked to know how everything was done. It was interesting to learn that the movement of the sea which looked so real was made with a piece of canvas manipulated by the hands of people beneath it.

Faust was my brother Albert's favourite opera; indeed it was probably the only opera that this most musical of the brothers Benois was really fond of. When he played it on the piano I sat spellbound beside him, and as he played he made a few rapid comments that gave me some idea of what the music represented. I was therefore able to go

through all the emotions of the opera without having seen
it performed, and cold shivers ran down my spine. Though
I knew nothing about old age I melted in sympathy with
the powerless misery of the old scientist, shedding tears as
he listened to the Easter songs echoing in the streets.

In view of this it can easily be imagined how excited I
was when I actually saw the opera at the Bolshoi in 1876!
Marguerite was sung by the famous Nielsen, and hers was
the only name I can remember among the artists, for it was
upon everybody's lips. I thought Marguerite very attractive
in a grey dress with her long fair hair, but I can only
remember that she flung herself in front of Mephisto on the
steps of the church, and fell down with a thud in prison
in the last act. Faust was splendid when he regained his
youth and appeared in a blue-black velvet suit with white
cuffs and a round hat with a white ostrich feather. But
the devil captivated me most. I felt a strange tenderness for
Mephisto, although I realised that this was wrong. His slim
red figure, the red feather in his little red hat, reminded me
of some of my dreams of the sweet-and-eerie type with
which Morpheus sometimes blesses his favourite children.
In the darkness of Faust's gloomy study, when the sharp-
nosed red gentleman, illuminated by a red spotlight, rose
from the floor, I welcomed him like an old friend and
shouted for the whole theatre to hear. Mephisto, like my
friend Harlequin, is endowed with the powers of magic.
At his command the wall of the study melts away and Faust,
to the music of a heavenly choir, sees Marguerite at her
weaving.

As the opera develops the devil reveals his evil nature.
How horrible that he should kill the good, kind brother of
Marguerite! Why is he so malicious towards good-looking
little Siebel, who has just brought a huge bunch of flowers
for Marguerite? It was also surely he who arranged that
poor Marguerite is finally thrown into prison? That is why

when I saw Mephisto at the end lying all screwed up under the Angel's sword, I decided that he had only had his due. A moment before the grandiose stone wall of the prison had fallen to pieces, giving way to the view of a large town seen from above. Over the slate roofs, over the steeples of the churches, a strange group wrapped in tulle rose slowly to the skies. It reminded me of the chandeliers covered with sheets for the summer. In this leisurely ascension of a shapeless something that was supposed to represent Marguerite's soul, there was something wonderfully uncanny. What I liked most about it was that one could not make head or tail of it! The solemn music of the finale seemed truly from heaven and aroused in me the same mood that Faust must have experienced when he knelt down to pray.

A few months after seeing *Faust* I was introduced for the first time to the ballet. As fate apparently predestined me to play a part in this field of theatrical art on an international scale, my first impressions of the ballet may be of some interest. Once more I was overwhelmed, not so much by the dancing itself (as in the opera it had not been the singing that entranced me), but by the spectacle, the fantastic blending of vivid décor and costume with the beauty of movement and the music. The actual dances, and especially those of the *corps de ballet*, I thought rather boring. On the other hand, the fact that there was no dialogue or singing in the ballet, only movement to music, appealed to some innate taste. Similarly, I had preferred the wordless pantomime to the spoken Harlequinade at the fun-fair theatres. As I sat, on that occasion in 1876, in a first-tier box with my cousins and stared motionless at the ballet of *La Bayadère*, I lived through moments that belong to the happiest in my life. Indeed they were almost prophetic moments, foretelling equal if not greater joys in the future.

By the age of fourteen I had become an inveterate balletomane, having managed to see all the ballets performed on the

Imperial stage. They were all spectacular and filled with a poetic romanticism. At first I used to be taken about twice a year to the ballet, at Christmas and at Easter, but later my visits became much more frequent. I saw the tragic ballet of *The Daughter of the Snow*, in which white bears devour a sailor who has scorned the love of a fairy princess; and also *The Butterfly*, which begins with a gay dance of animated vegetables and ends with the representation of a peacock spread over the whole stage. I also saw a very effectively staged ballet, *Pygmalion*, by Prince Trubetskoy, in which a sculptor falls in love with the statue he has created. I was rather disappointed by the ballet *Don Quixote*, which told the story of the hero of Cervantes who fought with windmills, stabbed the puppets of a travelling circus, and was finally overcome by a mysterious Knight of the Moon in silver armour. Some of the ballets I saw two or three times and always with unabated interest. Among them *Roxane*, performed in 1878, was an indication of the Russian attitude in favour of freedom for the Slavs in the Balkans.

Very different to the others were the comic and semicomic ballets like *Le Barbier* and *Marco Bomba*. One of the most popular Russian ballets, *The Hunchbacked Horse*, whose subject is adapted from a fairy-tale, could also be classed as comic. The chief part is not that of a prince but a simple peasant – a distinctly feeble-minded peasant. Nevertheless, he is the luckiest of mortals: having caught a magic horse, he transforms it into an obedient slave. Because of the difficulty of getting a real horse to perform on the stage, the composers of the ballet had to compromise. In the first scene Ivan the Simpleton catches hold of a cardboard horse which is dashing across the fields: in the second scene he flies over the clouds sitting astride it back to front. Later on, however, the audience sees not the cardboard hunchback horse but a little contorted manikin, dressed in strange clothes, who hops about ceaselessly. We children firmly believed that it was the same animal we had just seen, and in this way were convinced that the hunchback horse was endowed with great magic power. Ivan the Simpleton cracks his whip, and there is the little horse curvetting around his master, inquiring his wishes. Thanks to the horse, Ivan the Simpleton gets into the palace, into the presence of the Khan himself – a repulsively lecherous old man – and makes a journey to the fairy kingdom where a fountain throws up a jet to the sky and lovely creatures dance the famous valse; thanks also to the horse, Ivan the Simpleton descends to the bottom of the ocean in search of the Princess's wedding-ring, and finally manages to get the better of the Khan, becoming transformed into a handsome prince after being dipped into a boiling pot, while the Khan, trying to follow his example, finds death in the same pot.

The ballet ended with a grand finale. At the back of the stage rose the Novgorod monument of Russia's thousandth anniversary, and marching past it were all the nations of the Russian Empire come to pay homage to the Simpleton, who had become their master. There were Cossacks and Karelians, Persians, Tartars, Little-Russians and Samoyeds. I cannot understand how such freedom of expression was allowed by the strict censor of that time – and, what is more, on the Imperial stage. Obviously the protectors of the throne had missed the revolutionary element in it. As for us children, naturally we did not care so long as the horrid old Khan was boiled in the pot and Ivan the Simpleton, whom we had come to like, got a magic girl for a wife and came to the throne.

Taking part in the procession of nationalities was undoubtedly the most handsome of all the ballerinas of the day, Maria Petitpas, the daughter of the choreographer. She had made a great impression on me in *Roxane* in 1878, when I was eight, and now, at thirteen, I fell head over heels in love with her, especially when I saw her dance a

Ukrainian dance with great *brio* and give her partner a resounding kiss on the lips. This unexpected climax to the Ukrainian dance always aroused great enthusiasm and roars of 'encore'. From that moment and for many months Maria Petitpas became the object of my adoration.

My adoration reached its peak when I saw her in *Coppelia*, dancing the Mazurka and the Czardas. But I must confess that the long-legged, lazy and not very talented Maria was a bad dancer. In technique she was worse than the least of the *corps de ballet*. It was even an effort for her to rise on her toes, and she slipped down gratefully to the 'half toes'; her movements were clumsy and she lacked suppleness. That was why her father, the choreographer, would allow her to dance only character rôles in which she could project her sex-appeal in a mad whirl.

I am sure that my artistic development was immensely influenced both by the ballet *Coppelia* and by Bizet's music to *Carmen*, produced at the same time, 1883–84, though my reactions to these two works of art were entirely different. There was much less passion and pathos in *Coppelia*, but it was filled, without being sugary, with enchanting tenderness and sweetness. This ballet became my favourite one, not because I could not tear my eyes away from Maria Petitpas dancing the Czardas or the Mazurka, nor because the ballerina of the main part, Svanilda, the frail, slender and pretty Nikitina, enchanted me (not so much with her dancing, for she was rather weak in the leg, as with her slightly anaemic gracefulness), but because the music of Delibes penetrated my whole being with its enveloping warmth. The first notes of the overture carried me away into a magic world of sweet dreams. I might almost say that the moments of excitement which I felt during the prancings of Maria rather spoilt the picture: they infringed upon something much more valuable, something which, as I grew up and became more settled in my views, turned out to be my basic artistic convictions. Thanks to *Coppelia* my own aesthetic taste was firmly established, and a certain attitude began to take shape which afterwards grew richer and more mature throughout my life, while remaining intrinsically the same. I am on the whole a man of constant attachments but this was something more: I had found myself. And I was infinitely grateful for this discovery.

Such an admission may appear strange. The Delibes ballet is now so hackneyed and vulgarised that no one takes it very seriously; one even has to have a certain courage to do so. My own courage is derived from the force of those impressions which I experienced at the age of fourteen. Moreover, the conditions for such an appreciation of *Coppelia* at that time were very favourable. Everything was ideal about the *Coppelia* performance in Petersburg. The orchestra, directed by the fine musician R. Drigo, who worshipped Delibes, rendered beautifully the exquisite subtlety of the score. The naïve but ingenious intrigue was played with simplicity and conviction; the choreography of the Czardas and Mazurka was dazzling, as was also the charming 'Galop' finale. The solo numbers for the artists were chosen with great care; in fact, the scenes with the animation of the doll and its mischievous dances were imcomparable. Much later, in Paris – Coppelia's native town – I saw my favourite ballet in an unrecognisable and distorted form, but up to the end of the existence of the Imperial theatres it preserved with us the purity of style which I had the privilege of seeing in my adolescence. Obviously this performance was established on such a sound basis that not even the repetition through half a century could spoil it. The dancers changed, and the conductors, but the orchestra continued to produce the same stimulating effect on both dancers and audience. Always, at the beginning of the second act, one became the victim of a semi-mystical, semi-mischievous mood; in the scene of intoxication the dancers playing the parts of Franz and Coppelia continued to convince, as did also the feast in the third act.

A few more words about the third act. For a time it was not shown in Paris, out of a false deference to the memory of Delibes, as it was considered that this act was the result of collaboration between the Frenchman, Delibes, and the German, Minkus, and that it was difficult to determine which part was whose. Such deference is out of place. Certainly the third act is more of a spectacle than a ballet, a sort of addition to the main theme of the play, which ends at the moment of Svanilda's escape from the Room of Wax Figures, but it is an addition necessary to render the impression complete. Whoever the author may be, the 'March of the Bells', the 'Galop', the 'Dance of the Clocks' and the 'Prayer' are all musical pearls. As for the 'Peasants' Wedding', it is indubitably the work of Delibes – and there is hardly anything to touch the magic quality of this work. In watching the gaiety, grace and smoothness of this dance as performed by Litavkin, the eighteenth century came freshly to life for me, and I realised the very essence of that enchanting era which has been so ridiculously discredited and which in reality represents one of the culminating points in the history of culture.

In the same year that I discovered *Coppelia* I also learnt to know *Giselle*. This ballet, which has lately become a favourite of the whole world, was pushed into the background at that time. It was shown very seldom and ballerinas tried to avoid appearing in the main part. I saw *Giselle* quite by accident at a matinee in 1885. The star part was danced by no great star but by a bony, clumsy, ugly and rather tall ballerina, who was however quite a good technician. The audience was not enthusiastic, the auditorium was half empty, and the performance was probably merely a manoeuvre to satisfy a respected but not attractive dancer.

The décor was old and faded, the costumes haphazard. I wandered into the theatre alone, not out of curiosity but because of nothing better to do. The spectacle, however, proved to be one of great significance for me; in fact it so overwhelmed me that from that day I became a propagandist for *Giselle*. Later, in conversations with theatre managers, I insisted that it should be repeated, and when young Anna Pavlova appeared on the scene my dream was to see her in that part. At last I managed to persuade Diaghilev that the ballet should be included in the second season of our performances in Paris (with my décors and costumes) and with Pavlova. Actually it all happened quite differently. We did put on *Giselle*, but Pavlova, lured by a more favourable offer, refused to dance at the last moment and Karsavina took her place. However neither we nor the ballet suffered from this exchange. The success of *Giselle* with Karsavina was indisputable, and through this triumph this charming work of French romanticism, almost forgotten in its native land, became so fashionable that every famous ballerina became keen to include it in her repertoire.

I have jumped a long way in speaking of *Giselle*'s ultimate fate, but on that day, when I had the joy of seeing this ballet for the first time, I did not, of course, imagine all that would happen. This time I was not transported by the ballerina who danced Giselle but by the sad history of Giselle herself. The exceptional charm of this ballet lies in its story which, though an improbable one, has been rendered by Theophile Gautier with the utmost conviction and conciseness. Since then he has become my ideal author, and in one case my inspiration: the subject of my *Pavillon d'Armide* was inspired by one of Theophile Gautier's fantastic stories. I must not neglect to mention the music of Adam. It is not a first-class masterpiece, and it cannot be compared with the music of Delibes or Tchaikovsky, but several of the tunes are so arresting and attractive that in a considerable measure they contribute towards the exceptional effect the ballet has on the audience. This is particularly true of the famous *allegro*, which when it first appears expresses such love and tenderness and the elation of love, and which later in the second reprise, the scene of madness, arouses such emotions of unbearable sadness. It is difficult to imagine any other music that would reproduce a mood so poignantly as does this simple melody. I had, at the time I am describing, already lost the habit of shedding tears, but I found that the melody of the *allegro* provoked in me a certain tickling in the nose, and I had to control myself in order to refrain from bursting into tears – an effect which continues to this day.

My next theatrical-ballet infatuation was the last link in the chain of my artistic understanding. This time I was captured not by a particular work, as in the case of *Coppelia* and *Giselle*, but by an artist – Virginia Zucchi, who appeared in Petersburg in the summer of 1885. I had just reached the age of fifteen, but in many ways I felt older and more adult than most of my contemporaries. My feeling for Zucchi, therefore, cannot be considered merely childish infatuation.

I saw Zucchi for the first time in *Journey to the Moon*, an operetta performed in a suburban theatre. In it the Italian ballerina appeared in a modest dance which had no connection with the subject of the operetta. She was still unknown to large audiences and danced to a more or less empty auditorium. I immediately became aware of an entirely original quality in her dancing. I left the theatre in a trance, and repeated the long trip to the Islands outside Petersburg five times for the sole purpose of seeing Virginia glide across the stage with tiny little steps to the music of the popular but slightly common valse *Nur für Natur*. There was genuine poetry in that dance; the audience could not remain indifferent to it, and recalled her again and again. A month or so later I left for six weeks to stay with my parents in the Ukraine, and on my return I found a new situation. Zucchi had become the talk of the town. Seats were no longer available in the recently empty theatre, or only at exorbitant prices. This sudden leap to success was the result of her performance in scenes from the ballet *Brahma*. My former infatuation was renewed, and I lost my heart entirely. When it became known that after her appearance before the Imperial Family in Krassnoe Selo, Zucchi had been invited to perform in the Bolshoi during the coming season, I began to prepare for this happiness with feverish excitement. I arrived for the first appearance of Zucchi on the Imperial stage in a truly solemn spirit, ready, in case of need, to fight the gang of nationalistic ballet lovers who had, so we heard, threatened to sabotage the foreign star. But the enthusiasm with which Zucchi was greeted when she appeared in the rôle of the animated mummy of the Pharaoh's daughter was sufficient to discourage any opposition. The whole performance received a tremendous ovation, and from the box where the Imperial Family usually sat the sharp voice of the Grand Duke Vladimir resounded throughout the theatre with a 'Bravo, Zucchi!'

Indeed, what Petersburg saw on that occasion was something entirely novel, far from the academic stiffness which was considered the great asset of the Russian ballet school. Zucchi not only personified the life of a young girl with its passion, love and tenderness, but the emanation of her genius infected everyone around her. Even the male dancer, Gerdt, became unrecognisable. Abandoning the academic discipline in which he had been trained, he was in absolute unison with his new partner. *The Pharaoh's Daughter* was a clumsy, infinitely long and already old-fashioned ballet in which Sokolova had chosen to appear. The star, however, had fallen ill, and to save the situation Zucchi, who had just arrived from abroad, learned in one

week the part of Aspiccia – not a particularly suitable one
for her. When Sokolova returned after her recovery a few
weeks later and appeared in the same part, her performance
seemed so dim and uninteresting after that of Zucchi that
even her admirers were unable to conceal their disappointment. True, Sokolova played the part with a dignity more
suited to an Emperor's daughter, but it could not compare
with the exciting and vital performance of Zucchi.

Zucchi's power was due to the fact that she did not act a
part, she gave life itself to her impersonation of a given
character. Marius Petitpas, who at first tried to argue with
the new artist placed under his direction, gradually sub-
mitted to her charm and acknowledged the sacred fire
that burnt within her. The critics, however, raised their
voices, often very malicious ones. Most of them reproached
her with a lack of restraint in the expression of emotion
and with too much spontaneity, which was considered
common. There were also many technical criticisms,
accusing her of being too *terre à terre*, of having *trop peu de
ballon* and too little elevation. But how could one speak of
such flaws in the presence of what she gave, which was life?
There are some artists to whom the skies are thrown wide
open to allow them to converse directly with angels and
gods. This is true magic, and humanity is right in seeing
in them representatives of a higher order. Such are Sandro
Botticelli, Leonardo da Vinci, Michelangelo, Raphael,
Tintoretto. Other artists remain on earth, but though they
may be deprived of elevation, they make no less an impact
on our souls, and may seem even more accessible, more
closely related to us.

Zucchi, with all her poetry, belonged to these 'earthy'
ones. She was not a Sylphide, and I cannot imagine her as
an ethereal Willi in the second act of *Giselle*, but when the
scene demanded the impersonation of a real woman with
purely feminine charm, then Virginia was incomparable

and convincing. It was impossible not to believe that she experienced all the emotions she expressed to the full not only with the mime of her not really beautiful yet sweet and significant face, but with all the movements of her body, now impetuous, now soft and infinitely tender. I knew people who were moved to tears at Zucchi's performances, not because the dramatic situation in the ballet was so moving, but because it was so beautiful. This was art in which there was not a breath of artificiality. A miracle indeed!

CHAPTER IX

SISTERS AND BROTHERS

*

[A]

M Y parents had nine children, but my sister Louise died when she was one year old and my brother Julius ('Isha') at the age of fourteen. All the others, myself included, lived to a venerable age. We were very different from one another, with only a few family characteristics in common. As for racial characteristics, some of us inclined rather to our Italian origin, others to our French. The Germanic element inherited from Grandmother Benois was manifested in various ways. It was I who appeared to be most under the German influence in our family; but on the whole I have as much fondness for the English and their way of life, or for the Spaniards and even the Scandinavians, though there is certainly not a drop of English or Scandinavian blood in me. If there is a drop of Spanish blood (through the Cavos family) it must have reached me in a minute dose after three centuries.

The brothers and sisters Benois can also be classified according to the degree of their 'Russianism'. Though we have no drop of Russian blood in our veins, this has not prevented us from becoming purely Russian, not only by citizenship and language (I, for instance, prefer to write these memoirs in Russian as my native, most familiar language), but also in our ways of life and certain characteristics. My brother Ludovic – or Leontij, as he was called in the Russian style – became the most Russian of us all, since he was connected by marriage with a real Russian family, but the others all married foreigners, my eldest sister an Englishman of Irish descent and the youngest a Frenchman, three brothers married Germans, and one married his cousin, an Italian with a mixture of Russian blood.

My position in the family was privileged. Having come into the world after all the others, and since my parents could not hope to have any more children, I was their Benjamin. But not only was I the object of my parents' most tender care, I was the darling of my brothers and sisters also. My sisters were particularly fond of me. They were both old enough to be my mother, the elder being twenty-one when I was born, the younger twenty. My brothers also spoilt me in every way and each one had some suggestion to make about my upbringing, a situation which now and then gave rise to some misunderstandings and frictions. Sometimes I was so oppressed by excessive care and supervision that I rebelled and would not accept any infringement of my independence. But for the most part we were all great friends and my memories of my brothers and sisters are grateful and loving.

In my early childhood I preferred my sister Catherine, gay, pretty, slender, rosy Katia, to 'Camisha', my elder sister, who was not beautiful and who was slightly pockmarked, quiet and almost speechless. But in later years I learnt to appreciate the sweetness, the heart-felt wisdom, the absolute kindness and the self-sacrificing qualities of Camisha[1], and my feeling for her eventually developed into a kind of worship. If I adored anyone in our family apart from my father and mother, it was she; and it was Camisha who, after Mamma's death, could create for me the illusion that she was still with me. Mamma, however, had much more spiritual firmness, whereas Camisha's dominating feature was a Venetian indolence that often approached

---

[1] Translator's note. It is characteristic of the Benois family, as it is indeed of many Russians, to use diminutives of first names with variations of endearment.

passive resignation in an infinite submission to circumstances. She seemed unable to cope with the hardships of life.
She married Matthew Edwardes in 1875. Her husband,
an immensely tall, typical Briton, also knew the full value of
his darling Camilla, the gentle, fragile companion of his
life. He appeared on our horizon in 1874, as a teacher of
English; he fell in love with his pupil and won full response
from her – though his love could not have been expressed
very ardently! For a girl of our circle to marry a tutor was
not exactly a great catch and my parents were obviously a
little perplexed when Camisha asked their consent. But so
quickly and permanently did Matthew win our hearts, too,
that the hesitation did not last long; and indeed information
from Matthew's native country proved that the young man
belonged, if not to a wealthy, at any rate to a very respectable family. He was, in fact, the eldest brother of George
Edwardes, who became famous as the musical comedy
impresario of Daly's and the Gaiety. He had become a
tutor only by accident, having arrived in Petersburg to look
for fame, fortune and happiness and not knowing where to
turn. In fact he had no taste for teaching and at the first
opportunity (this being his marriage, which took place
very soon after his arrival in the Russian capital) he abandoned his pedagogical activities to apply himself to what
lay nearer his heart.

Nearer to Matthew's heart was 'business'; it did not
matter what kind, as long as it was honest and profitable
and promised quick and dazzling rewards, but he had
nothing of the aggressor or the profiteer in his nature. He
negotiated his business affairs with good will, through
persuasion and arguments, sometimes very lengthy and
complicated, which gave him immense pleasure. The
technique itself of negotiation, with bearded, uncouth
merchants and industrialists in pubs, drinking endless
glasses of tea, had an irresistible attraction for him. By this

means the well-educated Irishman who had taught English and English literature in Russia, finally learnt to speak Russian fluently, if not correctly, and could even use a few colloquial expressions.

There was nothing artistic about him, except his love for Tennyson, Shakespeare and Moore, whose works he mentioned less and less frequently as the years went by, but he took pleasure in listening to old English songs played by Camisha on their battered piano. He was totally indifferent to the creative art of the family of which he had become a member; he went to the theatre only when he was dragged there by force, and exhibitions and concerts did not interest him. Even less was he concerned about maintaining decorum in his private life which, with the assistance of Camisha's carefree nature, was run on distinctly bohemian lines.

I was deeply attached to 'Matt' I was impressed by his height, by his Herculean build, and at the same time I was not at all afraid of him; there was such kindness in his face. Up to the age of twelve there was nowhere I liked staying as much as in the Edwardes' home, not only because I was allowed to gobble juicy roast beef and the most delicious pastry (Camishenka learnt all the secrets of English culinary art), but also because their simplicity, the curious cosiness in the disorder (the cats and dogs appeared to run the house on equal terms with their masters) seemed enviable to me after the comparative severity of my own home.

But death was to separate this wonderful, sweet couple. Matt died in Petersburg, and a proof of the love which he inspired in his many subordinates is that his factory workmen volunteered to carry the coffin from the house to the Catholic cemetery, a distance of about five miles – and this at the height of the 1917 Revolution when the battle-cry was 'death and destruction to the capitalist exploiters'! Camisha emigrated three years after his death and ended her life in England, in poverty, in a cottage donated to her children and grandchildren by Matt's wealthy relations.

[B]

My second sister, Catherine, called Katia or Katish, was only a year younger than Camisha but seemed even younger. As a child, Katia was a charming tomboy and grew up into a pretty girl with a wonderful complexion, with swift and very graceful movements. But her manner was changeable, she was rather hot-tempered, and she liked to listen to gossip, even provoking it with an innocent air. What was worse, she passed it on equally innocently in the wrong direction, which often caused complications. There was no evil in her, but this feminine trick, totally absent in Camisha and Mamma, somewhat marred Katia's natural good-nature.

The destiny of poor Katish was far less fortunate and smooth than that of her elder sister. A few months before Camisha's marriage, Katish married the gifted young sculptor Eugene Lanceray, who early became famous. Their romance, which began in the summer of 1874, lasted unspoilt to Lanceray's death in February 1886, but he had been a doomed man from the very beginning, for from the end of the 1870s he had suffered from consumption. Katia was only thirty-six years old when her husband died and remained as attractive as ever, but she was faithful to him to the end of her days. Her own life, not too fortunate at its beginning, was to end dramatically through the intervention of war and revolution. Surrounded by children and grandchildren, she knew no want until those miserable days. But the Bolshevik Revolution, which broke out while she was living in the country, forced her to leave home, and when the Ukraine was recaptured her country mansion and its ancestral park were burnt to the ground. Katia was left like the rest of us without a penny, and she would have died had she not been saved by her children.

In 1920 we succeeded in moving her to Petersburg and settled her in the same apartment of our family home in which she had been born and spent the first twenty-four years of her life. Here she ended her days, but, oh God, in what sad circumstances! When the need for living-space become acute, Katia's apartment began gradually to fill up. At first this was still at her own choice, and the rooms she needed least were given up to friends and acquaintances, but afterwards complete strangers and unwelcome members of the new order invaded the empty rooms. Our poor parental home, witness of so many happy times, was transformed into a habitat of wild, miscellaneous elements, and its atmosphere was poisoned by intrigues and denunciations. 'Katenka', totally blind in the last months of her life, ended her days in one room and a communal kitchen.

[c]

My eldest brother Albert was born eighteen years before me. He was therefore almost old enough to be my father, but in spite of this difference in years I never conceived anything like a filial respect for him. To me Albert was always the same Bertusha, Berta or Albertus as the one I first learnt to love in early childhood, and up to his eighty-fourth year this wonderful man preserved the absolute freshness of youth. This was largely due to his temperamental (and on the whole enviable) incapacity to penetrate to the heart of a matter.

It must be admitted that Albert was a real charmer. His mission in life, the meaning of his existence, lay in his natural talent for fascination. He was in many ways remarkably gifted, but the greatest of his gifts was this *don de plaire*, and although a supremely egocentric being, Albert was unaware of its existence. It is impossible to imagine him feeling repentant or guilty. He was for ever 'picking the flowers of life'; often he broke their fragile stems and trampled upon their blooms, secure in the belief that he could do no wrong; never did he pause to consider that this charming occupation might transgress the limits of permitted behaviour. He delighted in and greedily absorbed the good things that life offered him, with never a thought that he might be disobeying the laws of God or man. And it was characteristic of him, too, that if he tasted forbidden fruit, he retained no memory of the misdemeanour. He was largely indifferent to the past: having turned a page of the book of life, he forgot what had been written on it. By contrast, the world of writing was to him a closed book. I do not ever remember Albert reading anything, unless it was a cursory glance at the newspapers.

Though Albert's charm was his outstanding characteristic, he had also a talent for musical improvisation. Long before, our great-grandfather Catarino Cavos had gathered together in the Scuola di San Marco an elite, enlightened audience which delighted in his spontaneous and magically constructed musical improvisations. Skipping two generations, our great-grandfather's gift was bestowed upon two great-grandsons – upon Albert, in a greater measure; upon myself in a lesser. I am therefore qualified to judge (indeed I began to do so almost in my cradle) the high quality of Albert's improvisations. Unfortunately nowadays this gift is not fully appreciated. Even Albert's wife, herself an excellent professional musician with a reverence for real, serious music, felt no admiration for and was even rather ironical about the music to which Albert's fingers gave life.

Nevertheless, his style of playing the piano (or the violin), his skilful touch, his original and brilliant technique, were magnificent. When he was young, he was invested with remarkable beauty at such moments. His fingers were long and strong and aristocratic (like those that

Sebastiano del Piombo loved to paint); nimbly and gracefully they developed the theme, the melody with its harmonious transitions and modulations emerging in a splendid
unity, rich and original. His hands produced these marvellous sounds as if they had been composed a long time
ago, instead of being completely transitory. It was remarkable that the moment the magic was over, Albert himself
was unable to recollect what he had just played with such
rapture. His considerable theoretical knowledge of music
should have enabled him to score his improvisations
quite easily, but he never did so, and was satisfied by the
pleasure he had given himself and others.

Albert would use his music as a secret language of love,
and it was amusing to watch the young women clustering
ecstatically round the piano, trembling at the alluring sound
of those ardent declarations! Albert seduced many daughters
of Eve by his musical love-making, which very often took
place in the most formal of drawing-rooms, crowded with
people, in full view of the mothers or husbands of the
transitory victims.

These improvisations of Albert's played quite a part in
the history of my balletomania, and indeed they were my
first inspiration. In the autumn of 1882 Albert settled down
in our ancestral home, in the flat above ours, and from then
on I became a constant listener to his music. As soon as I
heard the firm, melodious, luscious tunes, I flew upstairs to
the ballroom to interpret in movement my brother's music,
with my feet, hands, facial expressions, with the whole of
my body. I acted, I created, I was in a trance, I was choreographer and dancer in a *corps de ballet*, all at once. My little
nieces often joined us and then we could perform real acts
where the episodes were conceived and developed at a
remarkable speed, all at the whim of our inspirer.

Many of these invented ballets (which lasted about
twenty minutes) had a violent theme, such as murder, a

duel, rape, a curse. The central character would be threatened with terrible disaster; at the most dramatic moment the actors would lie prone on the parquet floor, a scene which was meant to express terror before the imminent catastrophe. But even as we lay there breathless, we knew that it would all end in joy and jubilation, that after the sinister and disturbing chords the music would suddenly rally and culminate in a frenzied gallop or a wild tarantella.

I continued to improvise dances to Albert's music right up to my student days, but I do not consider that these dancing exercises can be dismissed as entirely childish pranks. Inspired by the music, I felt I was creating something serious, and many years later, when I was producing *Pavillon d'Armide* on a real stage, with real ballet stars floating through the air, I seemed to be continuing a task I had started long ago; I had returned to the world, familiar from childhood, in which I found my inspiration in my brother's musical improvisations.

Later, this gift of Albert's was to be an asset in his career as an artist. In 1883 his water-colours were shown to the Emperor by Mr Charles Hiss, English tutor to the Imperial children, who was connected with us by marriage and was himself a clever painter. Their Majesties admired the pictures so much that they invited Albert to join their regular summer excursion round the Finnish islands; and thereafter not a cruise took place without Albert spending days upon the floating Imperial residence, the *Tsarevna*, where in an informal atmosphere he dined and afterwards entertained the company with his music. Alexander III was a great lover of pranks, and his whole suite laughed until they cried as they watched my brother give a one-man performance of a parody on a typical Italian opera, caricaturing the absurdity of its subject and the clichés which the composers used to describe the meetings of tragic lovers or the conspiracies, with a ballet suddenly thrust in at the most pathetic and inappropriate moment. The Italian influence was at that time the object of much scorn, but Albert's parodies not only had humour, they also had exceptional taste and spirit.

The endless adventures in love of our family Casanova were also improvisations in keeping with his gift for playing the piano. True, he had several serious love affairs and three of them ended in marriage, but these were punctuated with many transitory, casual affairs.

Albert was an architect by training. After finishing at the Academy he did some designs for buildings, but without enthusiasm, and he was constantly distracted by other things more in keeping with his nature. Most of his time was spent in painting, almost exclusively in water-colour from nature. In this field, which admirably suited his quick, impatient temperament and the light-weight quality that was natural to him, he reached in a few years a position which was unrivalled in Russia. In the 1880s and 1890s Albert Benois was one of the most popular Russian painters; his paintings were a great financial success, he was made an Academician and was given an appointment as professor on water-colour painting in the Academy. The Society of Aquarelle Painters elected him president and it was due to Albert that exhibitions of water-colours became one of the most prominent events of the Petersburg season and were visited by the members of the Imperial Family. Through Albert our family became more conversant with Court life, not with its gossip and intrigues (for which Albert never had any inclination) but with the spirit and atmosphere that surrounded Alexander III, which seemed to us fascinating in its simplicity.

With what ardour Albert could work! Not a day passed in the spring, summer or autumn without his making a sketch or even several sketches. And the freer and simpler they were, the better they turned out to be. Albert was particularly successful with transitory effects. Many of the famous Albert Benois sunsets, created in a kind of ecstatic trance, were real little masterpieces. Unfortunately his quick success somewhat impaired his artistic development. Albert remained a master in the full sense of the word until the end of his days, but towards the end of the first period of his creative activity the freshness and spontaneity of his work gave way to a certain excessive finish. Strangely enough, Albert's real gift had a brilliant renaissance in the water-colours he made during a scientific expedition to Murmansk in 1922, but from the moment he came to France in 1924 to live with his elder daughter and her husband, his art began to decline.

The sad fate that befell my sisters in their old age was shared by my brothers and the saddest of all was Albert's. Until he left Russia he continued to live in his own apartment, surrounded by the portraits of his ancestors which he had inherited and cupboards filled to the brim with all his works, accumulated during his long life. All this was left when he fled his country with nothing but a few clothes. At that time he still had illusions that abroad he could recapture the fine position which he had not completely lost in his own country even during the years of revolutionary chaos. But these illusions soon disappeared. An exhibition at the George Petit gallery, in the rooms where he had formerly exhibited with such success, passed unnoticed and there was no hope of finding a Maecenas among the Russian émigrés. So the situation arose which even to the lighthearted, childishly irresponsible Albert gradually became insupportable, and had it not been for his comparative superficiality, he would hardly have been able to bear the fate that befell him when at the age of seventy he lost the use of his legs and all his money and had to end his days at the mercy of an erratic son-in-law. Crippled, pathetic, tied to his chair, forgotten as a painter and

completely penniless, my brother accepted all these disasters
with a light heart and never lost his *joie de vivre*. He never
moaned or complained – not because he could control his
feelings, but because his nature was imbued with optimism;
and he never lost his childlike ability to live in the present,
looking neither backward nor forward, never really con-
centrating upon anything. He was also, it must be said,
impervious to the inconveniences caused to others by his
crippled condition. His daughter was a true martyr, but her
husband was resentful that his wife should give her whole
strength to looking after the helpless, unfortunate old man
and was almost openly hostile to his father-in-law. Albert did
not sufficiently appreciate his daughter's devotion and was as
exacting (in a childish way) as he had been when he was
master of his own house and head of the family. This was
not caused by any hardness of heart, but by his inability to
understand the reality of the situation. But as always this
old man, tied to his chair, charmed all who came within
his orbit; this ancient Casanova still made conquests. His
eyes would light up with the same naughty flame, rapturous-
ly he would kiss the ladies' hands and take an exuberant
pleasure in meeting his friends – though it must be admitted
that he included among these friends people whose names
he sometimes did not remember. But all this concealed the
tragedy of humiliating helplessness.

Albert ended his life in a small *pension* for invalids, near
Paris. From his window one could see a typical Île de France
landscape, only slightly disfigured by progress – probably
the same kind of landscape in which our ancestors had lived
and died. It was spring, nature was blossoming, but Albert,
who only a few weeks before had found joy in painting it,
now contemplated this beauty with the dim eye of a doomed
man. Thus ended the life of this 'prince of living', favourite
of Petersburg society, favourite of fortune, my dearest, my
never-despairing, joy-spreading Albertus.

[D]

My second brother was christened Ludovic, but this sounded
odd to Russian ears, and so our Ludovic was transformed
into Leontij. As a child I remember both Albert and
Leontij as grown-up men. Leontij was shorter than Albert
and his tendency to corpulence earned him the nickname of
Gros-gros.

His was a quiet, reasonable nature, neither violent nor
rebellious, yet at the same time ardent. He was a wonderfully
humane person, kind and honest, a man of good will in the
fullest sense, and he was loved and admired by everybody.
Like Albert he emanated charm but of an entirely different
kind. He was incapable of hypocrisy, guile or malice, and
although he was sometimes impulsive and hot-tempered and
even unfair in his judgements, his emotional outbursts
were spontaneous and he would calm down as quickly as
he had flared up. He lived according to principle, sometimes
perhaps wrong-headed, but always based on a genuine
belief. Even as a child he sided with the downtrodden. He
was fiercely opposed to any form of injustice and loathed
any kind of falsehood, and throughout his whole life his
capacity to feel indignation never diminished, whether
over world events, specific aspects of Russian life which he
considered disgraceful, or the idiocies of government. He
was disgusted by what he considered to be lapses of taste.
His wrath was especially directed against the Germans, in
matters of politics as well as of Art. As I grew up I realised
that Leontij was prone to oversimplify and to jump too
quickly to conclusions on mere hearsay, but even when I
disagreed with him I could not but admire the good will
which inspired his high indignation.

Our father had bestowed upon all three of us, Albert,
Leontij and myself, a gift for painting and a love for art,
but Leontij, I believe, was the most talented of us. Albert

was a great virtuoso as far as technique was concerned, but
his nimbleness of hand was not the basic trait in his art,
whereas with Leontij the dexterity was something inborn
and fundamental. The fact that this virtuoso of pencil and
brush chose architecture as his field was in a way the result
of that characteristic. His architectural designs displayed
this virtuosity in their tasteful rendering of detail and could
be admired also as pictures because, like Father, he would
populate them with hundreds of little humans and animals
of the most varied kind. Being a lover of racing and steeple-
chasing, he was particularly successful with horses.

Leontij's career as an architect started with an exceptional
triumph. He finished at the Academy of Arts one year before
the appointed time, and received the large gold medal out of
turn. The same distinction had been won by our father
fifty years before, but these were rare occasions in the life
of the Academy. Leontij did not take advantage of the trip
abroad which was offered along with the medal, for he preferred to marry the girl he loved. Maria Alexandrovna
Sapojhnikoff, who was to be Leontij's faithful companion
during his whole life, came from a rich merchant's family,
but they fell in love in the year when the Sapojhnikoff
fortune was in sad decline. Leontij was unaffected by
material considerations – indeed the match was considered
disadvantageous from his point of view, if not actually a
mésalliance – but later the marriage also brought material
prosperity when after a few years the Sapojhnikoff fortune
(derived from fisheries on the Volga) was re-established.
As by then Leontij's income as an architect had also
increased he and Masha were very rich indeed.

Leontij's first public work was connected with the
murder of the Tsar on March 1st, 1881. The Town Hall
invited him to build a temporary wooden chapel on the
spot of the murder, and modest though it was the chapel
had an exceptionally graceful quality and earned general

approval. A year later Leontij took part in the competition to design the church which was to be erected on the same spot. His plan, inspired by the work of Rastrelli and faithful to the style of Petersburg, was very beautiful and striking and was probably the best thing he ever produced. But the jury awarded him only third prize, the first two going to architectural designs in a more national style. However, the plan which received the first prize was never carried out, for the architect Parland (using his connections with the clergy and with various influential officials) managed to get his own extremely ugly but strikingly coloured design approved by the Emperor. While the 'Church of Blood' was being built the Academy of Arts insisted that some of the absurdities and flaws in the Parland project should be altered, but, alas, even in its amended final shape this pathetic imitation of the Church of St Basil in Moscow is a real blot on the general Petersburg landscape.

Other works by Leontij Benois are two bank buildings on the Nevsky Prospekt, the Insurance building on the Morskaia Street, the cathedral in the factory town of Guss and the majestic and luxurious cathedral in Warsaw which was destroyed as soon as Poland became independent. Of all these buildings I personally would be unable to recommend one as a model of architecture or even simply as a successful work. Leontij was a progressive architect for his time; he had nothing against new methods; he tried to freshen up old ideas and make them serve new requirements. His plans are cleverly constructed, his details beautifully drawn. But there is a lack of artistic direction in all that he has done. His work suffers from a casual quality. It lacks a convincing harmony. One wonders whether it was his very facility that prevented my brother from giving enough thought to his work and made him satisfied with the first apparently effective combination of lines. He never admitted second thoughts after he had conceived a plan and would at once get to work on his composition. With his good memory and considerable erudition he could complete a project in the shortest possible time, whereas the idea had perhaps only begun to ripen in the minds of other artists or architects. Also he was working in a period which was peculiarly unfavourable to architecture, in Russia as well as throughout all Europe. His education had not included the discipline of the severe classical tradition which was the basis of training for architects in the first half of the nineteenth century and which still had an ennobling effect on the architecture of the Romantic era. The era 1860–1960 was marked by unprincipled dilettantism, and the imitation of various styles of which there was no real knowledge reached a stage of genuine depravity.

But there may, perhaps, have been another reason why our charming and exceptionally talented Liovushka did not after all become a great artist. Perhaps it was due to his happy marriage – the happiest marriage I know of, except perhaps my father's and my own. Maria Alexandrovna was a plump little woman with a cheerful smile that never left her mouth and an expression both tender and cunning. She was well suited to her husband in appearance; she too was not very tall and had a slight tendency to corpulence. They were harmonious temperamentally and their attitude to life was the same. During the forty-five years of their marriage there were none of those petty quarrels, however brief, that are so difficult to avoid even in the most model unions. Nonetheless, Maria Alexandrovna Sapojhnikoff belonged, by breeding, education and way of life, to a totally different category from that which was truly *ours* and therefore her husband's.

In spite of her keen wit and her quite kindly nature, Masha upset me by her total absence of imagination. It irritated me for my brother's sake, for I loved and respected him and it seemed to me he was being overwhelmed by his prosaic existence. I was never at my ease in their house in my childhood. However sumptuous the dinners and delicate the wines, however animated the discussions in their warm company, the less I was interested, the more oppressive I found them. I would guzzle their delicious and expensive food, and then immediately try to get away, which I often succeeded in doing without much trouble since both hosts and guests would become so engrossed in playing cards that they failed to notice what was going on around them.

I was acutely conscious of our class differences the day Masha's parents first came to see us. She had just become engaged to my brother. Her father was a very amiable man with the manners of a British aristocrat, dwarf-like in size, with a grey, scented beard that came down to his chest. He had long, carefully trimmed nails and he was always fault-lessly dressed. He spoke good French and English and prided himself on his accent: nevertheless, he was still a typical Russian merchant. Indeed he emphasised this character with a kind of coquetry, using vulgar expressions and calling his wife, who was still quite young, 'my old woman'. As for his wife, she was one of those erratic Russian ladies who liked to squander her money in Europe and who as a result was pursued by a crowd of adventurers constantly flattering her and begging for favours. Among other valuable things in her possession were two colossal diamonds which were exhibited in a special showcase at the World Exhibition in Paris in 1900 by the jeweller Boucheron.

During the last few years of his life Leontij held the post of Rector of the Academy of Arts; but the revolution was coming nearer. A spirit of rebellion against the authorities in the students gradually turned to an open revolt in all strata of society against the government. But this rebellion was never directed against Rector Benois. He continued to inspire respect in the young for two reasons: they loved him as a good man regardless of his class, and also because he was an intelligent and careful tutor. He was never long-winded; he shared his knowledge in calmness and simplicity; he did not seek to impose his counsel upon anybody; his criticism was never resented. In artistic matters he was keenly interested in modern ideas; even if he had no firm convictions himself he knew how to stimulate the interests of others. His methods might now be considered obsolete, but those who experienced them derived satisfaction and pleasure from his instruction. Even after the establishment of the Bolshevist regime, Leontij, former favourite of the Grand Duke Vladimir and the Grand Duchess, former Court Architect, went on with his professorship, though the actual post of rector had been abolished. As evidence of his great popularity with his students, when he died in 1928 the Academy organised a funeral ceremony which it is hard to imagine being held for a survivor of the bourgeoisie in a proletarian country. His body lay in the round Conference Hall where he had once been acclaimed as one of the most gifted pupils. Academicians stood guard by the coffin and later an immense crowd accompanied him to the cemetery.

His lectures during the revolution underwent no change and were untouched by the disturbing reforms which introduced such chaos into academic teaching. But he suffered in his private life. He was able to face ruin with equanimity after the October days just as everyone else did. When a ship goes down, the loss of personal valuables has little significance. But what saddened him more was the burning down of the charming house he had built for himself in Peterhof and which in the first period of the revolution had remained by a miracle in his possession. He was further grieved by having to surrender a large part of his cosy apartment to complete strangers, and the forced communal existence caused much discomfort to my poor brother, so used to luxury and privacy. Then came illness and even worse affliction. He had to undergo two operations in the last ten years, which affected his outlook on life: he seemed to waste away, he lost his *joie de vivre* and grew despondent. Three of his children, in order to escape hunger and other dangers, left Russia altogether.[1] The youngest son, Shoura, a charming youth and a dashing Guards officer who escaped like his elder brother to France, joined the Voluntary Army and was killed near Kiev. Leontij himself almost became the victim of the Bolshevik terror. In the autumn of 1921, during the arrests in connection with Professor Tagantsev, he was arrested with his wife and children and put in prison. The family was released after a few days, but Leontij stayed in prison for six months. Intervention was useless; it was impossible to ascertain the reason for the imprisonment of a man so divorced from politics. We all trembled for his life, for the rumour spread that he was accused of being a spy, had been tried and was about to be shot; but he was ultimately set free owing to the influence of N. Sokolov and M. Gorki's first wife. When asked what his crime was, the magistrate replied: 'There must have been a misunderstanding'.

Leontij's attitude of mind in these terrible years was remarkably noble and detached. Bit by bit everything that he had loved crumbled to pieces, but he stood all these disasters with calm and an all-forgiving Christian meekness. Nevertheless Leontij did not feel strongly about religion, though he remained a good Catholic. He ended his life a truly pious man.

[E]

Of all my brothers I was least close to Nicholas (called Kolia by the family and friends). The reason why we under-

One of Leontij's daughters Nadejda—known in England as the artist Nadia Benois—has kept her maiden name though her married name is Ustinov. She went abroad not because of financial reasons, hunger or danger, but because she fell in love and married a young man who had come to Russia to search for his mother. Their only son, Peter Ustinov, has acquired world-fame as the author of remarkably witty stage plays and as a first-rate actor.

Photograph by Julius Edwardes

1. Alexandre Benois, on the eve of his 89th birthday, with his painting of Peter the Great by the sea at St Petersburg.

Drawing by his sister Catherine

2. Alexandre Benois at the age of 3.

Watercolour by Alexandre Benois

3. View from the Benois apartment in St Petersburg.
On the right, the Bolshoi Theatre.

Louis Benois
Painting by Courteuil

Catarino Cavos
*Lithograph after
a miniature by Osokin*

Alberto Cavos
Lithograph by an unknown artist

4. Alexandre Benois' grandfathers and great-grandfather

5. Nicholas and Camille Benois, the parents of Alexandre.

Bronze medallions by Arthur Aubert

Watercolour by Alexandre Benois

6. Nicholas Benois' study in the family house in St Petersburg.

Copy by Alexandre Benois of a watercolour by Albert Benois

7. Kushelevka: The Benois country house near St Petersburg (1877).

8. Two watercolours of St Petersburg by Alexandre Benois:
(*above*) the Winter Palace and (*below*) Rastrelli senior's statue of
Peter the Great with the Castle of the Archangel
Michael in the background.

stood each other so little was not so much the difference in age (he was twelve years older than I), or that he was less often at home than the others, or even that he was in the army. The reason for our lack of affinity was, I think, because Kolia not only chose a military career, but stuck to it undeviatingly all his life. I did not like his style, his hoarse, rough voice, his way of expressing himself in abrupt sentences, his noisiness. I don't think that I even liked his appearance, though at one time I was said to look very like him. I did not see much of Kolia even in my childhood, for he lived in the Cadet Corps quarters and in the summer went to camp; later, after joining the Imperial Uhlan Guards Regiment, he moved to Warsaw where he lived permanently and attained the rank of Colonel.

When Nicholas came on leave to Petersburg and stayed with the family, he was usually accommodated in Papa's large studio. As soon as he settled in, a special army smell spread through the flat, a rather pleasant mixture of scent, tobacco and leather. This smell became a fixture in our house during the two years (at the end of the 1880s) which he spent in Petersburg, having decided that his education ought to be completed by a course in the Cavalry School. He moved part of his personal belongings into our house, and the walls of the studio became festooned with fencing weapons and masks, sabres and daggers. When my brother first arrived, I used to feel much oppressed by his presence. I could hardly bear the row he made, not to mention the fact that sometimes he would recruit me into doing him various small services, such as helping him pull off his boots or fixing the silver band on his shoulder. My inability always to manage these straight away provoked impatient ejaculations from Nicholas which I found most offensive. But gradually I grew accustomed to him and learned to appreciate the good nature that was concealed under the layer of military roughness and odd behaviour.

Compared with his brothers Kolia married late. His wife, a widow with two children, was also not in her first youth, but she was of good family and as with her mother she owned a large estate, estimated at several million roubles, the marriage could be considered a good one from the material point of view as well as the social. But in the end his relationship with his wife deteriorated and they finally had to part.

During the years before the 1914 war Nicholas, who had already retired, was living with his favourite brother Leontij in Petersburg. Feeling lonely and suffering from idleness, he welcomed the opportunity to return to the army on the declaration of war. He was given the rank of general and sent to Siberia to recruit troops, but in December 1915 he had a stroke which ended his life. His body was taken to Petersburg and at Leontij's request buried in the vault which Leontij had acquired for his own family. The last time I saw Nicholas, his face dark but still looking very much himself, was through the glass of a coffin.

(F)

Many people still survive who were friends of my brothers Albert, Leontij, Nicholas and Michael, but this is not so with brother Isha; since the death of my parents and our close relatives there is nobody in the world, apart from myself, who remembers him. He left no trace of his stay on earth except for the remains reposing in our family vault, laid there in the autumn of 1874. I still think of him with great tenderness because of the great care with which he, who was ten years older than myself, surrounded my small person.

I resembled Isha very closely. In later years when I used to gaze at myself in the looking-glass I would imagine that I was seeing him, and this consoled me for his loss and made me feel more tolerant of my own appearance. Spiritually and artistically also Isha and I had much in common. Like him I was attracted by weird, even cruel pictures. I loved fairy-tales which described eerie happenings; I was lured by the spirit of adventure. I was never a fanatical devotee of sport like Isha, who was a wonderful skater, a fearless sailor and who devoted a large part of every morning to physical exercises in order to develop his muscles. But I loved to watch him skating on the pond in the Yussupoff Gardens; I caught my breath in rapture as he sailed his boat in Peterhof harbour; and I was filled with pride when he came first in a race.

His attitude to self-education and study also seemed to foretell my own. In the winter months he was never idle, but though he might be buried in a book it was never a textbook; when he sat scribbling on a piece of paper he was certainly not doing his 'prep'. In one of my earliest memories I am kneeling on a chair beside Isha, watching with bated breath the shapes that are springing from his pencil. They are of towering pyramids, on the gradations of which hundreds of little figures are hard at work operating cranes. A colossal stone drops from a great hook and tumbles down, squashing people on its way. Blood flows from one step to the next. In another picture warriors in golden helmets adorned with horses' tails stand in rows, resisting the attack of other warriors; or they dash past on horseback or in chariots to meet the enemy. Again blood pours in streams from their weapons or from their wounded bodies, the chariot wheels jolt over the heaps of dead and the wounded lie twisted on the ground. Sometimes it would be Roman legions or Attila's hordes, sometimes Napoleon's soldiers. In his youth Leontij also loved to draw battle scenes, but in Leontij's pictures everything looked tidy, even glamorous, whereas in Isha's tragedy and horror dominated the imagination. While he was drawing, he would go into a kind of trance, hissing with wrath, shouting, mocking and cursing.

Isha's death was totally unexpected. He caught typhoid, and after weeks of suffering which he bore with great courage, he died at the age of only fourteen.

[G]

Michael (Misha) was two years nearer to me in age than Isha. In those days Misha was a real schoolboy, but I remember him much less vividly than Isha. Like Isha, he was good at tricks, and at one time he set up a little theatre in which he tried to produce all the horrors of the *Valley of the Wolves*. He had the thick lips of a negro, slightly curly hair, black as coal, and a swarthy skin. He was unlike all his brothers in his childhood and only as he grew up did he acquire the general appearance of our family, and particularly of Leontij.

Misha wanted to be a sailor. Mamma was deeply upset by this, but Papa who had the greatest admiration for the fighting forces, gave him his blessing. After years of training in a naval college Misha passed out with the rank of petty officer, and eventually Ensign Benois was appointed to serve on a clipper. Preparations began in earnest. He got a brand-new uniform, and a very elegant black frock-coat and black tie to be worn on great occasions, with a belt of lions' heads and a little ivory dagger hanging from it, and by June 1880 he was ready to depart. Papa, Mamma and I went to see him off in Kronstadt. We had some difficulty in discovering where the clipper lay at anchor, but we finally reached it in a small boat to find that all these young sailors had been drinking heavily during the farewell celebrations and that the rest of the crew, to whom vodka had been distributed, were also tipsy. I was upset that Misha's ship had only one funnel, but to make up for this it had three masts. When night fell, families and friends moved to a specially chartered ship, anchor was weighed, and we set off in unequal competition with Misha's clipper, past the granite piers into the open sea. For two or three miles our puffing, rolling little boat tried to keep up with the clipper, but the distance between us kept increasing and finally the moment came when our ship turned back. This was accompanied by the traditional farewell ceremony. At the word of command the white figures of the sailors assembled on deck and to general cheering, a myriad of white patches were hurled into the water – the summer covers of the officers' caps which, according to custom, they had to discard on departure. A few minutes later the clipper *Plastoon*, silhouetted against a flaming sunset, turned into a faraway, silent shadow and after another few minutes seemed to sink behind the horizon.

Misha's voyage on this ship extended from months into years. Our parents subscribed to the *Kronstadt News* which reported the movement throughout the world of ships of the Russian fleet. When for some time there was no such information, anxiety grew. I could vividly imagine the enormous waves (like those in one of Jules Verne's books) hurtling against Misha's ship, which would be transformed into a miserable shell during the raging storm. But my brother's letters from Shanghai, Hong Kong, Nagasaki, Sakhalin Island, Honolulu, San Francisco, Tahiti, Melbourne and Sydney, all told quite another tale. Misha's descriptions were simple, truthful, precise, but they were not picturesque and did not stir the imagination.

Suddenly a telegram came from Kronstadt: 'Arrived safely'. Heavens, what excitement reigned in the house! Stepanida (Misha's wet nurse who had since served in our house as a housemaid), who was very free with her tears, began to mumble prayers of joy as if over a corpse. She was very worried by the idea that her favourite might have married a Japanese and we teased her about it at length.

This was June 1883. It so happened that I was staying with our English relatives, Matt Edwardes's sister Helen and her husband Reginald Livesey, who were sightseeing in Peterhof, and we arranged that after visiting the palaces and gardens we would make our way to Kronstadt. We did reach Kronstadt and the clipper, but by the time our noisy crowd arrived on deck, Misha had already left for Petersburg. However, the remaining officers received us with every honour, and I was particularly flattered at being entertained most lavishly by Misha's friend, Prince Putiatin. I drank to Brotherhood with him, sipping champagne and eating black radish in sour cream. After two glasses I was so drunk that I fell down the ladder that led from the captain's bridge.

By the time we reached Petersburg it was growing dark. As we entered our apartment Papa and Mamma hushed me – Misha was asleep and was not to be wakened. I was only allowed to glance at the sleeping traveller. Making my way on tiptoe to the bed, I gazed with astonishment. Instead of the former tender youth I found a huge, powerful, but nevertheless handsome man, quite black from sunburn. There was such a strange smell in the room: a spicy aroma, something eastern, alien, far-away. It came from the open suitcases, all nearly empty by now. Everywhere on tables and chairs lay parcels, and I wondered which of the treasures were destined for me, for in every letter Misha had promised me a surprise.

Alas, I was to be disappointed. The next morning after breakfast we all made our way to Misha's study and the distribution of presents from the trunks began. I was among the first to receive mine. Misha had obviously imagined his little brother as still a child for whom a mechanical poodle would make a suitable present and not at all as a smart thirteen-year-old boy. Aware of his mistake, Misha was confused and I felt so sorry for him that I pretended to be delighted with the toy, but the rest of the treasures that emerged from Misha's trunks that morning were so fascinating that I became quite engrossed in them and forgot my own disappointment.

There were a saw-fish's claw, a necklace of shells and birds' eggs from Tahiti, a magic Japanese mirror, an Indian casket with a mosaic lid which had a wonderful fragrance inside, a beautiful Japanese scarlet shawl with a peacock embroidered in yellow silk, little cups from the Satsuma factory and musical instruments that gave out odd, weird sounds, a tortoiseshell model of a rickshaw and masses of photograph albums, bright shawls and shells in rainbow colours. Out of the large wooden trunk also came endless jars with exotic preserved fruits and charming little bottles with sweet Cape wine.

The only thing that upset me was Misha's taciturnity; he told hardly any stories and only gave short replies to my many eager questions. And I wanted so badly to hear everything in detail – particularly how he had spent his time in Japan, where I had heard, the officers on shore leave soon found charming little Japanese wives. This rumour was widespread at that time and was one of the reasons why, a few years later, Gauguin decided to leave a decadent Europe and settle in Oceania. But I could get nothing out of Misha on that subject. I am convinced to this day that my pure-minded brother had returned from his three-year journey as innocent and chaste as when he left home. A girl in every port was an experience of which he knew nothing.

A few weeks after his return there was evidence that his heart had indeed preserved its freshness, and its capacity for love; his marriage to his cousin Olga Cavos (daughter of our Uncle Kostia) took place in the middle of September

1884. What a brilliant wedding it was! The blessing of the
bride and bridegroom took place in the summer church of
the magnificent Cathedral of St Nicholas. Uncle Kostia
'avait bien fait les choses'. The heavily gilded church looked
more like a ballroom; it sparkled with thousands of candles,
the clergy and the choir had donned their festive robes;
laurel and palm trees stood everywhere. Against a background of black evening dress the uniforms and light
dresses of the ladies stood out very effectively. Among the
ladies Grandmamma Cavos was the most outstanding in her
ermine cloak and a headdress of Venetian lace that hung
down to her shoulders. I must admit that I, too, felt festively
splendid on that day. I was wearing a new school uniform
made for special occasions, with silver braid on the collar,
and I felt sure that it made me look quite fascinating.

The first ten years of their married life, which had started
so brilliantly, was full of happiness for Misha and Olga.
Misha retired and became a Civil Servant, an occupation
which took up little of his time, and they lived comfortably,
on an income given to them by Uncle Kostia, in a large and
well-furnished apartment on the English Prospect. But
suddenly this happiness crumbled to pieces. Misha and
Olga, at first so much in love, began to quarrel and finally
parted, dividing the children: the son went with his father,
the girl with her mother. Then came the tragedy of war
followed by the revolution. From being rich people,
Misha and his children became 'have nots'. My brother
continued to live in the large flat to which he had moved
after his divorce, but gradually retired to his kitchen as so
many of his fellow citizens had done, while the rest of the
apartment was occupied by strangers. Misha's last days
during the Bolshevik regime were darkened less by illness
and poverty than by the bitterness of the undeserved
suspicions with which he was surrounded. He was arrested
on the same day as Leontij. Leontij bore the ordeal with

calm humility, but in Misha's nature there was bitterness as well as goodness of heart, and his unjustifiable and arbitrary imprisonment lasting six months had a destructive effect on his morale. When I last went to see him I found him in the room adjoining the kitchen making dolls' furniture. At that moment he reminded me acutely of my father who was also a great master of such things. But Papa created his pearls for his own pleasure and for the delight of his children and grandchildren. For Misha it was his only source of income. Death at last took pity on him and he died, three years after Leontij and four years before Albert, in Petersburg. We were already living in exile when we heard the news.

CHAPTER X

THE CAVOS UNCLES

*

MY mother had four brothers, Cesare, Constantine and Michael and Jean. Her only sister, adorable Aunt Sonia Zarudnaia, died a few years before I was born, and both the wives of Uncle Cesare and of Uncle Kostia also died before I was born. Uncle Michael remained a bachelor. These Cavos uncles attracted and fascinated me, each in a different way, but they were linked together by one outstanding characteristic which I would now call style. Though I was only dimly aware of this in my childhood, it none the less exerted upon me an irresistible charm. This elegance was part of their nature, unaffected and effortless, being neither imitative nor assumed, but derived simply from the fact that they had preserved the graceful manner of living into which they had been born.

Uncle Cesare was Mother's elder brother. I was only thirteen when he died but I remember him clearly as a dominating personality. I knew it was my duty to love him like all my other relatives, and I tried hard to do so, but I was not very successful since the feeling he inspired in me was not without an element of fear. Uncle Cesare was the most stylish of the three brothers but I thought him haughty, very pompous and inaccessible. I was embarrassed by the manner he reserved for children, rather supercilious and condescending. Perhaps he was not really like this, but I was an exceedingly touchy child, spoilt by the loving attentions of my family, and I considered any other attitude an insult. I tried to avoid crossing Uncle Cesare's path, which was not easy as I lived for part of the year in his villa with my parents. He was not a majestic looking man, being less than medium height, like most of the Cavoses; he had a quiet voice, was rarely angry and never shouted. True, he did once break an umbrella over his brother-in-law's back but this was due to such exceptional circumstances that even a mild and humble man would have lost his temper. The brother-in-law, who was as usual tipsy, was driving Uncle Cesare along the canal, and galloped his horse so hard that the carriage fell into the water. When Uncle Cesare climbed out, he thought that his son Genia, lying unconscious on the ground, was in fact dead. He was overcome with fury and hit out so fiercely at the unfortunate culprit that he actually broke the smart umbrella he had bought in Paris. But this was exceptional, and it became part of the family chronicle simply because it was so unlike my uncle's usual behaviour.

My image of Uncle Cesare is inseparable from my memories of the places in which he lived. I have always been like that. I visualise those who are close to me against an individual background – a room, an apartment, a villa. Even God I can only sense fully in His house, in church.

Uncle Cesare's house in Petersburg consisted of two apartments on two floors and a large basement, but it could perhaps be called three floors because of its attics, which were a unique feature in Petersburg houses at the time. The eyeholes, in baroque style, of the attic floor lent a foreign, almost Parisian look to the house. What impressed me most about the house was its splendid staircase. A wonderful fragrance invariably floated down the stairs (Uncle Cesare was a great lover of incense) and this alone made it exciting to my imagination. In my father's house we also had a fine staircase, one of the few remaining in their original condition from the time of Paul I; but we had no porter or central heating and the stairway was icy, its worn steps of Pudojh stone innocent of carpet. In Uncle Cesare's house you walked straight out of the cold of the street into a tropical atmosphere and your feet sank into thick scarlet felt.

Another thing that makes me remember that staircase is that we sometimes played there, strictly against orders, with my Cavos cousins and other children: it was most convenient for ambushes when we were playing bandits. I remember, too, the gatherings that were held there almost as a rite when guests were about to leave. Grandmamma Cavos would open the meeting on the couch while the servants were pulling on her winter boots. Mother would sit beside her and the conversation would begin; and although we were all ready to depart it was so pleasant to sit on, and the prospect of going out into the cold so repulsive, that the talk would continue. Other guests on the point of leaving would join in until everybody was sitting around or squatting on the steps. I did not understand much of the ladies' conversation, and often it would be switched to French or Italian with a *Pas devant les enfants* when the talk was of something that I ought not to hear. Nevertheless, though I was gradually stifling in my winter clothes with my head wrapped up in a warm shawl, I did not want the meeting to come to an end. The scene took on the appearance of a picnic, an amusing game which these boring grown-ups had suddenly decided to play. When the end inevitably came Grandmamma, supported by her son and by the porter, would descend the stairs, a long procession following her. Outside there would be frost and a dull drive in the darkness of the carriage through the town to our own house.

I had no exact contemporaries in Uncle Cesare's family. His youngest daughter, Inna, was two years older than I, and Masha, the next youngest, was about four years older. But we three were great friends in spite of that and played games without ever quarrelling. They were both kind, easy-going little girls, who never lost their tempers or sulked. The girls paid great respect to their father but showed none of the emotional tenderness that was so customary in my own family.

As well as Masha and Inna, there were in Uncle Cesare's family his eldest daughter Sonia and his only son Eugene (Genia). Cousin Genia, who was twelve years older than I was, was all good nature and good will. He was a close friend of my brothers Isha and Kolia and shared their sporting tastes. He treated me, not superciliously, but with distinct indifference. As for Cousin Sonia, her chief flaw in my eyes was her undisguised sense of superiority over the younger generation; she did not hesitate to reprimand us in the most offensive manner. Now as I look back at all this, having learned in the course of my long life how exacting life can be, I realise with how much tact Sonia did her duty as a sister who had also to be a mother to her brothers and sisters; but in those days 1 was an unruly child, very self-conscious and spoilt, and I easily clashed with anyone in charge of the household. Sonia was always controlled, she never allowed herself any outbursts of irritation, she was calm and even-tempered. But she issued orders and remained reproachfully silent when she could not scold me for my misdeeds. I did not like her haughtiness, her half-closed, myopic eyes, her manner that seemed to me unutterably conceited. I was supremely irritated when she galloped past in an elegant riding kit and a top hat, on her chestnut mare. I did not like her sing-song drawling voice.

Though Aunt Sonia died quite young before I was born, I was perfectly familiar with the appearance of the mother of Inna, Masha, Sonia and Genia, because an oval portrait of her, painted in the 1860s by the Italian artist Belloli, hung in the small sitting-room between the ballroom and the dining-room, surrounded by similar oval frames containing the portraits of her children.

Out of the window of this sitting-room and also those of

the adjoining ballroom, I could watch the children in winter playing below in Uncle Cesare's tidy courtyard, for in the winter months the whole courtyard was transformed into an ice-rink with, on one side, a snow hill built up against the house itself. Crowds came to skate there, and the dining-room was turned into a cloakroom where shoes were changed and special hats and coats put on, though the cadets and law students, of whom there were quite a number, paraded about even in the frost in nothing but their uniforms. Skates were usually screwed on beside the rink, but some of the virtuosos performed this operation upstairs, and then one could hear them thundering down the servants' stairs into the yard – not always without tumbling down on the way. One of the most dashing skaters was my brother Kolia, the cadet, who had already won many prizes at public competitions in the Yussupoff Gardens.

When I found that the people gathered on the rink were mostly strangers I preferred to stay upstairs and watch their antics from the windows. The spectacle of the dark silhouettes gliding gracefully against the background of white snow was particularly delightful at night when the lanterns were lit and spread criss-cross shadows over the ice and the walls. The silence gave a fairy-like quality to the scene, for the sound of voices, laughter and cries barely reached my ears through the double window-frames. I was delighted when I managed to attract the attention of my cousins by hammering on the glass. They made faces at me and naughty gestures, beckoning to me to join them, but what they screamed only reached me as a hardly audible murmur. I was a little ashamed of staying indoors, but I consoled myself by thinking that here was I, only a small boy, watching this feast as if I were a king or a prince. I had altogether too little inclination for sport. I was in fact rather a cissy, a typical mummy's-boy, and was often upbraided for this by my more belligerent and masculine brothers.

I remember Uncle Cesare's Peterhof villa as clearly as I remember his town house. He had decided not to design it himself, though he was a clever architect, and had entrusted the work to my elder brother Albert, who was just completing his training at the Academy of Arts. The work took about one year, and Albert must be given his due; he had done a splendid piece of work. Not only was the villa bigger than any other villa built in Peterhof during the previous thirty years, it was also the most elegant and glamorous.

Behind the main building, Albert had planned stables for six horses, coach houses, a laundry, guest rooms and apartments for the servants. This second building was constructed entirely of wood and was surmounted by a tall belvedere in a style which was a peculiar mixture of Moorish and Russian designs. The whole made a pleasant and elegant impression. These buildings must have cost my uncle many thousand roubles, but his hankering after splendour was satisfied. A covered verandah with pillars extended along both the southern and western fronts, and the verandah on the southern side served as a dining-room where grand dinners took place on warm days.

A very large, beautifully painted picture, that had once adorned Grandpapa's house in Venice, one of those panoramas that were attributed to Antonio Canale with figures by Tiepolo, hung in the sitting-room.[1] As I practised my dull scales on the piano above which the picture hung, I found consolation in its many details. I used to pretend I was strolling along the streets and squares of this imaginary town, meeting on my way the strange figures with which the artist had peopled it. Many years later, when this picture and its twin were hanging in the dining-room of our friends, the Olives, I had only to cast a glance

[1] Later this attribution was corrected: the landscape was the work of F. Battaglioli (1742–1789) the figures were by Zugno. Both pictures are now in the Hermitage.

during dinner at the familiar towers and palaces to capture at once the memory of a summer morning or of twilight in the sitting-room of the villa, and to hear again the sad little tune which my small fingers hammered from the keys.

The last time I saw my uncle was in the summer of 1883 in that very sitting-room where I had formerly practised on the piano and the large Canaletto used to hang. I had dropped in to see my cousins and found that they were waiting for the return at any moment of Uncle Cesare from Marienbad. The atmosphere in the house was morbid, and I understood from the family that Uncle was very ill; in fact, that he was dying. The idea that I would be facing a man doomed to death and probably unwilling to die was so unbearable to me that I was unable to go and welcome him when the excitement and noise in the house indicated that he had arrived. I sat down at the piano and, as I usually did on such occasions, tried to find consolation in improvising. Hardly had I time to run my fingers over the keyboard when I heard a great uproar, the shouting of orders, the stamping of feet. Uncle Cesare, sitting in an armchair, was being carried in by his devoted valet Timofei and Yermolai the coachman, followed by my cousins. Uncle Cesare, emaciated, altered beyond all recognition, rose high above the others, and this sorrowful travesty of a triumphal procession moved slowly past me towards the study. I will never forget my uncle's glance as it rested for a moment upon me: he tried to smile and with unexpected tenderness muttered: 'How are you, Shourenka?' His expression had nothing in common with the haughtiness that I had once resented. It was the infinitely sad smile of a man saying farewell to life and aware of the futility of earthly existence.

Before I leave this magic world enshrined in my memory, I want to add a few words about the other inhabitants of Uncle's villa. After his death I continued to meet and keep in touch with some of them, while others disappeared for ever from my ken. My two cousins and former playmates, Inna and Masha, appeared rarely at family reunions after a year of deep mourning; Masha, in fact, hardly at all. Soon after, Inna married Colonel Lashkevich: while poor Masha, delicate and pathetic, almost totally deaf and unable to stand her loneliness, went to live in Naples and poisoned herself with sulphuric matches.

Inna was the prettiest of the three girls. She was like a sister to me, but I started very early to be aware of her feminine charm. I was quite overcome when I found myself near her and even more so when I could touch her, as used to happen on the 'giant's stride' or when we played 'hit and run' and would clutch at one another and even embrace. Finally, during the summer of 1881, which we spent together at Uncle Cesare's, I believed myself to be definitely in love with her, and in my childish imagination pictured scenes of infinite bliss in Inna's company. But this romance, or rather whisper of romance, was never realised, and after my uncle's death we very seldom met and never again in the intimacy created by living under the same roof.

An important rôle in Uncle Cesare's household was played by Yermolai, the coachman, a striking and picturesque figure. Yermolai was no ordinary coachman; he was a celebrity, the pride and admiration of all Peterhof. The Imperial stables used to send out feelers, trying to win him over to their service, even promising him the honour of driving the Tsar himself. But Yermolai preferred to be the personal servant of Cesare Albertovich. He was treated in the house with the kind of reverence paid to an actor of genius by his *aficionados*. Well aware of his own worth, he accepted these attentions calmly, always polite and respectful yet not in the least arrogant. Now and then he would get disgracefully drunk.

Yermolai was then about forty. He was tall, powerfully built, with a perpetual smile lurking behind his square

black beard, and he had black, short-cropped, well-oiled
hair, which his spouse trimmed by placing an earthenware
pot ovei his head and cutting the hair all around the brim.
Yermolai, however, was composed of two men. One was the
cosy, 'backstage' Yermolai without any make-up; just an
ordinary peasant in a velvet waistcoat, from which peeped
the sleeves of his pink shirt. This Yermolai did not mind
scrubbing and brushing the horses and harnessing them
with the help of the groom, or washing the carriages and
raking the straw in the stables. This Yermolai held amusing
conversations with the horses, scolding or praising them.
His gait was undignified, he swayed from side to side, and
would stagger about the moment he had taken too much
drink. But there was another Yermolai – not the ordinary
mortal, but a being who belonged to a higher plane, whose
size increased in front of your eyes as the pillows were
pushed under his overcoat. At the slightest touch of the
reins the horses in his charge were transformed from
ordinary hacks into thoroughbreds; they pricked up their
ears, arched their necks and pranced about, filled with the
spirit of daring. It almost looked as though he were the
true master and hero, while those behind in the open
carriage were mere underlings. When he wanted to display
especial *bravura*, all he did was to smack his lips or whisper
to his horses under his breath, and in a moment we would
be dashing along like the wind, even passing Grand-ducal
carriages and thereby breaking all the rules. In 1881, during
the first summer after Alexander III's coronation, mounted
Cossacks used to do sentry duty at every cross-road; at the
sight of our approaching carriage they would prepare to
salute, assuming us to belong to the Imperial family. We
were always highly amused by this mistake, and I swelled
with childish pride at being taken for the heir-apparent, all
because of Yermolai. With a suitably gracious, majestic
smile, I would nod to the startled sentry who was trying to

control his prancing horse and raise his hand to his hat at the same time.

Less than ten years after these triumphant drives, Yermolai was taken to the cemetery. He was shattered by the death of his beloved master, whose heirs declared, a year afterwards, that they no longer required his services. The Cavos girls had decided to economise by getting rid of superfluous staff to enable them to go abroad when they wanted. Eugene had never been keen on keeping up appearances, and after his marriage he also went abroad and in his light-heartedness scattered most of his father's inheritance. How could they keep on this charming ogre? Yermolai took to drink in his misery and in a short time developed consumption.

Timofei, Uncle Cesare's pale, scraggy little valet, could not compete with the grandeur of Yermolai, but I had great affection for this gentle man. God had not given him an impressive appearance, nor bestowed on him any special talents which might have added lustre to his activities: his capacities did not go beyond serving efficiently at table, cleaning shoes and clothes properly, and keeping his master's personal effects in good order. But he performed these tasks with dignity and calm, despising fuss and obsequious zeal. He had many qualities, including a lot of common sense, and it was a pleasure to talk to him. He accepted tips without feeling humiliated, as he knew he deserved them. If I remember Yermolai as an Olympian god on his chariot, I recall Timofei, with a kind smile on his sad face, offering me a second helping of my favourite dishes of bisque or zabaglione. Timofei remained for a long time with my cousins, and this frail individual proved in the end to have more vitality than his Herculean colleague.

Constantine Cavos, my mother's second brother, was no longer young, as I remember him from my early childhood until his death in 1890. He had always the same, unchanging appearance – a smart little gentleman with a long nose, a short black moustache and black, wavy hair without a touch of silver. He was not such a dandy as his brother Cesare; he preferred conventional attire, but was nevertheless always faultlessly dressed. He used to wear a loose black tie *à la Lavallière*, and this single detail gave his appearance a slightly artistic character; and always floating around him was a whiff of good scent, which in Russia was rare among men. He walked with a firm and measured stride, stooping slightly, and with his toes turned out. He had an original manner of greeting the younger members of his family. He gave us his left hand *à la française*, not the right, at the same time proffering his well-shaven cheek to be kissed. One day, when I was about eight, I could not resist playing a joke in rather bad taste. Instead of kissing Uncle's cheek, I thrust forward my own cheek and they bumped against each other. Uncle only laughed, but for a long time after he held me off at a certain distance when greeting me.

I felt rather aloof from Uncle Kostia, but quite differently from the way I felt about Uncle Cesare. I was really afraid of Uncle Cesare, and sometimes my resentment at his remarks reached the point of hatred; whereas I never ceased to regard Uncle Kostia as a kind uncle of whom I was rather fond. These feelings I kept to myself; and indeed my affection for him was tinged with a respect which tended to lessen its ardour. Later, in my adolescence, I resolved to imitate certain characteristics of Uncle Kostia; I talked in the same measured way, and walked with my toes turned out.

Uncle Kostia considered himself a professional diplomat, though in reality he was merely an official at the Foreign Office, where he attained the rank of Privy Councillor and was entitled to wear the order of St Anne across his shoulder. But he was never given a diplomatic appointment abroad. For many years he worked as an interpreter, and being privy to all the deepest secrets of international relations he acquired a permanent air of mystery, almost of conspiracy, which eminently suited the diplomatic style of those days. Uncle Kostia behaved according to the school of Metternich and Gorchakov, making mysterious and apparently witty allusions that led one to suspect a hidden meaning in everything he said. Occasionally he would laugh softly, apparently to himself, with a slight snigger, looking slyly round as if afraid his significant laughter might be overheard, his smile clearly intending to hint at something sinister and dangerous. This Voltairean smile was particularly irritating to his brother Michael, a convinced liberal, humane and idealistic. Uncle Kostia, however, held the views suitable for a government official. He had no belief in human kindness or virtue, and saw only material interest in international relations; as for domestic policy, he stood for *la main forte*. His favourite historical figures were Thiers and Bismarck, and he had a certain weakness for Napoleon III.

Widowed early, Uncle Kostia entrusted his sister-in-law, Katia Campioni, with the education of his only daughter, Olga. Though bearing an Italian name, Aunt Katia belonged to a totally russified family of Greek Orthodox creed. She was a small, swarthy, very ugly woman with a look of benevolent importance about her. A constant smile played upon her tightly compressed lips and her arms were always crossed over her stomach under a warm, soft Orenburg shawl. This gave Aunt Katia a wonderfully cosy air.

To be honest, the atmosphere at Uncle Kostia's abode induced in me a positively lethal boredom. Cousin Olga, who was educated at the Smolni Institute, never came home except at Christmas and I had to spend hours in the company of Mamma and Aunt Katia. But one day, in this boring apartment, a new and unknown world was revealed to my eyes. For a long time I had been intrigued by a wooden box, with two round glass openings on its slanting lid, which stood in the dining-room, in front of the window. Aunt Katia usually attempted to divert my curiosity about this box whenever I asked what it was, fearful lest I should damage such a valuable object. This particular day, wanting to get rid of me and give me something to do, she made me sit on a tall chair in front of the box and invited me to look through the glass eye-holes. I was spellbound in ecstasy at what I saw. Curled up on a green armchair was a beautiful cat, asleep. Every single hair of her grey fur could be separately identified, yet together they formed an enchantingly soft surface. Long whiskers stuck out like fine crystal threads from her face; her closed eyes and blissful expression were evidence of the wonderful dreams she was enjoying. Every member of the cat species has always roused in me a very special admiration. This cat was all the more entrancing because she was inaccessible: I had no power to awaken and stroke her. There she was right under my nose: I could almost see her breathe. Yet it was all an illusion, and if I were to touch her the magic spell would be broken and she would be transformed into a mere photograph.

Besides the cat, Uncle Kostia's magic box contained much else that was of ravishing interest. I saw foreign towns, Paris, Rome, my 'native' Venice, Egyptian palms and the Swiss glaciers – there was everything in that fantastic box. Having had my fill of one picture, I would turn the handle and it dropped into the unknown and another picture appeared in its place. While the new subject was moving into place it seemed to be just a flat piece of cardboard, but when it reached the correct position reality confronted me, not merely an image. Apart from their subjects, it was the live quality of the pictures that entranced me beyond words, as well as their illusion of magic.

I saw over and over again the pictures that had been put into the stereoscope and remained there unchanged, and it never occurred to me that Uncle had a collection of them. But one day I got a surprise – all the pictures in the machine were new – and after that I became insatiable in my demand for new pictures. I soon learnt to replace them myself in their little wire frames, and would sit watching these miracles until my mind became a blur. I no longer urged Mother to take me home, but was furious when she tore me away from my favourite occupation.

In the early days of my childhood, up to 1880, Uncle Kostia was a shadowy person. I met him about once a month, usually at a family dinner either in our house or at Uncle Cesare's. He never entertained at home, probably out of a spirit of economy. On December 25th a small artificial Christmas tree, kept from year to year, was lit, and the celebration had a restricted and modest character, very unlike our own at home or that of other relatives and friends. In the summer he rented a villa in Peterhof – he did not own a house.

Then suddenly, in 1880, when Olga had finished school and become a potential bride, a radical change occurred in Uncle Kostia's way of life. He expressed the wish to move into our house, on the same floor as us. A whole chain of rooms was redecorated, and as soon as the work was finished, Uncle Kostia, Aunt Katia and Olga moved in and became our nearest neighbours.

Uncle Kostia himself now became a habitué of our own apartment. Every morning about ten he appeared and went straight in to Mamma, with whom he had long conversations, chiefly on financial matters. Under his direction Mamma bought and sold shares on the stock exchange, and we apparently acquired quite a considerable addition to our income from this. But towards the end of the 1880s there was a slump which the cunning Uncle Kostia had failed to foresee, and all this wealth melted as quickly as it had appeared. Uncle's affairs also suffered, but he soon recovered from his losses, and the capital inherited by Olga after his death allowed her to lead just as luxurious a life as the most well-to-do men of our family.

On the whole our two families lived in peace and friendship with each other, only disrupted by my own fault in 1887, after I had accidentally overheard a slightly ironical remark made by Uncle Kostia about my love for the girl who was later to become my wife. Mamma entreated me in vain to modify my attitude to her favourite brother, but I refused to relinquish the rather absurd position which I had taken up, and my ostracism of my uncle lasted for a whole year. In the end, shame at my own childish foolishness overcame what I had considered to be my duty, and the affair ended quite naturally.

Alas, I had little time after that to profit by the company of my dear uncle. He fell ill and died of a heart attack in the week after Easter in 1890. The last time I saw him alive was when I went with Mamma to wish him a happy Easter. He sat in his study, in a somewhat shabby dressing-gown, his face like wax, his cheeks sunken, his eyes dim, but with a Voltairean smile still playing on his thin lips.

At that time I was madly attracted by the Meiningen performances and had dreams of joining the Duke's troupe, which of course interfered considerably with my work at school. To begin with, in order to look more like an actor, I had shaved off my beard and moustache. Mamma was much distressed by my decision, but, true to her principles, she did not feel she had the right to oppose what I considered to be my calling. She had, however, asked her brother to reason with me. Having heard Mamma's tale of woe, Uncle Kostia became quite animated, his eyes sparkled with irony and he shook with silent laughter. Then he stretched out to me his dry left hand, cold as ice, and turning to his sister said: '*Ne t'inquiète pas, Camille, cela va passer, ce n'est pas sérieux.* It's only a childish whim.'

Thanks to that advice my whim – for it was indeed only a passing whim – evaporated, and if the world lost another Garrick, Rossi or Salvini because of it, I personally came out the winner. My uncle's words struck all the deeper for being his last instructions. A week later he was dead.

I did not learn to appreciate Uncle Misha until I began to pay more attention to the discussions of my elders at the family dinner-table. Till then Mamma's brother had been noteworthy only for his consistency in arriving late for dinner, appearing just as we were having our soup. We would hear his heavy tread outside, and there he would be in the doorway, looking guiltily at us with his myopic eyes. Papa never failed to scold him, since to Papa punctuality at mealtimes was a sacred duty. Uncle Misha, who never forgot how my father had once carried him in his arms, did not resent the scolding, but simply made his apologies and sat down at the table. This meekness, however, would give place to an altogether firmer tone if a controversial subject were broached.

On one occasion there was a terrible flare-up between Uncle Misha and the provocative Zozo Rossolovsky, who dared to mention without due respect the person of Baroness Uexkuell, who was the object of my uncle's adoration. Indeed, to put it plainly, he was besottedly and hopelessly in love with this enchantress. The Baroness, immortalised by Repin in his famous portrait *Lady in the Red Dress*, was then the talk of the town. Some people disliked her for her progressive ideas; others – the women – envied her beauty and her success. The gossip about her, which was both unfounded and malicious, was repeated one day during dinner by Rossolovsky and drove Uncle Misha, the

Baroness's knight-errant, into a perfect frenzy. This fierce outburst almost led to a duel; with a mighty effort my parents managed to pacify Uncle Misha, and Zozo was only too ready to beg his pardon.

It was about then, in 1887, when I was seventeen, that I really struck up a friendship with my fifty-year-old uncle. We had gradually been growing closer together through our mutual admiration for the Meiningen theatrical performances and for Virginia Zucchi. But now Uncle Misha became aware that the insignificant boy, of whom he was hardly aware at the family table, was as wholehearted and enthusiastic a supporter of the arts as he was himself. By 1887 my passion for books was growing more ardent, and we were further united by poring over new publications together. When I discovered Böcklin as a genius, it was enormously exciting to find that Uncle Misha already knew and admired him. We were also mutually stimulated by our enthusiasm for the new works of Arnold. My uncle no longer deserted the family gathering immediately after coffee, but came instead to my red room where, in the dim light of a paraffin lamp, we would study new works or the latest numbers of art reviews from abroad. Sometimes my brother Leontij, my nephew or cousin or school-friends who came on Sundays for tea would join us. My highly cultured uncle made a great impression on them all.

But it was these same friends who were the cause of some friction with Uncle Misha. He was irritated by their youthful arrogance, their uncontrollable desire to express opinions and impose them on others. My school friend Nouvel, with his self-assurance and bad manners, was the one who irritated him most. Gradually the gap widened between our group and Uncle Misha, and he began to be wary of us; he resented the fact that such schoolboys had such a high opinion of themselves. Then Bakst and Filosofov became the target for his sneers. He and I even started to quarrel. I remember one quarrel in particular when I tried to impress him with an edition of *Die Deutschen Malerradierer* which I had received from abroad. It included reproductions of three most striking *eaux-fortes* by Max Klinger. Far from sharing my enthusiasm, Uncle Misha criticised the *eaux-fortes* harshly and made fun of me. I was so hurt that I became quite abusive, and declared that I would remove his name from my list of friends. The quarrel was soon over, but a slight coldness persisted between us. My uncle expressed his disapproval of me by ceasing to show me his own treasures, including his comprehensive collection of the lithographs of Gavarni and Daumier, which I particularly admired.

I vividly remember one of my last meetings with Uncle Misha, which took place in 1894 or 1895 in the drawing-room of those famous poets, the Merejkovskys, whom I was visiting for the first time with my friend Nouvel. Though we tried to put on a brave front we both felt rather embarrassed in this ultra-sophisticated salon, especially as our hostess's manner seemed to us a little scornful. As soon as we sat down in front of the fire, she fired at us the question: 'What is your particular form of decadence?' Gradually we found our feet, and were able to respond suitably to her sharp remarks; an hour later we were even talking quite freely about our non-acceptance of all forms of decadence. Then suddenly our hostess jumped to her feet and ran out of the room, exclaiming: 'Misha has come!' She returned arm-in-arm with my respected uncle, whose myopic eyes immediately found us before the fire, very much at home. I wonder if it was a sight to please him: it is one thing to drink to Brotherhood in a slightly tipsy state with the famous Sappho of Petersburg and to allow her to languish gracefully in your arms; but it is quite another matter to find a nephew and his school-friend unexpectedly witnessing such a blow to your dignity! On the other hand he might have been flattered that we had seen him on such familiar terms in this sacred gathering, inaccessible to others.

Dear Uncle Misha! In spite of his sharp remarks he was good nature itself and his conceit was quite harmless. I believe it was because of this that he was a failure, in spite of his brains and erudition, for he was quite content with transitory, insignificant, drawing-room successes. Strangely enough this most cultured member of our family did not pursue any artistic career himself. But there is no doubt that I owe a lot to knowing so well in my early years a man with such an absolute regard for art and such a good judgement in his criticism of it. He died in the summer of 1897, in Petersburg.

CHAPTER XI

EARLY SUMMERS

*

As Court Architect my father was allowed to live in a Court villa in Peterhof, one of the 'cavalier' houses that lined the avenue running from the Palace to Old Peterhof; and every summer till 1874 the family moved to this villa from Petersburg. Built during the reign of Alexander I, these houses had the graceful simplicity characteristic of the architecture of that period. They consisted of one floor and were made of solid wood resting on stone foundations; they were brown with white bas-reliefs above the windows and green persiennes. I particularly remember those green persiennes.

Each group of houses surrounded a large courtyard and on the courtyard side each house had a small garden with lilac bushes and flowerbeds. Amidst these bushes Mamma and my sisters usually assembled at a round table to sew or knit or perform various household duties, like cleaning berries and peas, making jam, etc. On fine days we used to have our breakfast there too.

In Russia at one time I used to be called 'the bard of Versailles' because from 1897 I often exhibited sketches of Louis XIV. Versailles did indeed make a tremendous impression on me from the first day of my encounter with it in 1896; but it was nothing compared to the feelings I experienced when as a small boy, holding my father's hand, I walked along the paths in Peterhof and stood spellbound at the sight of the waterfall rushing down the golden steps at Marly or, at the foot of the Grand Grotto below the Grand Palace, was enveloped in spray through which I could watch the jets of the fountain flare up amidst the golden deities sparkling in the sun.

Among the wonderful Peterhof waterfalls were some that filled me with awe. I was afraid of the huge monstrous gilded faces above the white marble stairs to the lower basin. But I was even more afraid of the two Menager fountains that released their jets of water to form an incredibly powerful column that grew in front of one's eyes until it reached the limit of its height. If you gazed long enough at the perpetually seething summit you got the impression that this heavy column of water was tumbling down upon you. The black dragons above the Chess Mountain and the Neptune in the Top Garden were also among the fountains that frightened me. Neptune, wrought of iron, had a sharply serrated crown and a trident in his hand, and was more like Beelzebub than a classical god. Riders astride seahorses with fishes' tails clustered around him, and the fat snouts of dolphins spouting arches of water peeped out of the large basin.

There were also a few gay, amusing fountains in Peterhof; the fat, naked little urchins, for instance, that held trays over their heads upon which transparent cloches were formed by spouting water. Even more amusing were the Mushroom and the Christmas Tree near Monplaisir, particularly when one could watch someone newly arrived from Petersburg retire to rest under the cap of the Mushroom or on the bench by the metal Tree and become suddenly enveloped by a thick wall of water or be sprinkled from all sides by jets from the branches of the artificial fir tree. Women shrieked, men laughed, but some resented the joke. The best fun of all was the toy fountain hidden behind one of the marble pavilions by the basin of Samson. I was very fond of this simple spectacle, and when Papa refused to go there I would weep at being deprived of the joy of seeing the ducks swimming one behind the other with a toy dog pursuing them. The dog barked, the ducks quacked, and in the middle sat a shepherd apparently drawing from his flute a mournful sound.

It was probably these various Peterhof impressions, comical, terrifying and enchanting, that gave birth to my subsequent passion not only for Peterhof, but for Tsarskoe Selo, Versailles and the whole baroque period. It made also a great difference that the Peterhof of my early days was not the soulless, embalmed mummy of a museum nor the object of scientific investigation that it is now. It was a live body, fulfilling its functions. The Tsar, the Tsaritsa and their children lived in Peterhof, and to my childish imagination these exalted persons represented something fairylike, spreading a solemn radiance over the whole residence. Versailles must have been the same, when its true masters lived there, setting a pattern for the whole world.

In those days our summer residence in Peterhof meant far more to me than our town apartment in which we spent three-quarters of our existence. I loved the spaciousness of the rooms with their high ceilings, and the closeness of the trees which gave a perpetual shade to the rooms. I liked finding myself, after only five steps, at the table among the shrubs where Mamma and my sisters spent their days. I spent the whole morning there at Mamma's side until Nanny came to fetch me for a walk, drawing or listening to a book read aloud or to the stories told in broken Russian by my brothers' French tutor.

One early memory associated with Peterhof is of a small house, in the same group as our villa, which had a great fascination for me. When I passed by with my nanny I always stopped to look at the birds in the numerous cages hanging on both sides of the wide-open windows. Flower-pots stood on the window-sill, and a little old woman was usually occupied either in watering the flowers or in feeding the birds. Once this wrinkled old woman noticed me at the window and in a soft, thin little voice invited me to come in. My nanny seemed reluctant, but I liked the old lady and pulled my Filippovna so obstinately by the arm that she gave in and we mounted the porch and passed through the entrance into a deep, dark room, crowded with furniture. At close quarters the old lady proved to be an old gentleman, the mistake being due to the fact that his head was wrapped in a shawl; he seemed tiny even to me, who was only three. He was clean-shaven and his pink cheeks were soft and plump, and he was dressed in a faded, mended dressing-gown made of silk patterned with Chinamen, palms and peacocks. He was very, very old, and I could hardly distinguish from the hissing that came from his toothless mouth a vague invitation to partake of some food. I was drawn to the cages, particularly a golden cage containing a brightly coloured parrot. A monkey appeared from somewhere and jumped from one cupboard to another, making faces at us.

Further visits followed the first one. All these eccentric, exotic things were very alluring and the old man in his Chinese dressing-gown was very hospitable, offering me my favourite ginger cakes. When I came the next year to Peterhof, in the summer of 1874, I wanted to visit my friend at once, but alas – he was no longer there. The empty window covered with tulle curtains gave me my first feeling of irreparable loss.

Also in that year, 1874, I first came face-to-face with the terrible but fascinating mystery of Death. One bright day, walking with my father along the pier, I noticed some distance out a small boat floating towards us with two policemen in it. My attention was arrested not by the boat itself, but by what it was dragging behind it. At that moment Father met some friends, and they stopped to chat while I clung to one of the massive wooden stanchions of the jetty, and was able to watch what was happening below.

In the bright sunlight I could clearly see what was tied to the stern of the boat and quietly floating on the waves. It was rather like a huge doll with arms and legs spread-eagled. It was naked, and its pale body seemed to be slashed with coloured patches; the head was invisible, hanging in the water behind the boat. I felt no terror; on the contrary, I was riveted by the spectacle, I could not tear myself away. When the grown-ups stopped talking, I hastened to point out this interesting object to my father, but all he said was: 'Ah, it's a drowned man!' and detaching my fingers which still clung to the stanchion, he dragged me away.

This pier played quite an important part in the life of the summer residents, and I personally was very upset when it was destroyed with the rest of the harbour during the First World War and Peterhof lost one of its great sights.

The reason why my parents abandoned Peterhof for Pavlovsk in the summer of 1875, having spent every summer there for twenty-five years, was that Papa had given up his job in the Imperial Household at Peterhof, and had been commissioned to build a theatre in Pavlovsk. We moved in early spring, when it is still bitterly cold although the trees are covered with their first green down; for the Benois family were prepared always to freeze or be drenched in order to get out of Petersburg.

After much persuasion Lina, my German nurse, succeeded in enticing me into the Pavlovsk Gardens and to the palace; and after that I loved going to look at the monument erected to Paul I in the centre of the oval court in front of the palace, which in those days belonged to the Grand Duke Constantine.

This monument had a special attraction for me, apart from its artistic value. With a large tricorne upon his head, which is thrown back haughtily, his legs encased in heavy boots spread ballet-fashion, his right hand extended, and leaning on a bamboo stick, the mad Tsar is represented reviewing his Grenadiers. I was at that time crazy about military parades and marches, and I accordingly revelled in the attitude of almost absurd military leadership displayed by the statue. My childish infatuation with this statue of the Emperor must have led to the strange devotion I came to feel for the real Paul I, a devotion which I never lost. I had already been told in confidence by Papa that the poor Tsar, kind but insane, had been strangled by his courtiers. When we used to drive over to see Uncle Cesare our carriage passed Paul's Castle, and Papa would show me the window of the room where the murder took place. That one was forbidden to talk about it openly, that it was a secret, known to all but kept by all, gave a special aura of romance to the unfortunate Tsar. When I visited the Pavlovsk monument I would examine it from all sides, peering into the nostrils of the pug nose, admiring the fantastic high boots, the tricorne placed at an angle and the long sword emerging from under the flap of this opened top-coat.

The pug-nosed Emperor, comical and formidable, absurd and full of noble sentiments, exquisitely erudite and a tough and brutal soldier, unsuccessful master of the world's fate, head of the Maltese order without the aura of holiness, a model *paterfamilias* who at the end of his life became entangled in unsuccessful amorous intrigues – why does he still attract me so much ? It is even more astonishing that he was able to capture the imagination of a boy of five!

A few steps away from our villa stood the Paul Fortress. It was so meaningless, so obviously a mock fortress, with its useless towers quite unlike those of medieval times, its drawbridge, ravelins and counterscarps, 'toy' guns on gun carriages and statues of knights in niches by the gate, that it looked as ludicrous as its master. When I was five I used to go there almost every day. My governess would sit down on the grass and become engrossed in a book, while I would tirelessly climb up the soft grass of the trenches and then roll down, or clamber over the guns and peep, not without fear, into their sinister mouths. The fortress was a toy on a colossal scale, just as the Empire, bestowed on him by divine right, was itself a toy to Paul, and an inexhaustible source of the 'tin soldiers' whom he chased all over Europe and sent into battle to defend his so-called glorious and holy ideals. Like a spoilt child, also, he turned his wrath against those who did not immediately carry out his commands, deporting them to Siberia straight from the parade-ground as punishment for an unfastened button. And his supposed insanity, his bewilderment and fear, his thirst for heroics and untimely, ill-directed sense of justice – were they not the result of childish nightmares?

Of course in 1875 such thoughts did not enter my mind. On the contrary, like every other child, I was attracted mainly by two spots in Pavlovsk, the Rose Pavilion and the Net, which were the assembly points of all the local children, though the Rose Pavilion was rather far from our house.

I was not so much interested in the pretty country house, on the front of which was written 'Pavillon des Roses', nor the little garden in which a few faded rose-bushes were slowly dying, as in the games and amusements which had been there since the days of the Empress Maria Fedorovna. There you could ride a horse on the roundabout, or roll balls on the bowling green, or swing until you felt dizzy on every kind of swing, and you could also slide down a hill on a special toboggan or simply by sitting down on the smooth, sloping surface. Sliding was my favourite occupation, which I could indulge even in winter in our ballroom, where Papa had erected a hill in a rather primitive way by sloping a wide board covered with oil-cloth from a high stool to the floor.

The other Pavlovsk entertainment, the Net, was situated near the Palace in a copse given over to the naval exercises of the children of the Grand Duke, Admiral of the Russian

Fleet, Constantine Nikolaevich. It consisted of a mast with
rope ladders and rigging, with a tightly stretched rope net
underneath. You could perform every sort of convolution
on the rigging and the ladders without the risk of breaking
your neck, for the net caught you as you fell. Lots of big
boys (all dressed in sailor suits) ran from morning till night
up and down these ladders and performed acrobatic feats
under the supervision of two real sailors who were always
on guard by the Net. We small children, both boys and girls,
had to content outselves with jumping up and down on the
net on to which we were lifted by mothers, nurses, governesses or the sailors on duty. I can still remember the
enjoyable sensation of stamping on the unsteady surface
full of holes. It was such an intense pleasure that when the
moment came to go home there was general howling. All
my contemporaries howled, but I loudest of all.

I distinctly remember Papa's work on the building of the
theatre in Pavlovsk (which was to stand there for fifty
years until it was burned down in 1930). I have to confess
that I did not like his design in the pseudo-Russian style
demanded by the prevailing fashion. In spite of its four
tiers, from the outside the theatre looked sprawling and
squat, its front composed of balconies supported by pillars.
These balconies led from the outside to the boxes and
corridors. The pillars were joined by arches of carved
ornaments and this gave the building a fussy and frivolous
look. The colour in which it was painted was also a bad
choice, a dull, dark brown which combined disagreeably
with the green foliage of the gardens. The theatre reached
its final stage only at the end of our stay, but while the work
was in progress I loved to climb on the scaffolding, accompanying Papa wherever he went, mounting up the steps
and boards to the very sky. On the pediment above the
stage Papa placed a huge clock (as in the Mariinsky Theatre),
but its mechanism was not ready for the opening of the

theatre and a great head of Apollo was at first fitted into the frame as a substitute for the clock-face. I was allowed to help Papa with the head when (chiefly for his own amusement) he decided to paint it himself. How wonderfully well he did his work, according to all the rules of the classic school! I was entrusted with the colouring in yellow of the rays of light radiating from the god's head, which I did meticulously with great success. How proud I was when I saw our Apollo fitted into his place: he seemed to me both splendid and beautiful.

Papa's theatre was erected a few steps away from the station,[1] which for the permanent grown-up population of Pavlovsk was a rallying place, a sort of club in the open air. In the evenings, partly to listen to the music and partly to have a good dinner at the celebrated station restaurant, a crowd arrived from Petersburg which was not interested at all in Pavlovsk itself and its rural beauty. I, too, later on in my student days, went through a phase when I constantly frequented the Pavlovsk concerts, which by then took place in a separate hall. In my childhood, however, I really loathed the station and its surroundings. It is hard to imagine the boredom that overcame me when my governess succeeded in getting me there and I had to stay in the broiling sun tramping about the dusty paths or sitting quietly on a bench while she gossiped with another governess.

But one day as we arrived on the station square, where there was not the smallest shade and instead of lilac bushes tropical plants in green boxes withered away around a fountain that never worked, we found a far greater crowd than was usual during the daytime, an exceptional, a very smart crowd. The silk of the ladies' long trains rustled as

[1] In Russian every station is called *vokzal* – a word coming from the English Vauxhall. The one in Pavlovsk was the first railway station in Russia and had a concert hall next to it as well as a restaurant, in imitation of the London Vauxhall.

they protected themselves from the sun with tiny, coloured sunshades, while the men, monocles jabbed into their eyes, played with their walking-sticks. There were also a number of officers in snow-white uniforms. And on the platform, where on other days I had watched the bearded Hlavač wave his baton, there now stood a slender, upright gentleman of foreign appearance, whose hair was dressed in a most peculiar style. With a wide gesture of his right hand, or with reassuring movements of both hands, he conducted the musicians in the waltzes which were driving all the grown-ups so crazy that ladies continued to whirl to in their partners' arms until they actually collapsed. Although it was the middle of the day, this elegant gentleman wore a tailcoat (tails were worn then at every opportunity, even for morning visits) and his charming face was adorned with a handsome moustache and small side-whiskers.

It was Johann Strauss himself – the god of all Europe, the dictator at Court and of private balls, the conqueror of a myriad women's hearts. It was my good fortune on this summer morning to see and hear Strauss at a rehearsal for nothing (you paid nothing to go to the station square). But what did I care about Strauss then? It mattered only that I could boast later of having seen this famous man with my own eyes, a man whose portraits were familiar even to me. At that time I hated his celebrated waltzes, which was my first expression of musical idiosyncrasy. Although I did not then know the meaning of the word vulgar, I was acutely conscious of vulgarity, which was what I did not like in his music. Later I changed my mind about *Die blaue Donau*, just as I changed my mind about *La fille de Mme. Angot* and *La Belle Hélène* when my taste became more debauched. But while I was still unspoilt I loathed that music, typical of the time; it gave me a strange feeling, almost of nausea. Apparently I was even then not a child of my times. I hated, for instance, the whims of fashion, especially for men, like the coiffure *à la Capoule*, and flat round hats, and shirt collars wide at the neck and trousers wide at the bottom. As for women's clothes, I detested the extremely ugly fashion for masses of material, lace and ribbon built up at the back of dresses and for chignons drooping low down the neck.

Our Pavlovsk summer of 1875 ended rather sadly for me when I caught scarlet fever from the children of our handyman. I remember very little else about the illness. I remember better the days of slow recovery, sitting up in my parents' big double bed, surrounded with books and toys. A large piece of cardboard was spread on my knees and I placed on it my new presents – little tin figures representing a hunt. Amidst transparent trees, elks were running, hunters dressed in green were firing at them, with smoke and flames at the ends of the guns to indicate the firing, while other hunters on horseback chased hares and boars. Or I would turn the pages of the newly arrived copies of *Münchener Bilderbogen*, with its funny stories about burglars breaking into a house or the poodle Caro who found a silver coin in the trousers of a strolling artist or the athlete falling through the floor on to the lodgers living below.

Towards the end of my illness I almost had to undergo an operation – what a terrible word! A huge abscess had formed behind my left ear, and Dr Pavlinov who looked after me in Pavlovsk insisted that it should be lanced. Mamma, against all surgical interference, protested and delayed the operation; but the day was eventually fixed and the doctor arrived with his instruments. I was saved, however, by a manoeuvre which I always remember with the pride of an astute diplomat recalling a successful political move. When I heard the doctor's cab arriving I turned my face to the wall, shut my eyes and pretended to be fast asleep. Dr Pavlinov tried to rouse me, at first with words then by shaking, but I went on sleeping. Then the doctor turned to cunning. 'Shourenka, look what I have brought you. Such a marvellous drum! And tin soldiers!' It was torture for me. I wanted desperately to have a look at these wonderful presents, but the fear of the operation predominated and I did not open my eyes and even tried to snore. Then I heard Mamma's reassuring words: 'Leave him, Doctor, he is sleeping so well. Sleep is beneficial, anyway – he did not sleep during the night. Let us put off the operation till tomorrow.' And the doctor gave in, took his bag and proceeded on his rounds.

When the sound of his wheels had disappeared, I opened my eyes and shouted: 'Where's the drum? Where are the soldiers?' There was nothing there, of course, and I realised that the doctor had deceived me. Mamma put a compress of dry figs on my abscess that night and towards the morning it burst. Pavlinov arrived to find me sitting up, my neck bandaged, radiant and gay, for all my torments were over and I knew that there would be no operation. I was very much amused at the idea that I had pulled the leg of this large, bearded gentleman who wore a uniform with silver epaulettes; and it was funny to see how embarrassed he looked and how proud Mamma was of her victory.

Two days later I was up in a dressing-gown and a day later allowed into the sitting-room. But at my first attempt to walk I almost fell down, and for a time I could move about only by holding on to chairs and tables. It was quite an experience. But it was not at all amusing to sit for days in the darkened sitting-room. In spite of the stove, alight all day, the room was damp and a persistent rain poured down outside, transforming the roads into such a swamp that the few cabs whom I could see beyond the bare branches of the trees in the garden floated on it like boats on the sea. Through the last yellow leaves I could see distant buildings and hedges, of the existence of which I had had no idea before. The days dragged on, I was already bored with the new toys, I knew my picture-books by heart, and I was surfeited with the taste of my favourite egg-nog. I was happy, therefore, when the day of departure arrived and I left Pavlovsk without any regret.

In the summer of 1876 my parents installed themselves again in Peterhof, but this time Papa did not get a grace-and-favour apartment and we had to content ourselves with renting a villa. In April I celebrated my sixth birthday, and though as yet I could neither read nor write I observed my surroundings with more conscious eyes and had my own judgement about many things.

Our villa was not very far from the 'Cavalier' houses but in quite a different setting. There was a large meadow across the road from us where the cadets exercised, and it was amusing to watch these small soldiers in their light linen jackets with red shoulder flashes exercising in even ranks and performing acrobatics on the trapeze and other gymnastic equipment. One day some friends whom I had made among the cadets took me, with the permission of their captain, into their pavilion, where in spite of my protests I was forced to eat a piece of warm, soft chocolate from the trouser pocket of one of the hospitable boys. I was enchanted with the little brightly coloured 'joke' table that stood in the middle of this summer-house, on the dark green background of which were painted a box of matches, three cigarettes, a pack of cards and two matches one across the other, giving the impression that someone had just left it all lying there. The author of this, a small pink-cheeked cadet, beamed with pleasure at my enthusiasm for his *tour de force*.

It was a long way from our villa to the Lower Gardens, but only a stone's throw to the Upper Gardens, spread out by the Big Palace. We used to go there, not through the Palace as was the custom, but through a monumental gate that led to the high road. The tall stone pillars of this gate were ornamented with Rastrelli's favourite squiggles and lions' heads painted in the official colours – bright orange and white. Near the gate, to right and left of the main alley, stood large, sprawling, round summer-houses with benches outside, and farther on, past the wicked Neptune and the aromatic lilacs, in the shade of the old gnarled limes, one reached the flower-beds beneath the windows of the Big Palace. But it was not the flowers here that were the attraction; it was the changing of the guard that took place every day. A detachment of soldiers marched swiftly from the Palace guardroom and stood at attention while another detachment approached from the distance. There was a brief command, the band played, another command, and the soldiers from the Palace marched off and those who had arrived on duty lowered their rifles and settled down in the guardroom. Only one soldier of the newly-arrived detachment remained outside to pace up and down the wooden platform with a rifle across his shoulders. The inaccessibility of this platform served as a symbol of military discipline and impregnability; and I was warned that if anyone did dare to step on it, the sentry had to kill him on the spot! Some demon seemed to challenge me to take the risk. I made my Russian nurse, who had replaced the German one, go right to the very edge of the platform, and there I raised my foot as if on the verge of taking a step up. The sentry, on the alert, made a stern face – and I walked away to admire the sundial near-by. A minute later, in spite of the entreaties of my clumsy old nanny, I repeated this silly game until the soldier threatened to hand me over to the Court negro who, in a splendid uniform, was standing at the Palace entrance displaying his dazzling teeth in a wide grin as he chatted with the liveried lackeys.

Peterhof's greatest point of interest was Montplaisir. Even as a little boy I had had a special tenderness for this spot with its low, small, brick-coloured houses hiding in the shade of the lime trees planted by Peter the Great himself. In the main central building, topped by a high purple roof, Peter the Great had lived. My elders talked about it with reverence. I could dimly distinguish, by peering through the thick uneven glass of the old-fashioned windows reaching to the ground, what was inside – the black and white checks of the floor, and the long corridors with painted ceilings and the pictures hanging upon dark oak panels. The room I liked most was charmingly decorated with white and blue vases on golden consoles. If I looked at this enchanted world long enough, it seemed to me that the door would suddenly open wide and the huge Tsar would pass from one room to the other with long strides across the stone floor to gaze at me with stern eyes.

Through one of the windows of the side wing one could see the large, almost empty assembly hall lined along the walls with chairs like those in Papa's study, looking as though they were waiting to receive an audience. The tapestries in that gloomy hall were covered with a design of Red Indians in feather head-dresses, crocodiles, rhinoceroses and wild horses, all of which by no means inspired gaiety.

But Montplaisir meant more to me than history. Just by the Palace near the sea was the famous Marble Square, whose surface was composed of marble slabs surrounded by a white balustrade of fat pillars lined with green garden benches. As you sat on them, you were supposed to be admiring the view of the Finnish Bay and especially the natural fireworks laid on by the Divine Firemaker over the western evening sky.

This was a favourite spot of the governesses of varying nationalities. 'So beautiful!' sighed the English, as they walked on the marble slabs. '*C'est ravissant!*' announced the French. '*Wunderschön!*' murmured the German girls. As for me, when I felt the smooth marble under my feet I was overcome by a theatrical sense of magnificence. I imagined

myself a Prince, the ruler of the world. The atmosphere of
solemnity was enhanced by Peter the Great's lime trees
that spread their powerful branches over the square, and
by the splash of the waves against the stones that supported
it. The Court orchestra played in the open air not far away,
by the Imperial bath-house, and the music reached one's
ears in a sort of enchanted resonance. The whole population
of Peterhof gathered to listen to the orchestra, but I was not
greatly pleased by the concerts, especially on cool, damp
nights when I had to sit quietly, wrapped up in the carriage,
and let the grown-ups listen in peace. I did not altogether
believe that they were enjoying themselves, for often, at the
start of some familiar and exciting operatic air, they would
order the coachman to leave the row of carriages and do the
round of the Gardens. On returning to the music, we naturally got into the back row, from which we could hear but
little. Often, too, the horses in the carriage next to ours
would become restive, and their stampings would interrupt
the most enchanting passages. Now and then I would
succeed in liberating myself from the yoke of the enthralled
grown-ups and be allowed to get down from the carriage
with one of my cousins. Then – oh, joy – the whole space
of this open-air concert hall was at our disposal for every
kind of childish entertainment, the only restriction being
that we must not go too far and must return at the first call.

From that moment of freedom the music itself became a
magic accompaniment to our games. I always found children I knew and we would play hide-and-seek and hit-and-
run and, when the boys happened to be in the majority,
a more violent game of bandits. What a lot of good hiding
places there were! You could squat with some beautifully
dressed, sweet-smelling little Lidochka behind a glass bird-
cage and feel a special delight in knowing that some Peter
or Paul would be quite unable to find you. Or, in spite of
its being strictly forbidden, you could catch frogs in the

thick grass; frogs had a particular liking for this place, which was intersected with little streams hurrying towards the sea. Nowadays I would probably feel too squeamish to pick up a frog in my hand, but then I loved to hold the slippery, twitching, frantically pulsating creature and frighten my little cousins or any other casual playfellow with it.

We might have found a more suitable place for our silly games than the Promenade in Peterhof, but there they took on an added spice of pleasure because of the festive atmosphere. The rippling water under the bridges and the rustle of the trees mixed wonderfully with the sounds of the orchestra; and the reverent silence of the audience seated on the benches ready to receive the offerings of its favourite, Hugo Wahrlich, the conductor of the Court orchestra, added to our pleasure. The old buildings around also contributed to the décor, with the 'Dutch village' of Montplaisir beside the more impressive yellow and white Court buildings of the Elizabethan era. I loved the rotund summer-house, which in the time of Peter the Great had been an aviary. Its glass doors did not open in the usual way but had to be lifted, and the great heavy green cupola on the top made it look like a lady in a crinoline. On the other side stood the Tsar's bath-house, with painted niches with vases in them. The paintings of landscapes that could be seen through these arcades had faded with time, but that only added a poetical character to this folly of the Catherine the Great era.

There were two more pavilions in the Lower Gardens which attracted me and which I insisted on visiting during our Sunday strolls with Papa – Marly and the Hermitage. In Marly the most interesting feature was not the little white house with its tidy little rooms but the goldfish in the pond in front of it. It was amusing to watch the little fish – hundreds of them, sparkling with gold – dash for the crumbs of bread thrown to them by an infinitely old

Court lackey. To attract the fish to the edge he rang a bell, and the gluttons would appear immediately and snap up the food.

What I liked best about the Hermitage, a charming little house of simple cubic design, was the ditch that surrounded it like a fortress. To reach the house one had to cross the ditch by a drawbridge. The pictures that adorned the walls of the top ballroom, among them one of the Poltava battle, also interested me. But the peak of enjoyment was reached when the guard demonstrated the mechanism that sent dishes up and down for meals at the Hermitage without the help of visible servants. The kitchen was on the lower floor, and there the servants on duty, who were not allowed access to the top rooms, received the dirty plates and replaced them on the lift with clean ones.

It was from my visits to this toy palace on the shore that I got my first faint sense of familiarity with Peter the Great. I saw nothing ridiculous or despicable in the Emperor's enjoyment of such childish things. On the contrary, in this way I was able to understand something of his mighty personality, and I felt the same kind of respect for him as I did for conjurors and magicians. Indeed, the idea of Peter the Great entertaining his courtiers in this room of glass looking out over the wide spaces of the sea, around this magic table that dispatched its dishes and plates to fetch their own food, had as great an appeal for me as any magician. I had then no idea what the grown-ups said or read about him, but I was already filled with devoted enthusiasm for this gay giant with his broad, flat face with small moustache and upturned nose who, I was told, was taller and stronger than anybody else.

My first clear memory of picnics belongs to this year, 1876. These picnic expeditions in Peterhof, in which the whole family used to take part, together with other friends, usually took place at the 'Babigons'.[1]

[1] Word of unknown origin, probably a corruption of a Finnish word.

A regular caravan would proceed there, with servants, samovar and huge baskets. One of the baskets contained food and wine, another prizes for the competition winners: silk ribbons, kerchiefs, beads, bits of cotton material and also for the greedy sweets, gingerbread, caramels, nuts. The destination of the Babigon picnics was the village on the crest of a hill a few kilometres south of Peterhof. Tradition demanded that one should stop at Oserki on the way, where all except Grandmamma and the other old ladies climbed out of the carriages and went to look at the sleeping marble lady. This beautiful sculpture stood under a pergola overgrown with ivy; if you wanted to see the face of the sleeping beauty you had to tip the Court lackey, who would then raise the linen cover that prudishly concealed her nakedness. On the pond here, nearly twenty years before my birth, the Emperor Nikolai Pavlovich had entertained his guests with the unforgettable spectacle of the ballet, *The Mermaid and the Fisherman*, in which Cerrito gave a dazzling performance and the décor was supplied by the landscape lit up by the moon as well as by lanterns.

The next traditional stop was by the Belvedere Palace, that dominated the landscape with its colonnade of blue marble, and there everybody except the old ladies dispersed on the terraces of the gardens. The view from the balcony was magnificent, not a sad Finnish landscape but a true Russian one, with the tender shadows of the clouds on the soft golden fields, green meadows and dark forests. The Russian character of this harmonious drowsy view was intensified by a church in Russian style rising on a near-by hillock, and a little farther on by the two-floored dwelling known as the Nicholas house.

When we reached this house, built by a German architect in the style of a Russian *isba* to satisfy a whim of the Emperor Nicholas I, we established our camp, unloaded the baskets from the carriages and gave them to the old man with a wooden leg and side-whiskers who served as caretaker to this little palace, and then proceeded to choose a cosy spot on the slope. While the coachmen were unharnessing the horses (this operation added a bohemian touch to the excursion) the children rushed off to the unharvested fields to collect poppies and cornflowers, and the young people went to the village to recruit more girls for the competitions. If the picnic happened to coincide with haymaking or the harvest the village appeared quite dead; you could make your way through the empty sheds and yards as though round an agricultural exhibition, and it was seldom that you saw even an old inhabitant. But at the sight of carriages the village children soon gathered timidly round our camp, giggling bashfully, hiding one behind another. Gradually the crowd, like an opera chorus, formed a thick wall around us.

On the whole this seignorial entertainment was not in the best of taste. It seems strange to me now that, in a society so conscious of human dignity as was the Russian intelligentsia in the 1870s, such serf-like habits were still tolerated. But at that time I was hardly conscious of sociological theories, and my enjoyment in the 'chasing of women' was not obscured by sinister stirrings of social conscience. There was certainly no sign of noble indignation on the part of those whom we invited (they were by no means compelled) to entertain us by running in our races.

What excitement those competitions caused! What scenes of envy, or resentment, or triumphant victory! Everybody shouted, quarrelled and indulged in riotous gaiety. It was beautiful, like a scene from Russian ballet, to watch those girls form themselves in rows, adorned with the newly-acquired kerchiefs, beads and ribbons, and whirl in a dance on the meadow, singing folk-songs. Against the background of the Nicholas house and the Nicholas church it all acquired an unreal theatrical character.

But the blue of the sky was genuine, our northern transparent blue; we were surrounded by genuine peasant buildings, and the wheat, now golden in the fields, had been sown by real peasants, not characters in an opera. By the end of the feast the peasants had returned from the fields with their scythes and rakes, and, singing, surrounded our camp in a gay crowd.

When I remember those picnics, it seems as though it all happened only yesterday and not nearly a century ago. Do the 'Babigons' still exist, I wonder?

I must include in my story of the Peterhof summer of 1876 an account of the illuminations which used to take place there every year. In 1876 the illuminations – possibly to celebrate the visit of some prince or foreign monarch – were exceptionally magnificent and this is why I remember the occasion so clearly. Our villa was situated not far from the centre of the celebrations, which were being prepared on the edge of the lake upon whose two islands – Tsaritsyn and Olghin – stood the curious pavilions of the Tsar. The week before the illuminations the shores of the lake were covered with timber; everywhere men in red or blue shirts were planing, sawing, chopping, and large carts arrived with loads of cunningly made screens with pieces of painted canvas nailed to them. As these wings were raised, sometimes higher than the trees around them, one could see that they represented some of the most famous palaces and churches of Europe. I was delighted when I recognised the Palace of the Doges. The grown-ups criticised this gigantic décor very severely, saying that the splendid monuments had been caricatured by reducing their size, but to me the sight of a Venetian palace rising from Peterhof soil was pure joy.

Those unprivileged mortals not invited to the gala on the island had to admire the illuminations from the wings, making their way stealthily between the stands on the swampy shore where the lanterns gave out a terrible heat and a strong smell of burning grease. But close to the water the sight was magnificent. In the light of the lanterns and against the background of dark trees, the palaces and churches did not seem at all small and insignificant: reflected in the water they were transformed into huge and splendid buildings. In my excitement at this sight I demanded that my parents should take me round the lake, which was not easy, as we had to make our way through the crowd and risked slipping and falling into the water.

Unfortunately the merciless Peterhof weather proved most unfavourable; the fireworks had not yet started when a strong wind got up and extinguished the lanterns, and rain began to fall. The entertainment was no doubt a failure, but I was fascinated by what happened to the illuminations. Suddenly a part of one of the palaces would disappear, and as soon as some of the lanterns were lit again the wind would blow out the next lot. The magic buildings seemed to crumble to pieces before my eyes – and what could better please a child's imagination than such a scene of destruction? (How I used to long for a fire to break out in our house! What fun it would have been to see Papa and Mamma and my brothers and the servants snatching anything that came their way and breaking through the smoke and the flames! The piano, no doubt, would be thrown out of the window on to the pavement.)

That night I saw the Tsar for the second time in my life, and this time I fully realised the greatness of my happiness. The first time had been in Pavlovsk, when he rode with his suite past our villa and made a friendly gesture to show that he recognised Papa. That, and the glitter of silver and gold on his uniform, had left an indelible impression on my memory.

This time I saw the Tsar quite clearly in the dazzling illuminations from my perch on somebody's shoulders.

The Emperor was sitting in a queer straw carriage with six white horses ridden by jockeys dressed in gold, which was called an *équipage à la Daumont*. The lady in a white dress and white hat with a feather must have been the Empress, and standing behind on a kind of bench were two immovable footmen, their arms folded. The Tsar and Tsaritsa bowed constantly to the right and to the left and people came so close to the carriage that they almost touched the wheels. Other carriages followed, among them some curious hunting brakes on which people sat back to back. This procession was so long, there were so many ladies, generals, chamberlains with gold braid and Ministers in three-cornered hats with white feathers, that I got very bored after the Tsar's carriage had passed.

It was during this summer of 1876 that a dog, a golden setter, appeared suddenly in our midst and soon acquired an important position in the family. Mamma, who was afraid of dogs and protected me from every contact with them, seemed not at all inclined at first to welcome this new inmate and tried to get rid of him. But it was no use: however many times our handyman took Sultan to the farthest corners of the park, the dog always found his way home again, wagging his tail as he ran into our garden with a cheerful air not unmixed, one felt, with irony. I intrigued for all I was worth to keep Sultan. I liked his dignified bearing, his smooth, silky, golden hair and handsome tail, his patience, his affectionate nature and good manners; and I was constantly in fear that his real master would turn up and take him away.

Mamma's attitude to Sultan, and Papa's too, improved after he had performed a truly remarkable feat one stormy night. Rain was pouring down and branches were breaking from the trees in the gale – but the cruel human beings would not let Sultan in for the night and left him in the garden. Usually he found shelter of some kind, but this time, whether because lightning and thunder frightened him or the cold was unbearable, he forced his way into the house – not through the door, but by leaping through the window of a bedroom where the shutters had not yet been closed. The extraordinary sight of Sultan, crashing head-first into the room with the window-pane broken to smithereens, remains clearly fixed in my memory. The poor dog had cut his nose and paws and was bleeding profusely. My parents' kindness of heart then revealed itself: not only did they not scold him for such impudent behaviour, but Mamma hastened to wash his wounds and even bandaged one of them, while Papa arranged a cork bed for him on the carpet by the warm stove. Sultan, with a guilty air, licked their hands and showed himself deeply touched.

However, when the day came for us to move back to town Mamma decided that we must part with Sultan, and left him in the care of the handyman. At the moment of our departure he was locked in, in spite of my protests, and as we drove to the harbour I wept the whole way, reproaching Mamma for her cruelty to Sultan. We were already on deck, the gangway had been removed and the screws were churning the water, when my brothers shouted: 'Look, there's Sultan running!' He was not merely running, he was flying, and at the very moment the ship drew away from the pier Sultan jumped straight on to the upper deck. Mamma surrendered. She had been reproaching herself for doing what she considered her cruel duty, but now she realised that Sultan was no ordinary dog, but an unusual creature of rare instinct and with feelings uncommon even among human beings. Such a gift of fate could not be discarded.

From that moment Sultan became a member of the family. Unfortunately, a year later an accident befell him, as he was trotting round my brother-in-law's rope factory. His tail got caught in a screw, and in a flash our handsome dog lost half of his finest ornament. He lived to the end of his days with this blemish, but it in no way affected his position as favourite in the home and it won him general sympathy. Gradually Sultan built up useful connections in the district: he became very fond of our chief yardsman, and later extended his affection to the policeman who lived in a wing of our house; the cooks and housemaids spoilt him, and so did all the coachmen and grooms and indeed all our close neighbours. He achieved his peak of popularity when he discovered a thief trying to steal the alms box hanging outside the Cathedral and helped to capture him.

The end of this wonderful dog, which occurred in 1886 or 1887, was not quite worthy of the high position he had acquired. He did not die in our house, in his favourite place in the hall or on a carpet in front of the stove; but, feeling that his end was near, he retired to the woodshed to wait for death, maybe not wishing to inflict upon his masters the sight of his corpse. I truly believe that it was his natural tact, his good manners, that moved him to do so. In his last days he would wag his crippled tail in a guilty manner, and it was with an effort that he stood up on his hind legs when we greeted him with affectionate words. He seemed to be apologising for being unable to serve us any longer or to express properly his unswerving devotion to us.

CHAPTER XII

KUSHELEVKA

*

THERE were two reasons for my parents' decision to settle in Kushelevka for the summer of 1877. In the first place, my sister Camisha, who was living there with her husband Matt, was expecting her second child; and secondly, Papa had to supervise the building of the church steeple near the Catholic cemetery. Kushelevka was a villa near Petersburg belonging to the Counts Kushelev-Besborodko, and was one of a number of luxurious villas on the Neva, among them the magnificent colonnaded villa of the Durnovos, which became a headquarters of the victorious proletariat during the revolution.

In the 1850s at Kushelevka, the home of his famous ancestor the Chancellor, the luxury-loving, spendthrift Count Kushelev had entertained Alexandre Dumas in a manner befitting its traditional splendour. Since that time an English cotton factory had been built alongside Kushelevka; and its red building with a chimney belching out smoke and its ceaseless noise had entirely altered the character of the district. Furthermore, Count Mussin-Pushkin, heir to the Kushelevs, had decided to make a profit by breaking up his estate and selling the land off in lots, and had thus disposed of the major part of it. On one of these plots near the Palace yet another factory, the 'Slav' brewery, had been built, of a similar kind to the paper factory, with the same belching chimney and perpetual noise.

My uncle Cesare Cavos profited by Count Mussin-Pushkin's eagerness to realise his land; for Uncle Cesare, a man of initiative, had fallen under the influence of my brother-in-law, Matthew Edwardes, who persuaded him to put some capital into a rope factory, and Uncle Cesare bought a large section of the Kushelevka park for the scheme. The building was started in 1876 and in a few years it had expanded into a whole settlement.

The brewery and the paper factory, situated on the shores of the Neva, encroached on two sides upon the private estate created for the leisure of the *grands seigneurs* in the time of Catherine the Great; but even in 1877 the Palace, which had been designed by Quarenghi, the granite quay with its monumental stairs descending to the Neva, and some of the other buildings distributed through the park were still intact.

The former owners had built a few villas in the grounds at some distance from the Palace, partly for their own house guests and partly to let. The most charming of these houses, near the entrance gate, and adorned with a balcony supported on four pillars, was rented by my parents, who allotted part of it to my recently married brother Albert. Some friends of Matt Edwardes lived in the other Kushelev villas; a Scot called Nethersall, a charming German family, the Ludwigs, and a few others who did not disturb the prevailing peace and harmony. There was only one slightly discordant note during that first year in Kushelevka; the largest villa was let as a community centre for foreign workmen who were employed at the rope factory. But even they behaved quietly and modestly; nobody ever saw them in our part of the grounds; they went early to work, when everyone else was still asleep, returned at midday for two hours for food and rest, and came home late at night along a path far from our house. I do not remember any scandals or drunken orgies.

We lived in Kushelevka in 1877, in 1878 and then again in 1882, and these three summers meant a lot to me. Of course I was unaware that I was witnessing the disintegration of a glorious era. But when Papa condemned the mercenary spirit of Mussin-Pushkin; when he recalled nostalgically the Kushelevka of his youth; when the Ludwigs described the feasts in which they themselves had participated not so long before; and when old retainers told me of the statues and vases that had once stood in the garden, and how meticulously clean had been kept the canals upon which the golden gondolas used to glide – all this evoked in me a vague feeling of sadness, and the sight of things still standing in their places awaiting their end aroused in me a sort of anxious foreboding of more destruction to come.

A year before we settled down there, I visited Kushelevka, at the time when the brewery was being built. What impressed me most then was the Ruin. This Ruin, built in the eighteenth century, in the time of Catherine the Great, by the famous Quarenghi (there is a reproduction of it in his complete works), was a romantic folly intended to represent the ruins of a castle with a round tower still standing. I knew nothing then about Quarenghi, and the Middle Ages were a vague and fantastic period to me, but, like many children, I was easily excited by anything that had a mysterious character. If Papa had not taken me by the hand I would never have had the courage to surmount those noble columns and cornices lying on the ground, nor to climb the musty-smelling, shaky steps of the interminably winding staircase. But fear vanished with Papa by my side, and the view that stretched before me from the highest platform of the Ruin was magnificent. On the far side of the Neva, and reflected in it, sparkled the roofs of the Smolni monastery and the fine buildings of the Besborodko Palace; on the near side the gardens blended with the distant forests, and here and there could be discerned the white shapes of statues and pavilions.

The Kushelev Gardens, called also the Besborodko estate, occupied an irregular quadrangle which stretched on one side along the Neva and continued for at least a mile. Almost in the middle of the quay was (perhaps it is still there) the Summer Palace of the Chancellor Alexandre Besborodko, consisting of a massive three-storeyed building with a portico and a round tower at each side. The Besborodko Palace had a terrace with railings of wrought iron leading into the garden. A long avenue of lime trees leading from the front of the garden was lined on both sides with marble busts of Roman emperors; it reached the bridge, also ornamented with lions, and ended, after 1877, with a wooden fence that separated the plot of the factory 'Neva' from the rest of the garden. To the left of the Palace, under the trees, there was a graceful summer-house, the so-called 'Coffee-house' that resembled the Turkish Pavilion in Tsarskoe Selo. Inside the walls were painted with birds and arabesques on a yellow background, but by 1877 it had become a storehouse for all kinds of junk; and if you looked through the chink of the locked door you could see a heap of broken statuary, benches, tables, bits of railings and garden tools. Farther to the left of the Palace, until 1876, was the Ruin, which was intended to serve as a belvedere; beside it was the bailiff's house, built in the English Gothic style, in which in our days Mr Nethersall brewed his porter and ginger beer. Near the Gothic house was a simple triumphal arch through which, according to legend, Catherine the Great herself used to drive on her way to the festivities arranged by Chancellor Besborodko. To the right of the Palace the gardens were enclosed on the side of the quay by a wooden fence with stone pillars. The nearest gate led to the settlement in which we lived. Almost at the gate, near a small two-storeyed yellow villa, was a granite pedestal on which, once upon a time, there had been a vase, the stone lid of which still lay in the grass; another beautiful vase of polished granite the size of a man was preserved near my brother-in-law's factory. An overgrown path led from the gate, through gardens filled with trees of every kind, to a Chinese wooden bridge of which very few Chinese fragments were left. One day the rickety railings of this bridge gave way under the weight of an imprudent guest of ours and he almost broke his neck falling into the shallow waters of the canal. Since then the old carved railings have been replaced by simpler, stronger ones, and the whole bridge has been modernised.

Behind the curve of the canal the view opened on to the main attraction of the Kushelev Gardens, the Quarenghi rotunda, perhaps too big for the site but nevertheless a model of classical architecture. It consisted of a low granite foundation and eight majestic pillars with magnificent Corinthian capitals supporting a flat cupola richly ornamented inside by sculptured panels. In the 1860s this impressive pavilion had served as a shelter for the monument to Catherine the Great in the guise of a Sibyl; but in my time the statue was no longer there and it was said that Kushelev had made a present of it to the Emperor. The Quarenghi rotunda itself remained standing in good condition without any repair until the 1890s, and was then pulled down for a paltry sum.

To the left of the rotunda was situated a once-famous, but now completely neglected orchard; farther away, behind the main avenue, by the bridge with the lions, a view opened on to a large pool, in whose waters were reflected the two pavilions connected by one common marble staircase. The buildings, now on the land belonging to the Slav factory, reminded one of the Peterhof landscape. The first pool was linked by a canal with the second, which was owned by my brother-in-law and was famous for its white and pink water lilies. Here and there along the banks one could see the remains of granite wharfs embellished with terracotta sculptures, and here too was the farm, a large building painted red with a round tower, that resembled the farm in Tsarskoe Selo. Beside it, over broken marble bowls and steps of porous stone, flowed the waters of a small canal, rusty from its iron source in the neighbouring village. This village spread inland for about a mile on both sides of the canal, whose waters became redder and redder as they neared the source. At the source itself the canal grew wider and was shaped like a chalice; on the bank stood a long building painted in dark red, the Mineral Waters Factory, which had had a great reputation in the 1840s and 1850s but in our time had fallen into decline. In the overgrown gardens of that institution all that remained of its former glory was a kiosk for a band and some decrepit little booths. The villas in this village, once inhabited by the rich, were now rented by the poor. Behind the village began the forest, a real forest, where we went to collect blackberries and mushrooms and in which, it was said, there were wolves and foxes. On the other side lay a large open space, fields and orchards, and in the distance on the horizon sparkled the cupolas of churches and gunpowder factories.

Our comparative proximity to the factories had for me a most disturbing attraction. The Ludwigs told us that all the windows in the villas of the Besborodko Palace, in the village and along the river had been broken from the force of a great explosion which took place a few years before we arrived, and that the earth had trembled as if from an earthquake. I was never able to share such a rare experience, but the mere sight of the factories allowed full rein to my imagination. On the one hand I was afraid that an explosion would take place; on the other I wanted to live through such an explosion for myself.

I clearly remember the day of our installation in Kushelevka in 1877. We moved early in the year, I think at the beginning of May, when the trees were still bare and the grass, recovering from its winter lethargy, was only just starting to grow, though a few tender snowdrops and purple crocuses were breaking through to give a little colour to the sombre background. The air was cold and here and there the snow had not yet melted. The rustling park around seemed empty and unwelcoming.

I can also remember our first evening there. Large cases filled the empty ballroom; the straw and hay that had been in them to protect the crockery from breaking lay in heaps alongside the sad groups of plates and dishes, glasses, bowls and pans that stood on floors and window-sills and chairs. On the faces of Mamma and the servants there was the expression of despair that they always wore on such occasions. 'One blue sauce-dish is broken.' 'Heavens, we've forgotten the coffee-pot.' 'Are all the napkins there?' 'Is the sugar-bowl safe?' Mamma, with assumed severity, and our old servants Stepanida and Olga, urged me to sit quietly, to stop throwing the straw about and not to fiddle with breakable objects. I, on the other hand, seemed to find a malicious pleasure in those house moves because of the disintegration which resulted from them, and I was unable to control a very special kind of excitement. As it grew dark I continued to flit between the cases and trunks or to gaze out of the three tall, curtainless windows into the large courtyard shared by several villas, where I was not allowed to go because of the cold, but which lured me all the more on that account. I was fascinated by the flocks of rooks circling with wild cries round the tops of the trees whose bare branches were clearly outlined against the pale evening sky.

Early in the morning I was wakened by the noise of the cotton factory starting work across the road behind the hedge. From the open windows on every floor came the crackling sound of hundreds of machines, and at a certain distance they blended into a single, not unpleasant, blur of sound that resembled the noise of a waterfall. You soon got used to it, so much so that it seemed at times as if the factory had stopped working and was silent, whereas in reality its clatter and rumble went on from morning till night with untiring frenzy.

I started to investigate our surroundings from the very first morning. At that time it gave me a special delight to be in a place I had not seen before, and even now it fills me with eager curiosity. It was a clear warm day. Though there were no leaves on the trees yet or flowers in our own flowerbeds; though it was a weekday and not a Sunday when there would have been no noise in the factory; although the house was still upside down because of the move and I could find no corner for myself – yet it seemed to me that a festive atmosphere reigned over Kushelevka.

My investigation started with the villa itself. Not very impressive from the outside, it was big and roomy inside, an impression emphasised by the ballroom which formed the whole centre of the house and whose windows looked out into the courtyard on one side and on to the front garden balcony on the other. The row of rooms to the right, empty for the moment, were to be occupied by brother Albert's family; of the rooms to the left I chose for myself one coming between Mamma's and Papa's bedroom and my governess's.

The kitchen was in a separate building linked with the main one by a covered passage with shaky boards, for the villa was ancient and had not been restored for many years. I used to run to and fro along this passage all the time, for through it I reached a small yard separated from the real garden by a trellis. I immediately appropriated this secluded spot, which later became particularly so, when the runner beans covered the trellis and formed walls around it. In fact I liked this place so much that I began to plan my own garden there: I made paths, fit only for Lilliputians, covered them with gravel, dug ditches and ponds, and to the annoyance of my governess always emerged from it with my clothes filthy. The first rain, alas, destroyed my efforts, after which a real gardener planted mignonette and sweet peas there, transforming my mud plot into a charming aromatic place which became my permanent residence. Here at my little table I drew and looked at picture books; here, on exceptional occasions, I gave cups of chocolate to the Nethersall girls and the little daughters of a factory manager. Sometimes we put up a tent in the garden, for which we stuck a broom into the ground, threw an old rug over it and tied the corners to four pegs. Mamma did not very much approve of this game because once I got under the tent with my guests I was able to escape the surveillance of my elders. In those years, however, any suspicion that Shourenka would think of fooling about with girls was quite unnecessary. In any case all my little girl friends were very timid and modest; it was quite an effort to rouse them, and after genteelly consuming the chocolate and sweetmeats they would hurry back home so as not to be tempted to look at picturebooks or have a game of Lotto. My passion for the tent was so strong that on rainy days I put it up in the half-dark hall. If I stood the broom straight up it looked more like a large umbrella and was too open on all sides, but if it was inclined and the rug tied to chairs placed half lying down it produced an effect like a Bedouin's shelter and seemed the peak of seclusion. Inside it was warm, even hot, in spite of the fact that a damp draught of air came from the open door on to the balcony where it was raining. One day, however, I almost set the house on fire when I tried to add an element of cosiness to the interior by lighting a candle which I took from the piano. Mamma suddenly became aware of a smell of burning wool and came rushing in terror. All ended well, and only a large hole in the rug remained as a reminder of what the grown-ups called 'Shoura's mischievousness'.

The installation, a few days after our own arrival, of brother Albert and his family added great animation to our lives, but deprived us of all peace. Albert himself could never lead a quiet life, and as it was difficult to organise picnics in Kushelevka his eagerness to undertake something or other expressed itself in home entertainments. Papa's birthday, Mamma's, Camisha's and his own wife's names-day offered opportunities for illuminations, fireworks and festivals. I remember particularly well the celebration of his wife's namesday on July 22nd, when my enterprising brother decided to improve upon the traditional illuminations by making the numerous lanterns at home out of coloured cotton. Some of the young people whom he recruited cut out the pieces of wood for the bottoms of the lanterns, others sewed the material, others still (including me) made holes for the candles. The material had to be nailed to the pieces of wood, the candles had to be wired in and cut to fit the holes when they were too thick. There was a lot of fuss, a lot of waste, and in the end the effect justified neither the effort nor the expense, for the lanterns were so dim and shabby that we had to resort to the traditional paper ones.

Brother Albert's favourite spot for sketching was the fishing centre on the Neva situated not far from the gates to the gardens, which consisted of a wooden platform over the water, on which there was a capstan for rolling up the net and a wooden hut where the fishermen lived. From this platform there was a wonderful view; opposite were the churches and chapels of the Smolni monastery, on the left was the surburb of Okhta with its church and huge old wharves, and to the right were the distant steeples of the Petersburg churches and the tower of the town water works. The brightly coloured barges lining both sides of

the river or being pulled along in Indian file by a tug made
the landscape even more picturesque. Albert was untiring
in returning again and again to these truly incomparable
subjects. If the evening was clear, as soon as he returned
from his work about six o'clock he would snatch a hurried
meal, collect his painting gear, and rush off to this spot.
The intense excitement that filled him at such moments
contributed much to his work. That summer was the most
important period in his development, and I consider the
Kushelev water-colours of Albert Benois, painted with a
rare assurance and simplicity, the best of all his work.
There is no trace in them of the influences he acquired later
when he became a popular celebrity.

On the whole Albert's activities were never a nuisance to
others, never noisy or restless, though he always managed
to drag along with him whoever happened to be around.
As a result he worked surrounded by a group of people,
a fact which he did not mind in the least. Albert's young
wife interrupted the peace and quiet of our home in quite a
different manner. The morning after their arrival in
Kushelevka, a large Schroeder piano arrived, and barely
had it had time to settle down than she started to practise
exercises and to work out difficult scores. This technical
and educational music filled Kushelevka for six hours a day,
and the distant waterfall noise of the red factory was nothing
compared to this thunder in our midst. The playing of a
professional pianist was also quite a different matter from
the marches and quadrilles which Papa played by ear or
the timid playing of Mamma or even the brilliant improvisations of Albert. Every note was struck with rare precision,
resounding as they whirled in the half-empty rooms of the
villa and poured out like hail into the garden. Even when I
strolled some way from the house I was followed by the
sound of the *arpeggios*, trills and roulades. What irritated
me most was that even the things I loved, like Liszt's

rhapsody or Rubinstein's waltz, she dismembered, stopping half way and returning several times to the part she found difficult. This music prevented me from listening to my governess or taking part in any coherent conversation, for I already suffered from my inconvenient idiosyncrasy that any music, exercise or the simplest tune immediately plunges me into a state of absentmindedness and inability to think of anything else. In later years when I listened to my sister-in-law I used to delight in her repetitions. But the seven-year-old boy, though responsive to music, understood nothing of it. Though I disliked going for good healthy walks under my governess's supervision, I used to agree to go just to get away from the house and that cataract of sounds. Besides, there was some personal friction between my sister-in-law and me.

When my brother Kolia, who had just been promoted to the rank of officer, arrived to stay with us at Kushelevka, together with his horse, he suggested to Mamma that it would be a good idea for me to have riding lessons. Mamma, who always hoped to improve my very inferior physical education, asked me whether I would like this, and in spite of my fears I agreed with joy. I thought it would be rather smart to trot about on a horse like a general.

But we never reached the stage of trotting. Kolia's riding lessons lasted an even shorter time than the music lessons of my sister-in-law. Regardless of my character and of my size, he assumed towards me the manner which was common in the regimental riding school, where the novices regularly fell from their horses like so many sacks. Having seated me on his mare without a saddle and pushed the reins into my hands, he let go the rope, standing in the centre like a horse-trainer, cracked his whip and the horse started circling round. To my horror I found myself at once slipping down over her smooth back. Kolia did not reach me in time to help me up; I was already lying on the grass when Mamma, who had been watching this exercise anxiously from the balcony, came running to my help.

What is astonishing is that I did not cry. I got on to my feet by myself, shook myself and, summoning all my courage, declared that I was ready to continue on condition that I was given a saddle. But this was outside Nicholas's educational programme. He seized me by force, placed me on the horse, pushed Mamma roughly aside and again let go the rope. My courage vanished at once. Clutching the horse's mane and clinging to its neck, I shouted insults at the tyrant and demanded to be allowed down. Kolia tried to subdue what he considered to be my insubordination, but Mamma sternly ordered him to let me dismount, and eventually to my relief I found myself in her arms, her hand stroking my head. I sulked at Kolia for a long time after that. There was no further question, of course, of continuing my riding lessons, and after that unfortunate day I have never attempted to climb on the back of the noblest of all animals, though there have been many temptations to do so during my life and my family were all good riders.

The cemetery of the Catholic church, where Papa had started to build a steeple, was about three miles from Kushelevka, nearer to the Finnish station. The church itself, very simple but elegant, was built by my father in the 1850s in Romanesque style. The lower floor was supported on vaults, in the western angle of which was our family grave where lay my sister Luisa, who died in early childhood, and my brother Isha. For that reason alone our family was closely linked with this church. It was also the parish church of the Edwardes; my brother-in-law Matthew, a fanatical Catholic, never missed a Sunday without going to Mass, sometimes with the whole family. The former façade, without the church tower, was, it must be admitted, more compact and harmonious. Papa had obviously imagined it that way. But now, thanks to some newly found capital

and to satisfy the ambition of the Polish colony, who wanted
the church to be more prominent in the neighbourhood, it
had been decided to build the steeple which, according to
Papa's plan, would rise above the main entrance into the
church. In 1877, I believe, the work had not yet started,
and the foundation was laid only in the spring of 1878,
but Papa was busy with it all the same and often went to
the cemetery to consult the Catholic priest, Franziskiewisz,
who also used to visit our villa.

I rather liked priests, though I was afraid of some of the
Polish Dominican priests of St Catherine, whom Papa used
to rebuke gently for malice and cunning. But I loved Father
Franziskiewisz with all my heart and I believe he returned
my love. Unfortunately, our friendship did not last long:
the authorities took the view that this kind and harmless
man was dangerous because of his popularity and sent him
to a remote Siberian parish.

In appearance this priest was a typical yet comical 'Jesuit',
so comical indeed that as a child, in spite of my respect for
Franziskiewisz, I could not help imitating his mannerisms;
even my parents, who usually did not encourage such
impudence, laughed good-humouredly at my imitations.
My kindhearted Mamma would laugh till she cried, vying
with me to reproduce the funny grimaces with which
Franziskiewisz refused all food (though he would soon give
in and reveal an unexpectedly large appetite). I could also
mimic rather aptly his mannerisms of speech, his own
peculiar French and Russian expressions which he had to
use in our home where no one understood his native
Polish. All this was most amusing and would have been
useful to an actor playing the part of Don Basilio in *Le
Barbier de Seville*. But perhaps Franziskiewisz's mannerisms
might have appeared too exaggerated on the stage!

Father Franziskiewisz's most unusual characteristic was
his way of walking and particularly of entering a room.

Other priests that we knew adopted a somewhat noble and majestic manner with which to impress their parishioners; their bearing suggested that, in their capacity of Divine representatives, they were honouring simple mortals; and the touch of humility assumed as they stretched out their hands to be kissed arose only from a sense of Christian decorum. As Father Franziskiewisz appeared in the door, he bowed two or three times in every direction, his hands raised above his head, palms outwards, as if expressing by gestures something like 'unworthy', 'too much honour', 'forgive my impertinence'. Had he been an old man, these mannerisms might have meant something different, but he was only just over thirty. His face was youthful, always clean-shaven and a little purple about the cheeks; he was a little taller than average, very thin and gaunt, and appeared even more so because of his tightly fitting black cassock.

This 'comic-opera' Jesuit was a pure, disinterested man of angelic kindness. He looked particularly spiritual when he officiated at Mass, which he did very simply, gravely, even sternly, without any grimaces. He seemed transported at such moments with a deep sense of religion and to experience each time a new feeling of ecstasy. It was a moving sight to see him talking to the poor, almost weeping when he heard their complaints, apologising when he could not help them as much as he would have liked. All his income was spent on helping the poor, and of the money he received (which was not inconsiderable, for the dead bring regular profit) he distributed the greater part – after which, it was said, he often had nothing to eat himself for days.

Franziskiewisz was incapable of malice or intrigue or venality. He was, moreover, a man of erudition, with a good knowledge of lay as well as theological literature and, rather unusually, also of the history of art. It is probable that it was these exceptional qualities which caused his enemies to draw up the denunciation which was to take him away from the capital to a remote exile.

I remember Father Franziskiewisz especially clearly at Kushelevka, walking with his strange, staggering gait along the alley leading to our villa. When he took a step, it was as if the wind had thrust him along; he always seemed to be struggling with it, and his long, voluminous cloak flapped all round him even if there was no breeze. As soon as he saw the son of the 'highly venerated Sir Professor' busy catching frogs or building castles on the garden paths, he would begin his ritual of greeting, bowing low and raising his palms upwards. This made my return-ritual more difficult, for I had to catch his hand in the air in order to kiss it. He always murmured gentle and affectionate words, unfortunately incomprehensible to me because they were in Polish. At the sight of Mamma he would repeat the cere-mony with even more zeal, uttering an elaborate greeting in a strange French jargon, and when Papa's turn came he was treated to a real St Vitus's dance. But as soon as they turned to business he would become quite natural and serious.

That first Kushelev summer is also memorable because of the odd friendship which I formed at the age of seven with a young man of twenty. I don't remember his surname and am not sure whether I ever knew it; the entire house-hold called him simply Monsieur Stanislas. He still lives under this name in my memory. I never knew where he came from, what evil fate brought him to the Russian capital, how he got to Okhta, who were his parents. Mon-sieur Stanislas seemed to avoid such subjects. Possibly he was the son of a rebel who came to a tragic end during the Polish mutiny of 1863. He certainly belonged to the upper classes, judging by his manner and accent. He spoke Ger-man and English, and French of the kind one speaks when one has learnt it as a child. Mamma decided to make use of his knowledge of French and suggested that he should become my tutor. This he could not undertake because of his poor health, but he gave me occasional though rather inadequate lessons. He did not teach me to speak good French, but my conversations with him enriched me in a different and more spiritual manner.

Monsieur Stanislas looked a truly poetic figure, like one of those martyrs in Bolognese pictures who die at the hand of the executioner, gazing in ecstasy at the open heavens above them. Gaunt, terrifyingly thin, deathly pale, with dark, slightly curly hair, he resembled a ghost. He used to dress like a beggar (that shocked no one, because in those days students often resembled vagabonds), and he washed his only shirt himself. One day I caught him at this occupation and was struck by the incredible leanness of his naked body.

Of what our conversations-cum-lessons consisted I do not remember, but I was certainly not bored by them, though I loathed most lessons in the summer. The first lessons took place at the villa, but one day he did not come and Mamma sent me with the governess to find out the reason. Monsieur Stanislas lived in the attic of the large villa, of which the lower floors were used as a dormitory for the workmen. To reach him one had to go through the only door of this building, which was otherwise empty during the day. When we had climbed to his low-ceilinged room we found him lying on an iron bed, with his head towards a semi-circle of window that came down to the floor. A few books were scattered on his blanket and on the floor around, but the poor invalid was apparently unable to read and was prostrate with fever; his eyes were burning and his arms lay limp. At that time people did not know that consumption was infectious, and in any case Mamma was sceptical about the possibility of contamination, so that even after this first visit had revealed my tutor's critical condition I was allowed to come to see him daily, and with-

out my governess, as the villa where he lived was only a
few steps away from ours and Mamma was confident that
I could not lose my way.

I would like to think that these visits of mine were not
too much of a strain for poor Monsieur Stanislas. There is
no doubt that there was great affinity between us. He was
one of those grown-ups who have retained the magic gift
of a child-like spirit, and for whom the company of children,
especially interesting and precocious children (in which
category, without unnecessary modesty, I include myself),
is sometimes more agreeable than that of their contemporaries. I almost always found Monsieur Stanislas lying on his
uncomfortable bed, but even in the words 'Come in!'
which he uttered in answer to my knocking I could sense
his delight, and as soon as I entered the room I could see
that a contented smile had replaced the usual bitter expression on his blue lips. On the days when he felt less ill
he would get up and pace to and fro across the creaking,
boards of his attic, while I sat on the tattered grey blanket,
often for hours at a time, firing every kind of question at
him. I collected so many and was so impatient to hear the
answers that I asked more and more without fully listening
to his explanations.

Part of our conversation touched upon religious and
philosophical subjects. Thoughts of life after death, of
ghosts, of eternity, of stellar space, of the infinite, greatly
preoccupied me at that time. Sometimes we passed on to
natural history. Monsieur Stanislas was, I believe, a student
of natural history, but had been unable to continue his
studies because of lack of means and illness. He would tell
me fascinating stories about insects, which was a special
subject of his: he had a collection of them in boxes which
he had made himself. A few of these boxes with glass tops
were attached to the shabby, carefully patched wall. His
sole possessions were these boxes, a few dozen books and

an old suitcase. Matt Edwardes had provided the necessary furniture, and it was he who had arranged for Monsieur Stanislas to live in the attic of this workmen's lodging. Sometimes Monsieur Stanislas would remember the educational duties he had undertaken, and then we would take up Margaux's *French Grammar*. This dull and serious book, however, had the effect of sending us into peals of laughter; we laughed over some of the sentences until we cried – but Monsieur Stanislas's laughter invariably turned into a wracking cough and was followed by a severe haemorrhage.

Towards the end of the summer my attachment to Monsieur Stanislas became intense. He treated me, a comparative stranger and a mere boy, like his own brother or an equal. There were days when he suddenly grew animated, younger, and could talk for hours eloquently and intelligently. On the other hand, when his condition was worse he asked me to leave him, but with such tact, such touching courtesy, that though it upset me I obeyed at once. On rainy days I would run over to see him (as a child I loved to run about in the rain) and on such days our conversations were particularly cosy. We could hear the rain patter on the iron roof below and the caretaker scolding some trespasser, and see the grey foliage through the window-pane against which the rain streamed down. In the meantime my friend and I would be wandering in India, admiring monkeys darting through the lianas, hunting wild beasts, listening to the teller of tales on the market-place. Matt Edwardes had a fair-sized library and many illustrated books which Monsieur Stanislas was allowed to borrow, and we could go on endlessly turning over the coloured illustrations to Shakespeare by Gilbert or the pages of the *Encyclopaedia Britannica*. He could tell wonderful stories of his own about most things, but if he struck an unknown subject he would translate for me the corresponding text. It was with my dear, unforgettable Monsieur Stanislas that I went for the first time to visit a waxworks exhibition, introduced into this Hoffmann world by a man who was himself a 'Hoffmann' character. The 'human doll' theme has always had a great attraction for me; it has appealed to my mentality and been reflected in my art. I need only to remind my readers that the subject of 'Petrushka' is based on all the moods and meditations ever induced by 'automatons'.

You entered the waxworks museum through a porch which housed several uncanny-looking, congealed ladies and gentlemen. One of the ladies did not seem to me to be so uncanny as the others: she was constructed with greater care and was kept prisoner under a glass case, dressed in a bright raspberry-coloured blouse and a pink skirt with silver spangles. Holding one hand on her hip and the other in the air, with her head thrown back, she balanced a sword on her nose and on the tip of the blade a glass filled with wine. When she was wound up this beauty began to bend at the waist, her free hand waved about, and the glass on the blade trembled but did not fall and the wine did not spill.

This exhibition also prided itself on a remarkable lady at the cashier's desk. She sat under a poster of foreign origin and foreign inscription, between two incredible monsters, one of which was supposed to represent Edward, Prince of Wales, and the other a famous bandit. This lady was the same 'Julia Pastrana' whom I had seen before in the Zoo at the fun-fair; not the original famous bearded woman, who by that time must have been in her grave, but a similar young female with a large black beard to provide her with a source of income and glory. This pseudo-Julia Pastrana was dressed in a costume similar to that of the beauty with the sword; she sat on a velvet divan embroidered with gold and when not distributing tickets she did some sewing. The charming artificial equilibrist and the very much alive Julia Pastrana gave me a foretaste of the exceptional pleasures I might expect in the museum itself. But, alas, there was disappointment to come after such a promising beginning. We were shown round the museum by a totally drunken guide, fetched on Julia's instructions by a small messenger boy, who in broken Franco-German delivered a speech of the most arrant nonsense. But two out of the hundred or so other figures in the house made a considerable impression on me – those of a deadly-pale Napoleon lying in a moth-eaten frockcoat with a decoration on his breast, and of a long-haired young woman whose large bosom rose and fell most gracefully to create the illusion of breathing. There was also an amusing conjuror who made different objects appear from under glasses; when sometimes nothing appeared he shook his head disapprovingly. A number of scenes were quite hideous and pitiful; for instance, one of policemen catching bandits in a public house, or a family quarrel with broken crockery on the floor and a chair wedged over the head of the master of the house. One whole room was devoted to the war. That year had seen the beginning of the Russo-Turkish war, and the owner of the museum had hastened to display something topical. But even my childish eye detected that the collection consisted of old and decrepit junk displayed in utter disorder – probably the remains of some pantomime dating back to the Crimean campaign. As we returned on top of the tram, Stanislas and I exchanged impressions and tried to persuade one another that what we had seen had been of some interest.

Alas, one of us was destined to become, a few months later, as motionless a figure as the ones we had seen that day. My dear friend lasted through the winter and died of consumption in the spring. He died, according to my brother-in-law, in possession of full consciousness, having received extreme unction from Father Franziskiewisz. As though illuminated from within, he clearly repeated several times: *'Que c'est beau! Que c'est beau!'*

CHAPTER XIII

KUSHELEVKA – *Continued*

*

I WOULD like to save from oblivion another small group of people who are linked with Kushelevka in my memory. Not because these people were remarkable in any way or different from millions similar to them, but because in my imagination they were part of Kushelevka's surroundings, imbued with its poetry. I never saw them anywhere but in their small villa, which stood inconspicuously in a corner not far from ours.

For many years this house had been rented by an old-fashioned German family called Ludwig. Papa Ludwig was a respectable-looking, grey-bearded old gentleman, who worked in an office on the Nevsky Prospect: his life's companion was a round, wizened, busy little old woman. The rest of the family consisted of three sons, Kostia, Fedia and Sasha, and two daughters, Katia and Ania, who lived with them.

Papa Ludwig left home early to go to his office in town, accompanied by his eldest son, a man in his late thirties, who worked in the same concern as his father. Long brown side-whiskers gave Kostia an impressive appearance, though he had a squint and was often drunk. I can see that pair as if it were today, in bowler hats and dark old-fashioned frock-coats, walking from the garden gate to their villa with brief-cases under their arms. There they would find comfortable dressing-gowns and a filling German meal – a *bier suppe* and a roast with a sweet jelly. Of the two girls, Katia, an ungainly, ageing spinster, was a creature of unusual kindness of heart. She used to spoil me, and although I tormented her with all sorts of childish pranks, I was genuinely fond of her. Ania was considered by the family to be pretty, and this was confirmed by the fact that she had a fiancé, who, unfortunately, was one of the oddest and most hideous creatures I have ever come across. Hunchbacked, with a little red, pointed beard, he dressed with a pretence of smartness in brightly coloured ties, striking-looking waistcoats, and light grey check trousers full at the bottoms; gold pince-nez on a long chain were perched on his red nose and were perpetually slipping from it. The marriage between Ania and Victor was to take place when the financial conditions of the future husband became more secure. This, however, did not prevent the two love-birds from kissing each other uninterruptedly. My presence in no way embarrassed them; on the contrary, in the intervals between kisses, Victor would give me a playful wink, half apologetic, half ecstatic, while Ania shook her little finger at me and begged me not to give them away. Shamelessly I rushed at once to Mamma Ludwig to report on what I had witnessed. But the old lady merely nodded to me and went on with her cooking, murmuring: '*Lass sie doch, sie sind ja verlobt.*'

Besides Katia I was also fond of the two younger Ludwig brothers, tall, fair-haired Fedia who was preparing to be a clergyman, and Sasha, who was only fourteen and with whom I therefore felt an equal.

Fedia was very witty, and had the gift, invaluable for a buffoon, of remaining imperturbable while all the others rolled about with laughter. He would put on a long, black cassock, take a book in his hand and preach to us in a way that made us hysterical with laughter. This was perhaps a little surprising in a man who was preparing to become a clergyman, but his comic sermons were of a perfectly harmless nature and only underlined all that can be pompous and ridiculous in the bearing and manner of a parson.

Alas, an early death five years later put paid to Fedia's ambitions. I must admit that I cannot imagine how he would have behaved at real weddings, christenings and funerals.

Sasha, who had the same name as my own, helped me to forget the deep sense of loss which I felt on the death of Monsieur Stanislas in 1878. He was a remarkably pleasant youth, and in many ways reminded me of my dear brother Isha. Whatever he undertook he approached with great earnestness, very different from the buffoon Fedia. When I watched Sasha at work, whether mending something or planting flowers or preparing for a family celebration, I was lost in admiration; he did everything so neatly, so quickly, so skilfully. He was a schoolboy, but I never saw him in uniform; he always wore a clean, striped linen shirt, and when he went shopping by the river he pulled on a coloured jockey's-cap with a peak, which very much appealed to me.

Sasha dreamt of becoming a fireworks designer in the distant future and was already preparing for his career by making up various kinds of fireworks according to text-books on the subject. For this reason I classed him with the magicians and the conjurers. I could listen for hours to his stories, told in a soft whisper, about the fireworks he had seen and the fireworks he would manufacture as soon as he has mastered the science; tales of special charm because of the spice of danger connected with fire and explosives. About three times a year Sasha would put his knowledge into action. He would buy some gunpowder, sulphur and saltpetre, which were weighed in proportion on a small pair of scales and then mixed together with a spoon: the mixture was put into special cardboard cornets and finally packed in coloured paper. If anyone were to appear in the room with a lighted cigarette during this proceeding Sasha, with his usual calm, would warn him of the danger, while I would be seized with panic and hustle the careless visitor with his cigarette out of the room. For birthday celebrations Sasha would arrange magic lighting among the bushes of the little garden, illuminating the leaves of the trees with multi-coloured lights. Fountains of fire would spurt and hiss, Catherine wheels would spin, Roman candles and rockets flare up, while familiar figures were made monstrous by the distorting shadows.

Sasha's greatest achievement was the manufacture of some 'naval' fireworks. He took several weeks to prepare this supreme surprise, during which he locked himself in his room, leaving me hanging about outside asking tedious questions. On the appointed day Sasha emerged from his room with a beautiful three-masted ship in his hands; along the deck protruded tiny copper guns and the frigate was decorated with fireworks like a Christmas tree. A real ship from the land of Lilliput! In the evening, after all the guests had arrived, the ship was carefully launched in the canal that ran by the Ludwigs' garden. A gunpowder rope from the shore set fire to other similar ropes fixed on to the mast, and the whole ship was soon ablaze with Bengal lights as her guns began to fire, one after the other. But one of them must have been too heavily loaded. There was a terrible explosion and the ship capsized and very nearly sank. The causes of the catastrophe were discussed for many days. Sasha was embarrassed, but he was consoled by the assurance that the spectacle was far better that way, as the explosion was just like the one that had destroyed a Turkish monitor on the Danube.

This explosion of the Turkish monitor was also represented in a grandiose style on the lake of the Tivoli Gardens, recently opened near the Slav factory. We waited for two hours on the other side of the lake for the explosion of the monster of wood that had been nailed together to represent the Turkish warship, but finally it was announced that the fireworks had gone damp and the explosion would be postponed. Disappointed, we strolled back home through the dark park.

With Sasha and Katia we boated on the canals in a little boat that belonged to the Ludwigs and was moored at the jetty next to their villa. Unfortunately the water in the Kushelev canals became very shallow in later years, owing to some mishandling of the levels where they joined the Neva, and these trips were usually accompanied by many mishaps. Sometimes the boat stuck completely in the mud and we had to climb on to the shore and drag it out on a rope.

I have one romantic memory of these excursions on the Kushelev canals when, in the summer of 1878, the Kushelev Palace was placed at the disposal of a State girls' school. During recreation hours or in the evenings after work, if our boat reached the bridge connecting the main path to the Palace, we would see several charming schoolgirls on the bridge and on the shores nearby. They were dressed in the pretty, old-fashioned dresses with open necks and short sleeves which was the uniform of these little State prisoners in the reign of Nicholas I. It was a light blue colour and was worn with a white apron and sometimes a white pelerine. From afar we could see the girls on the Lion bridge, some of them leaning against the metal lions or the balustrade, others strolling on the bridge or sitting on the grassy banks. When they saw our boat, those who sat on the grass would jump to their feet and run to join those on the bridge, and the whole group would come to meet us, silently, with smiles and timid gestures of greeting. As we rowed under the bridge this lovely picture would disappear, to emerge on the other side to smiles now sadder and gestures registering grief. An hour later we were rowing back, and if the schoolgirls were still by the bridge, the scene would be repeated.

After a few such meetings both sides became bolder. Those in the boat would make such remarks as: 'What lovely weather!' or inquire: 'Wouldn't you like to come with us?' 'Will you be here tomorrow?' and so on. The answers were barely audible. If Sasha's sisters were with us the schoolgirls gathered enough courage to exchange a few words, and on those occasions our boat would linger a little.

We ourselves were to blame for breaking up this charming idyll, which was repeated almost every day, when we suddenly decided to offer flowers to our secret friends. As we approached the bridge with our sheaves of flowers, plundered, in spite of her timid protestations, from the flowerbeds of Mamma Ludwig, Sasha and I were as excited as if we were going to a secret assignation. When we reached the bridge, with unusual agility I jumped ashore with the flowers and started climbing. Reaching the lions, red as a lobster and dumb with confusion, I placed our gift at the feet of the blue beauties, who were so touched by my exploit that they rushed forward and began to hug me and, forgetting all caution, to chatter loudly. Others, older and more cunning, took the opportunity to start a conversation with Sasha who, standing in the boat and holding on with the boathook, shook them all by the hand. Everyone was so preoccupied and noisy that we missed the signals of the girls posted to give warning of the approach of the schoolmistress. Suddenly the gay banter stopped, faces became solemn, and when I turned round I saw the figure of an elderly, severe-looking lady. I stood frozen to the ground in terror, not knowing what to do. Without a word the lady took me by the hand and led me to the canal-bank and, feeling desperately ashamed, I climbed down into the boat. As we rowed away we could see that two more mistresses had joined the first. They were examining the flowers, expecting to find a note, and then, stiff and dignified, they disappeared with the crowd of schoolgirls towards the Palace. From then on the girls were not allowed to visit the fatal place and we never saw them again. In later summers the Palace remained empty, and the bridge was destroyed after my brother-in-law bought all the gardens behind it.

One of the superb features of Kushelevka was the view that opened upon the Neva. It was blocked, however, by a tall fence, so Papa decided to build a kind of balcony out over the fence from which one could look at the panorama. To sit on this belvedere was just as pleasant as rowing on the canals and I used to spend entire days there, either alone or in the company of Mamma or my governess. One could see from inside the villa what was going on in the belvedere, so that when I was there no other vigilant eye was needed. When I had had enough of the vast outlook on the Neva or of what was going on on the quay below I would turn to a book or draw any nonsense that came into my head. My brother Misha also liked this belvedere. He was preparing for the Navy and often came to visit us with his friends, the tall Baron Klupfel and the painfully short-sighted Vinogradov, who was remarkable for having at the age of only seventeen a thick black beard. All three considered themselves to be old salts, and as drunkenness is in the tradition of old salts these nice, well-behaved young men, after two bottles of beer among the three of them at luncheon, would pretend to be tipsy, singing songs at the tops of their voices to attract the attention of passers-by. They also ate sunflower seeds like true sailors, spitting out the husks into the street. I hardly recognised our timid Misha, and was immensely entertained. The youths did not always misbehave on the belvedere, however; sometimes they would bring a pile of text-books and would study conscientiously, examining each other in their work. I believe they all three failed to passed their naval examinations the first time, which was not surprising.

The centre of the panorama that spread out before our balcony was the Smolni monastery, standing on the shore

of the Neva opposite us. It is the most beautiful and
poetical building in the whole of the Russian Empire.
Proudly and magnificently the colossal mass of the main
Cathedral rises above the rest, its five cupolas, like deacons
officiating at a solemn liturgy, grouped around four completely similar churches. All round this holy settlement
extends a high wall, interrupted at regular intervals by
intricate towers. At all times of day and in any weather there
is a fairy-like quality about this scene that is particularly
moving on clear summer evenings, when the buildings
seem to dissolve in the crimson rays of the setting sun and
the blue roofs of the cupolas and steeples shine with the
gold of the crosses and sculptured garlands with which the
luxurious phantasy of Rastrelli has adorned them. It seems
to me now that it was Smolni that first made me realise the
beauty of architecture set in landscape, and before I ever
sensed my link with Petersburg's past I drank in the marvellous beauty of this unique view.

Looking from the Smolni to the left, the view extends
over the river and the church, around which are clustered
small wooden houses with green and red roofs; farther on
are the black gaps of the old ship-building wharves and,
where the Neva bends, the towers of the Alexander Nevsky
monastery shimmer in the distant mist; there also is a
church built in the Russian style by an architect friend of
my father's. Looking to the right, on the opposite shore,
behind the hedges and wood-sheds, is the Tauride Palace
with its flat cupola and beside it the dark red mass of the
water-tower; farther still the cupola of the Isaak Cathedral
shining with gold, and a mass of different steeples. Papa
liked to give them all their names, and as I studied Petersburg from the Kushelev belvedere I learnt many of its
features and remembered their characteristic outlines.

This distant view of Petersburg was motionless, without
life; but close to us, occupying the whole forefront of the

picture, was the perpetual movement of the river, still only at moments when there was no breath of a breeze. Then the buildings of the opposite shore were reflected in the waters of the Neva, though even on such days the blue stillness was constantly interrupted by the life bubbling on its surface, by the heavily laden Schlüsselburg ship or a tug-boat dragging a line of barges, or by hundreds of brightly coloured yawls darting to and fro in all directions, or the fishing boats that disappeared up-river with their nets.

The traffic on the quay along the Kushelev boundary was not particularly exciting on ordinary days and was certainly not of a distinguished appearance: its proximity to a workers' suburb was obvious. Seldom did one see a private carriage belonging to a foreign factory-owner or to a land-owner with property farther away. The usual sight was of endless rows of carts or simple peasant vehicles on the way to Petersburg or coming from it. Pedestrians were mostly workmen. In the mornings the milkwomen marched in detachments, their metal pails of milk clinking on the ends of their yokes, baskets of butter and curd behind their backs. They were either genuine Finns or Russian women who tried to imitate the Finnish accent – for Finnish butter was considered the best. They advertised their produce with cries that described it as something exceptionally alluring. Often their regular progress was interrupted by some scandalous scene for which, secure in my sheltered position, I must confess I had a great predilection. I was sometimes even annoyed when a budding quarrel ended too quickly owing to the arrival of a policeman or caretaker.

But one day, towards the end of the summer, our quay was transformed. It was August 15th, the feast of the Assumption of the Virgin, usually celebrated with a splendid church procession that covered the whole district. Excitement on our quay was intense. From early morning crowds of men, women and children, workmen, fishermen, sailors, soldiers, artisans, shopkeepers, petty officials, hurried in one direction, away from town towards Okhta or farther to the gunpowder factory. Towards 11 a.m. the church bells began to ring, and the procession appeared round the corner. Sitting on the belvedere with the rest of our house party, I waited for that moment with mixed feelings, partly with exhilaration, but also with something like fear. The slow movement of the procession to the funereal singing of the priests, the choir and the crowd gave the impression of something sinister and infinitely sad. Not being Orthodox, indeed having a bias against Orthodoxy, in which I was encouraged by my governesses who spoke of the Orthodox Church with a tinge of contempt, I felt no pious emotions, but instead a gnawing fear. It seemed to me that these approaching banners, waving, dipping and lifting again, were launching a sinister attack upon me and that I was in danger. When the procession reached our balcony the fear vanished as the holy banners, causing no harm, trooped slowly past. As they did so the attention of all of us on the belvedere was engrossed by a scene of truly medieval character. A number of pious people had tried to pass or crawl under the image of the Virgin which, shining with gold and precious stones, was carried on the shoulders of some parishioners pouring with sweat and obviously exhausted. Suddenly there was a shriek and several strong men pushed their way to the ikon, dragging a hysterical woman who was struggling and shouting violently. In spite of her resistance she was thrown on the pavement and held there, so that the ikon in passing could have its miraculous effect. And indeed the hysterical creature pulled herself up without help, so completely calm that everybody around, even our servants on the belvedere, were struck by the miracle and made the sign of the Cross. Such scenes occurred many times that day along the route of the procession.

The centre of that primitive method of fishing known as the 'tonia' was situated close to the Kushelev Gardens, and was a great attraction in those parts. We lived a mere stone's throw from the 'tonia': you walked out of the garden gates, crossed the street running by the river and went down a wooden stairway on a steep slope, and there you were on the platform of the 'tonia', which reeked of fish. When the Edwardes came on Sundays, it was customary to visit the 'tonia' about three hours before luncheon so that Matt Edwardes, who was a great gambler at heart, could order a 'tonia' in the hope of a magnificent catch. Sometimes there would be salmon and perch and pike in the net, and on lucky days there would even be trout. But more often the net returned empty or with only small fry, and then Matt lost his money and would leave the river grumbling good-humouredly, while Mamma, with a sly look, would tell him: 'I was sure that would happen and took my own precautions: I bought a wonderful fish this morning.'

For us children the long wait for the return of the net was unbearable, and we preferred to spend that hour on the beach paddling in the water, carelessly wetting our clothes and collecting tiny fish in our little buckets with our hands. Sometimes a passing ship would stir up the waters and the wash, reaching the beach, would splash us from head to foot. The girls would shriek, lifting their skirts. But the water by the beach was warm and we never caught cold after such fishing adventures. We collected shells as well as fish, and also red fir bark, out of which Papa would cut beautiful little boats and ships. The greatest luck fell to the one who found a bit of driftwood or a long spar. Sometimes we made our way along the beach as far as the granite pier of the Besborodko Palace and watched the fishermen there sitting round the fire boiling fish and eating it on the spot, each dipping his wooden spoon into the common pot.

When we returned to the 'tonia' we would find the

fishermen breathing heavily, sweating hard, shouting and egging each other on as they hauled in the last ropes dragging the net – and if their exertions were considerable it was clear that the net was heavy with fish. Matt would be radiant, and on the faces of the others there would be as much tension as if their own fate were in jeopardy. As the floats that supported the nets appeared on the water, the fishermen seized the edges and dragged, with one last pull, the contents on to the platform. On a good day Matt would have no more need to repeat to his mother-in-law as he had done for the last hour: 'You watch, Mamma, you just watch!' – for we would see a real miracle: a twenty-pound salmon beating its tail and twisting in the net. The sparkling, silvery catch and the king of all these doomed brethren would be let loose on the boarded floor and some time would be spent sorting and laying out some of the fish in vessels of water and killing the others. But Matt would have his catch, ending its life by hitting it with a stone on the head and holding it by the gills, as he searched for a silver coin in his pocket. Once again his heart's desire of a good catch would be fulfilled and we would be supplied with a dish such as we had not seen for a long time. The salmon would be cooked at once, taken to the cellar and put on ice, and would then be ready for serving at dinner, fragrant and fresh, garnished with vegetables, parsley and dill in its open mouth, as the main, delicious feature of our festive meal.

The Neva was not always as lovable as on the days of the miraculous catches when, sparkling, shining like blue satin, she bore her waters solemnly and smoothly to the sea. There were days when we saw her dark grey and sullen, bristling under gusts of wind, covered with white horses. Perhaps I even liked the river better like that. After such days the evenings would sometimes be really spectacular, especially if the sun on its way to the horizon pierced through the accumulating clouds. Then a bright orange glow lit up the factory buildings, and Smolni burnt like a fire against the background of dark, leaden clouds and the deep blue of the Neva. On these evenings, so particularly tantalising for the artist, Albert would rush to his favourite spot by the 'tonia' and feverishly try to reproduce the scene on paper. Though usually calm when he worked, on such days he showed extreme excitement: he could not possibly fail when nature itself was offering him such exceptional, such moving opportunities.

On one of these stormy days my brother Michael and I almost lost our lives. There were several means of reaching Kushelevka from town. The simplest was by droshky (but that was expensive, and economy dominated our household) ; otherwise there were two horse-tramway routes. Unfortunately the one that went all the way to the Kushelev Gardens was appallingly slow, stopping for ten or fifteen minutes at every station. It took an hour to cover the short distance from the Finland station – an hour during which one had to breathe foul air and listen to the irritating rattle of window-panes and the excruciating noise of wheels. The other tramway from the Mikhailovski Square went only as far as Smolni and from there you crossed the Neva on a ferry. The latter way was pleasanter because the carriages, just imported from Germany, were clean and even pleasing to the eye. If we were travelling with Papa we climbed on top and from there had a splendid view. I loved crossing the Fontanka with its view of the Engineer's Castle, and the journey past the Church of St Simon and the view of the Gothic Evangelist Hospital and the round Greek Church above the pond. I liked to drive by the walls of the Smolni, to pass its unique towers, and after the last turning to see the Neva.

On the day of the nearly fatal incident Misha, who was in charge of me, and I reached the monastery safely, but this time after the turning we were faced with an unexpected and truly sinister sight. The waters of the Neva were an angry purple and brown, rough and disturbed and covered in white horses, and lashing about as though in a violent rage. The heavy barges loaded with timber that lay in three lines by the shore were bumping into one another, and the ferry-boats by the pier jumped up and down in a crazy dance. It was a real storm, which we had not realised while travelling along the streets in town. None of the ferry-boatmen would agree to take us across in such weather. Misha, however, though that for him, a future sailor, it was unseemly to surrender to the elements, and when all his persuasion failed he pulled out of his purse a green three-rouble note. At the sight of such riches one youth agreed to take us across the river, and I had hardly time to grasp what was happening before my brother, seizing me in his arms, jumped into the quivering ferry-boat and we started on our way.

While we were in the lee of the barges the danger we were running was not apparent, but hardly had we left behind the last barge than our boat was tossed up in the air with a force that took our breath away and we were able to realise the horror of the situation. I remember how the boatman sitting in front of us was at one moment high in the air above us, and the next moment, as we rolled down from the top of the wave, far below us. The violent waves were breaking over the boat, Misha was baling out the water as quickly as possible, while I sat, in a sort of stupor, clinging to the side and to the thwart. The boatman's hat flew off; there was an expression of terror on his face. It was a terrific strain to steer head-on to every approaching wave, but a side blow would inevitably have capsized our shallow little vessel. At last the exhausted oarsman begged Misha

to take one of the two oars, and as soon as my brother –
who was obviously a true sailor and showed great strength
and self-control throughout – had done so our progress
became more definite and at last, after twenty minutes or so, we
found ourselves in the passage between the timber barges
along the opposite shore – and were saved. Misha, who was
by nature extremely truthful, asked me to help him to conceal
our adventure from Mamma. So we arrived at the villa
as though nothing had happened, maintaining that it was
by the rain on the way home that we had been drenched.

A crossing of the Neva in the opposite direction provided
a contrast to this adventure. This time I was in the ferry
with my father in the autumn of 1882, at the end of the last
of our Kushelev summers. The weather was fine and so
warm that even supper was still served on the balcony, the
lighted candles protected by glass shades. But, fine as the
weather was, the holidays were at an end and I had to
return to school – and if Shourenka had to be reinstalled
in urban life, how could his parents remain in their summer
residence? The carts arrived, and with them the packers
came clattering in their boots to spread their own peculiar
odour through the empty rooms, a mixture of sweat and
tar which is considered essentially Russian. Papa, who
sometimes had odd ideas, suddenly suggested that the others
should go ahead with Mamma in the hired carriage; he and
I by ourselves would return home by a roundabout way
across the Neva and then take a droshky from the Smolni.
Mamma protested, but seeing that I was fascinated by
Papa's plan she surrendered, and while the carriage clattered
off in the direction of Petersburg Papa and I walked, by
way of the bridge that separated Kushelevka from the
suburb Okhta, through the miserable streets, to the
distant crossing just opposite the church.

As we walked along the unpaved, dingy little streets, Papa told me stories about the happenings here in his childhood; about the hand-to-hand fights on the ice, and also about the rich merchants who used to live in these same decrepit wooden houses, some of which they painted in two colours so that it would be clear, when the will was read, who would get one part and who the other. More than by anything else I was surprised to hear that ships used to be launched here in the day of Alexander I; and it was probably this memory that compelled Papa to suggest to the ferryman that he should cross the Neva higher up, instead of direct, so as to pass under the ancient wharves.

It was quite dark, with a wonderful stillness, the water was smooth, there were no lights in the windows of the Smolni monastery, which stood like a dim phantom against the greenish sky. In the purple autumn twilight the two huge sheds, from which the frigates and corvettes with their golden sterns had once slipped into the water to the sound of trumpets and gunfire, loomed fantastically large. But the days of their glory had vanished long ago. The immense empty interiors were dark and decrepit, the roofs were full of holes, only the rows of pillars and the architectural ornaments on the façade overlooking the Neva still testified to the magnificent architecture produced by the builders of those times. Over everything loomed the giant Poseidon, carved by Martos out of Kasan oak, which was situated in the gap between the two slopes of the wharves.

It was an unforgettable sight. Seeing my enthusiasm, my father asked the ferryman to row nearer to the slope leading from the gigantic docks into the water. From below the God of the seas, his beard fluttering in the wind, hand stretched out to control the elements, looked wonderfully sinister in spite of a broken sceptre. From the ancient buildings came the sound of something crumbling and falling with a dull thud, as on the opposite shore the street

lights suddenly flared up and in the Alexander Nevsky
monastery the bells rang out for late Mass.

Though my parents no longer lived in Kushelevka after
1882 the family used nevertheless to go there often. Sometimes I even went alone, and in the winter I might spend
the night or stay a few days there with my sister Camisha.
The easy happy atmosphere of Kushelevka and the variety
of walks in the neighbourhood were great attractions;
and also I had two lots of playmates there – my nephews
and nieces, the Edwardeses and the Lancerays.

It was natural that the Edwardeses should live at Kushelevka, for Matt had to be close to his factory; but in
addition my other brother-in-law, Lanceray, had to move
there because of his health. The villa which had housed
the workmen, with the attic which Monsieur Stanislas had
occupied during his last summer, was now rebuilt for him.
The small Edwardeses, who grew up almost without
supervision, were rather wild; the meek, frail Lanceray
children on the other hand were the objects of their parents'
and governesses' constant care. Both groups fell under my
influence, or rather put themselves at my disposal, which
considerably affected their behaviour. I allotted to each his
part, quiet or boisterous; I introduced them to the games of
robbers and rounders. There was no need to worry with the
Edwardeses where we played. I would take them far into
the gardens, or rowing for hours in the boat, or wandering
about the factory. Indeed, the small Edwardeses had a
whole gang of playmates among the children of neighbouring factory-owners and workmen, and in such company
our games naturally became boisterous and unruly. Our
expeditions then extended to the more neglected parts of
the park, and the rowing parties in particular were often
quite dangerous. It is in fact remarkable that we did not end
up at the swampy bottom of the ponds. We were very

mischievous and did a lot of damage; we chased cats (whom I loved, in spite of it); we went birds'-nesting; we teased dogs, turkeys and geese. But what delight there was in all this! Hot and sweating, we would return home with huge appetites when we heard the factory whistle or the bell of the villa calling us for lunch or dinner. I had acquired a taste for the English specialities of Camisha's table, and at meals at Kushelevka I devoured so much that I could barely get up from the table. Everything was delicious – indeed exceptionally luscious. I have never since eaten such roast beef, such turkeys and geese, such *pâté de foie gras*! In many things that have happened in my life I feel I was specially privileged by fate, and chief among these was the fact that, thanks to the Edwardeses, not only did I learn the way of life of 'good old England', but I somehow became personally associated with it. That part of Kushelevka owned by Matt – his factory, private house and garden – was a true piece of England, miraculously transferred to Russian territory. I know nothing more attractive, cosier and more homely than this adorable Dickensian life; and I am grateful that red-haired Matt, a true Briton and a pure-bred Celt, should have married my sister Camisha, a Franco-Russian-Italian who quickly adopted her husband's way of life and became a true Briton herself – not a pillar of respectability, but a model country-housewife such as you meet in English novels and indeed in real English life.

Matt's and Camisha's lives ran on broad and simple lines. There was no formality in the Kushelevka household; rather, there was a complete lack of restraint, a state of perfect ease, together with limitless hospitality. It was sufficient to pass through the wooden gates from the high road on a wintry evening and see the two-storeyed house with its windows lit, to feel oneself in a wonderful realm, unlike anything in Petersburg. Because of the tar used in manufacturing the ropes a special smell pervaded not only the factory building itself but also the rooms and the courtyard of the house. This smell belonged to the sea, to ships on the sea, and therefore to England.

Matt's factory was typically English in appearance, too, quite unlike the usual huge barrack with tall smoking chimneys and a dreadful noise of machines. It was a low, rambling building on one floor, more like a little town of wooden buildings. There was little smoke, and as soon as you crossed the threshold you were assailed by the mixed smell of tar, tow and rope. It was of course noisy, but its noise was gentle and monotonous, soft, natural, with frequent intervals of silence. The factory did not employ thousands of workmen; indeed, not more than a hundred, counting women and children; but the workers did not look in the least like disgruntled slaves exhausted with too much work. One felt sorry only for the three or four women who day after day ceaselessly turned the wooden wheels upon which the thread was rolled; but even they performed their job cheerfully. In fact, it was a model factory, with discipline maintained by patriarchal good will rather than by stern measures.

I loved to walk round the factory; to visit the shed filled with innumerable coils of twisted rope; to climb up and settle down comfortably on top of a closely packed heap of the sweet-smelling coils; to weigh myself on the huge weighing machine that hit the wooden floor with a thud every time the colossal weights were placed upon it; to walk into the hot main room where a large flywheel turned ceaselessly and where the stokers, black from the coal, fed the glowing stove. It was exciting to see all these operations, and terrifying to go near the whirling belts and rapidly turning wheels (it was one of these wheels that tore off our Sultan's luxurious tail). But the chief attraction was the wooden gallery, two hundred yards long and seeming even longer because it was so low and narrow. It was so long that when a grown-up person's silhouette appeared in the bright square of the doorway at the far end, it looked no larger than a midge.

A railway stretched the whole length of the gallery, and along the rails ran a special machine imported from England, at the back of which were hooks of different sizes: when the machinery was put into motion the hooks began to revolve rapidly, weaving several threads into a thick rope, then several thick ropes into one still thicker, then several of these into a cable of incredible thickness. In the course of this operation the machine moved farther and farther away from its starting point till it reached the other end of the gallery. Its journey was accomplished at a steady crawl, accompanied by ear-splitting noise. But when the operation was completed and the coiled ropes removed from the hooks, the machine made the return journey at astonishing speed, like a horse scenting its stable.

One of the great entertainments of Kushelevka was a return journey on this machine. We children were great friends with the men who operated it, and they enjoyed giving a ride to the owner's relations. And how my heart swelled with pride when I drove 'my own' engine along the seemingly endless tunnel!

Kushelevka was wonderful in the summer, but it was no less so in the winter. I remember the magic of the moonlit nights in the old gardens when the blue shadows of bare trees lay on dazzling white snow, and of days when the landscape, covered in exquisite hoar-frost, stood in spellbound immobility. It was fun to ski with the Edwardes children and to disappear to places where the grown-ups could not follow us. Christmas celebrations at Camisha's were a joy; the tree would be lit after dinner, the drinks – a special punch – would be brought in and Matt, slightly tipsy, arms folded across his chest, would start dancing a jig with remarkable lightness considering his size.

But nothing can compare with the delight of tobogganing that I shared with the other youngsters at Kushelevka. A rather steep wooden slope was built on the edge of the nearest pond, one end of it extending on to the ice for over a hundred yards. When guests were expected the slope was cleared of snow, so that two high banks rose on each side and the neatly swept ice glittered like a mirror. Tobogganing either in moonlight or in complete darkness had a special fascination. Against the white snow of the starry night the icy path was quite black as it disappeared into the darkness. Matt had enough sledges for everybody, though some of us liked to slide down without one, on a mat or on our own bottoms. But the most exhilarating of all was to go down the slope one behind the other, landing in a real mess at the bottom, with sledges tumbled on top of each other and nothing to be heard but squeals and coquettish complaints of the girls and wild laughter from the boys.

These entertainments lasted for hours, and ended only when limbs began to ache from tiredness and we were covered with sweat and drenched from the snow which had penetrated our clothes. But in Camisha's house the fire was glowing so brightly that we did not bother to change – a few minutes by the fire and steam would rise from us like a pillar and we would be dry to the bone. We would find Matt at the fireside, sitting with his paper in a comfortable chair whose back was embroidered by Camisha's own hands, with the dogs and cats obediently disposed around him. The dogs and cats at Kushelevka were of no particular breed; indeed, they were all rather uncouth specimens of the animal proletariat, having found shelter under heaven knows what circumstances with my kind sister. But they were devoted intelligent and charming animals, and were considered almost full members of the Kushelev gang.

CHAPTER XIV

THE MAY SCHOOL

*

FOR the five years from 1885 to 1890 I lived under the influence of the May School – not that school occupied all my time and thoughts, but my social standing was expressed by the words 'a pupil of the May School'. Also, although I progressed with varying success, it was here that I received the more or less firm foundations on which my further education was afterwards built. And it was at this school that I made those friends who remained for a great part of my life my loyal companions, and with whom I achieved considerable success in the field of culture. I have kept the memory of the May School fresh, and I have a feeling of profound gratitude to it.

I had tried to persuade my parents to send me to the Lycée, because two of my schoolfellows had already gone there, and also because at the Lycée I would find companions belonging to select aristocratic society. I was tempted, too, by the delightful uniform – black with red and gold, a three-cornered hat and even, I believe, a sword. Moved by some childish ambition I imagined that on completing my studies at the Lycée I would without any difficulty attain the highest posts in the diplomatic service, for, having read a number of historical novels I was attracted by the possibility of entering the ranks of the elect who decide the fate of States. I would be a representative of my own country and confer with foreign monarchs on an almost equal footing. It seemed to me that I possessed all the necessary qualities for this: intelligence above the average, sufficient cunning and an evident talent

for acting. Even my still unspent inclination for lying seemed
to me a kind of professional gift required for this career.
However, all my entreaties made no impression on my
father and my dreams of becoming, thanks to the Lyceé,
a second Gorchakoff, Bismarck or Metternich were dispersed like smoke.

But I very soon accepted this defeat, and promptly
forgot it when, on entering 'May's', I found out that
this new school was entirely to my taste. No uniform was
worn, the majority of my schoolfellows belonged to the
middle classes, the school did not open the way to any
particularly brilliant careers, but I found there something
much more valuable. I found homeliness, an atmosphere
which pleased me, in which it was easy to breathe and which
supplied all that was missing at the State institution; I
found moderate liberty, warmth and contact between the
teaching staff and the pupils and respect for the individual.
There was no trace of formality at the May School.

Everything depended on the personality of the founder
and director of the school which bore his name – K. I.
May, a man who, at the time I joined the school, was no
longer young but still active and alert. The atmosphere of
the school was entirely his own creation, the result of his
qualities of mind and heart, as well as of his principles and
theories. Karl Ivanovitch was firm in his belief that one
could achieve anything with young people by trusting them.
Clearly there were among us many boys who abused this
trust and even laughed behind his back at Karl Ivanovitch's
credulity, but the majority of the pupils respected and loved
their director and experienced these feelings almost immediately on meeting him. I myself felt a liking for 'Kar-
lusha' from the very first day and remained true to it till the
end of my schooldays.

I was at first sight won over by his peculiar, I would
almost say eccentric, exterior. He was a very bent, thin little

old man, invariably dressed in a long black frock-coat, and carrying in his thin, fragile hand a snuff-box of which he made frequent use; as was proper for a snuff-taker, a large red and yellow handkerchief hung out of the back pocket of his frock-coat. His raven-black hair (naughty boys maintained that he dyed it) was coquettishly cut and fell in a straight fringe on to his forehead; below it gold-rimmed spectacles assisted his slightly inflamed, short-sighted eyes; his red nose protruded to the point of caricature; and his chin was decorated with a very black goatee. His little old legs moved quickly and he took uneven mincing steps.

This mixture of extreme old age, almost senility, with comparatively juvenile traits in his appearance corresponded to May's character. The normal state of Karl Ivanovitch was one of limitless good temper. His thin, hardly noticeable lips, which seemed constantly to be either chewing or whistling, smiled readily in greeting. But this good humour was not a sign of weakness: he could be wrathful occasionally, though only with good reason. When distressed he stooped still more, his spectacles slipping to the tip of his nose while over them his bleary eyes looked sorrowfully at the culprit. This did the trick. Moreover, the wrongdoer was debarred from shaking hands with Karl Ivanovitch – a ceremony with which every day at school began. Karl Ivanovitch would stand on the top landing of the staircase which we passed on our way to the school hall and our classroom, keeping his almost lifeless hand proffered for everybody to shake. The boys walked hurriedly past this immovable figure one after the other, snatching at rather than shaking the hand and muttering a greeting. But Karl Ivanovitch's indifference was feigned; he knew very well who was greeting him, and when it was the turn of yesterday's culprit the wizened hand would be withdrawn.

The boys believed that Karl Ivanovitch was a Scandinavian, either a Swede or a Dane; in appearance, notwith-

standing his black hair, he resembled a Finn; but in reality
I believe he was a pure-bred and typical German. His
native tongue was certainly German, and though he
spoke Russian correctly and even perfectly, there was still
the hint of a foreign accent in his speech. Besides his duties
as director he taught us geography, and at these lessons he
displayed not only an actual gift for teaching but also a kind
of poetical quality which was natural to him. We all liked
his lessons, his original method of teaching and those
descriptions of nature, countries and towns which made
his lessons so alive. His system was founded on the simplest
of schemes. He would draw on the blackboard a combination of three lines and then, pointing to one of them, he
would turn to the boys and ask: 'What is this?' The boys,
already acquainted with this method, would answer: 'These
are the Fichtelgebirge'. 'And this?' 'The Main' and so on.
Gradually the basic design would be decorated with diverse
additions – mountains, towns, tributaries of rivers. My
acquaintance with Karl Ivanovitch started at such a lesson
on Central Europe, but I had to attend the same lesson
several times over, owing to the institution of joint lessons
by which elder boys found themselves in the same classroom as their younger schoolfellows.

These joint lessons were a part of Karl Ivanovitch's
educational system. It was probably based on economic
reasons: the same master could simultaneously teach two
forms – an economy in time and salaries. Sometimes it was
because a master, teaching also at another school, could not
find the time to attend to us twice a day. The joint lessons
were occasionally the result of certain casual circumstances,
such as the sickness of one of the masters, when his form
would be allotted to another one. All this presented Karl
Ivanovitch with manifold worries.

Some of the masters were always with us, even living in
the same building, but most of them came only to teach

special lessons. The permanent staff, as well as teaching, also acted as class-masters. Our own world, the world of the upper school, was ruled by the director and his assistant 'Inspector' Krakau, and also by Mr Emil Mohl and Mr. Wind. Mr Mohl immediately won my sympathy. He was a huge man whose clumsiness made him seem stout, with the fine face of a Jupiter, though perhaps it actually reminded one more of a hippopotamus. He was a new arrival in Petersburg and was born in Swabia in the town of Tübingen (he pronounced it Tibingen). He had a kind of gentleness, a sentimental sociability, typically German (in the pre-Hitler sense of the word). He was sociable in that he preferred sitting among the boys to throning it on the rostrum; usually he would settle on one of the desks, his enormous mastodon legs squeezed into the space between it and the seat. But this normally kindly man could turn into a wrathful thunderer when the boys whom he himself had spoilt overstepped the bounds of the permissible. Then Mohl would jump up, take up a position between the rostrum and the desks and glare at the boys in a way which he probably considered to be paralysing, whereas in reality it was only comic, for he was terribly short-sighted, and this was very obvious in his vague, purblind gaze even when he considered it necessary to transform himself into the personification of wrath. These fits of rage were quite customary with Mohl, but on extraordinary occasions he could be provoked into a positive paroxysm by mean and stupid tricks, and his fury would be expressed in wild uncontrollable gyrations. He would turn round on one spot with a skipping motion (a skipping hippopotamus!), hurling terrible words at us all: *'Ihr seit alle unverschämt! Ich schmeisse euch alle heraus!'* A moment later after such an eruption he would be once more sitting on a desk, his nose and right eye buried in a grammar, or in Xenophon or in the *Niebelungen*, and his Swabian speech would purr again, low and cosy.

Mr Mohl taught us – that is, the boys in the fifth, sixth and seventh forms – German literature and classics. I am thankful to him for the knowledge I acquired at his lessons, always a little muddled and unsystematic but also lively and fascinating. I am also indirectly obliged to Mohl for inspiring me then to become a passionate collector of books. Once he brought us the two volumes of the newly published *Kulturgeschichte Deutschlands*, by Otto Henne am Rhyn. This was one of the first popular works on historical research; it contained many illustrations, reproductions of old engravings and pictures of monuments depicting the morals and ways of life of the past. I was so struck by this book and took such a liking to it that I immediately begged my mother to buy me a copy, and my friends Nouvel and Filosofov followed my example. This was the beginning of our serious libraries and my introduction to the noble but ruinous hobby of book-collecting.

In contrast to Mohl, Mr Wind, a native of Vienna, was a man of smart appearance with well-groomed hair and beard. Wind was what is called a good-looking and even an elegant man. He was never angry, never lost his temper, but there was not the slightest hint of warmth about him: he completely deserved his reputation of being a dry stick. He did not conceal the fact that teaching bored him, and though we were reading with him the most entertaining of all works in classical literature, the *Metamorphoses* of Ovid, gloom and drowsiness reigned in his classroom. He disliked and rather despised his pupils. Only once did I see him in a gay mood – when, quite unexpectedly I met him in his native town, Vienna, in the Ring, and had a cup of coffee with him at the nearest café.

These two men were not the entire staff of classics teachers. On the contrary, Mohl and Wind only prepared us for Parnassus, on the peak of which sat enthroned Mr Malchin and Mr Blumberg. Blumberg did not make a pleasant impression on any of us. True, by some special kind of training he taught us to read Homer without any preparation (his lessons consisted exclusively of the reading of the *Iliad* and the *Odyssey*) but he was a man of a disagreeable appearance – yellowish complexion, with a small plucked sandy beard and green eyes concealed behind thick glasses. His breath was bad, and he was moreover rather capricious and trivial – trivial certainly in his refined attempts to *improve* on Homer. We all know that the poet of the Trojan War uses some very picturesque and now obsolete expressions and epithets: we were supposed either to omit entirely those words which shocked Mr Blumberg or to replace them by others. In no circumstances was it permitted to apply to Hera the epithet of 'ox-eyed' or to say about Ajax that 'he marched like a bull'. Blumberg was prepared to give a bad mark to anybody who through haste made such a mistake, and he would sulk during the whole lesson if anybody repeated it.

A real cultural abyss divided this Russian 'Greek' from his German colleague, Mr Malchin. My memories of Mohl are of a sentimental nature; even his most comical traits were somehow touching; he was a type straight out of a painting by Spitzweg or Schwind. My memories of Malchin, on the other hand, are full of the deepest respect. Of all my teachers my greatest respect and schoolboy loyalty went to Malchin. He was my ideal of a professor, not only because he taught me to grasp the subtleties of grammar and to understand Plato's philosophy, but also because he had an unshakeable sense of duty. Only under his direction did I understand why classical education exists; how it serves us in life, how it influences the processes of our minds and our critical capacities.

Malchin appeared on our horizon only when we moved from the sixth form to the seventh, but as I and my closest friend, Valechka Nouvel, were not allowed to sit for examinations and therefore did not move up to the next form, we had the luck to work under Malchin for three years instead of the usual two.

Malchin's most noticeable features were a shortish, thick, fiery beard, and a fierce, penetrating gleam in his green eyes. In his teaching he usually followed the peripatetic system, walking up and down the classroom and enunciating every word – German, Latin or Greek – very clearly and harshly. He suffered from chronic pleurisy which caused him sudden sharp bouts of pain, but even at such moments Malchin never stopped his promenading, but only pressed his hand to his side, moaning intermittently, his suffering reflected in his eyes. When the fit was over his lecture went on. There was nothing mechanical or dull about his teaching (this was most noticeable in his interpretation of Plato): everything had to pass through one's consciousness, every new conception could be established only by his interpretation. I and my particular friends readily accepted this and Malchin treated us because of that with particular benevolence.

On the other hand, he did not conceal his contempt for dullards and sluggards, even if their answers to prepared questions rated full marks. He even hated some of the pupils for their stupidity or laziness, and some for their complete lack of talent which they attempted to disguise by rather mean tricks.

Another curious figure was the teacher of Mathematics Obrastzoff, a tiny man with a long, fair beard, nice, kindly rather weak, and absolutely incapable of disciplining the gang which had been thrust upon him. He was considered to be a very learned mathematician; there was even a rumour that he was a corresponding member of some famous foreign scientific association or academy. It is possible that for this reason his teaching was so poor: he could not adapt himself to the level of our mental capacities. Obrastzoff was the first to examine me on my entering the school and he did this in such a kindly, careful and benevolent way that he earned my everlasting gratitude. Even in the periods when I became one of his worst pupils and quite deservedly received bad marks, I never stopped liking him. At the same time I somehow pitied this small, slightly ridiculous dwarf. We kept up relations after I left school – he was the only one of the masters who used to come to my house. Examining my books on art he disclosed surprising naïveté and a great readiness to learn and understand, and if I had not gone abroad in 1896 we would probably have exchanged rôles: Obrastzoff would have become my pupil and I his teacher, in the history of art.

We did not make any better progress under our teacher of Russian and Russian literature, Mikhail Evgrafovich Dobropistzeff. The surname Dobropistzeff is, of course, merely a translation of the Greek word Eugrafos, from which it could be concluded that our teacher was of clerical extraction; it was customary in theological seminaries to give that kind of surname to boys who had entered them 'nameless'. In any case our Dobropistzeff was a typical seminarist – a man who even if he did possess the necessary knowledge had not properly assimilated it, and who in no way belonged to the intellectual and cultural strata. He was a typical proletarian – put him into a cassock and he would be an ideal model for a village deacon; put him into a long Russian coat with an apron tied round his waist and he would become a counterhand in a small village grocery. He had a small red nose, a longish red beard and tufts of red hairs stuck out over his eyes. His clumsy, long, scraggy figure revealed his lowly extraction. His speech and his angular gestures – somehow always rectangular – were definitely those of a peasant. He taught us Russian history, keeping strictly to the text-book, and seemed to have no knowledge of anything beyond it (except that he was enthusiastic about Peter the Great, which had my approval). However, he held very independent opinions on Russian literature: he worshipped Pushkin and had studied him well, and he appreciated Gogol and Lermontov, as well as some older masters. Every one of his sentences he started with 'you – eh', accompanying it by a movement reminding one of a cobbler overcasting a shoe. Poor Mikhail Evgrafovich was burdened with a family, so he was obliged to teach in all forms, beginning with the most junior, and in other schools also.

Being a Roman Catholic I was not obliged to attend any Scripture lessons at school, neither those given by the deacon Postnikoff attached to the Church at the Academy of Arts, nor those of the Lutheran pastor Jurgens, but I met them constantly and sometimes remained in the classroom during their lessons. It was interesting to compare their teaching methods. The Orthodox priest was a man of about fifty, stoutish, with a protruding stomach, with curly hair going grey and a well-kept shortish beard. He seemed somehow juicy, affable and gay. The pastor, too, did not give an impression of asceticism. He was rather tall, with a clean-shaven face resembling that of a fearful old woman.

In making friends at school it is natural that at first I just looked round. For one thing, I was ashamed of appearing to be older than the others (I was beginning to grow a beard) and only later learnt that Kostia Somov, in spite of his childish appearance, was seven months older than me. During these first weeks I was persecuted by another future great friend, Dima Filosofov, who in spite of his angelic face was full of malice. He made fun of my ungainly suit (made on somebody's advice out of a rug), my shaggy hair and dirty nails; but most of all was I mortified by his disclosures concerning my family.

Through a cousin of mine, who gave music lessons to the Filosofovs, Dima was well acquainted not only with the existing ramifications but also with the past of the Benois family. In my childish ambition, I wanted to add weight to my personality and talked nonsense about our French ancestors, the marquesses, and my Venetian grandfathers, the doges and cardinals. I began to loathe Dima intensely. My hatred was exacerbated by his open contempt for the rest of the class, except perhaps for his bench-partner, Somov. With him he behaved like a lovesick flapper, embracing and nearly kissing him – though I saw nothing unseemly in this at the time; such effusions seemed merely ridiculous and not suitable between men.

Valechka Nouvel was very different. Though he shocked me by his pretensions at dressing smartly and by some of his habits – for instance, he smoked cigars just to show off – there was a lot in him that appealed to me, such as his western ideas.

He was a lazy boy, and always ready for mischief. He had an excellent memory, and a lot of shrewdness which was a great help to him, so that he could slack without the risk of joining the ranks of the out-and-out sluggards. These qualities, along with an insatiable curiosity, made him an interesting companion. He was a precocious boy, like myself, and interested in all human activities; he was just as addicted to the theatre as I was and a great reader, so it was natural that a friendship should rapidly grow up between us. Another factor contributed to our friendship: he was a serious music lover, he played the piano very pleasantly and had great facility in reading music. He was, like me, very fond of Italian opera (which was in its heyday on the Imperial stage in Petersburg) and under my influence became, a little later, interested in the ballet, particularly in ballet music. The only thing that I criticised in him was his dry intellect, and his easy acceptance of ready-made ideas. This provoked violent discussions between us and I did not spare Valia in my holy indignation.

Gradually my friendship with Valia, our discussions and

arguments, began to attract other young men, and in the sixth form my friends and I formed a little circle, akin to a school club. This circle did not represent anything serious or learned, and even later when we were in the seventh form and started for fun calling ourselves the Society for Self-education and drew up a constitution, our club maintained its lighthearted character with a tendency to burlesque entertainment. Any tinge of pedantry was ridiculed and excluded. In the seventh form we held our discussions more frequently in my house, to which my friends were attracted since I could provide many means of enlightenment in the form of *objets d'art* as well as books and reviews. The atmosphere of our house was imbued with art, which none of my friends found in their own homes. I have to confess that I started very early to feel a kind of proselytising fervour, a need to rally around myself people who thought along the same lines as myself.

My friendship with Kolia Skalon and Grisha Kalin began in the seventh form. Both young men were unusually erudite for their years: there was no subject you could not discuss with them, particularly literature, without finding both pleasure and profit. These new friends were very different in character and personality. They were also very different in appearance. Skalon was a typical Russian whom the proverb 'Scratch a Russian and you'll find a Tartar' suited perfectly, with a fundamentally wild element beneath a layer of civilised human being. This wild element is often noticeable in Russia, both in the features – pleasant maybe, but coarse and somewhat shapeless – and in the gestures, in a clumsy gait and in fact a total lack of grace. Kolia Skalon was that type of Russian.

In other circumstances, if Skalon had not had a gentle, almost feminine nature, he might have developed into a nihilist, a 'narodnik' as demanded by the political fashion of the time. Intellectually he was inclined to be analytical, and it must be admitted that his logical deductions had a remarkable, sometimes even a deadly infallibility. He was an intelligent young man, perhaps the most intelligent of us all. His opinions were direct, absolutely sincere and idealistic. He was a good dialectician and in the twinkling of an eye had the most convinced opponent with his back to the wall. Almost always he veered towards the moral in his views according to the spirit of the one to whom we then paid obeisance – Leo Tolstoy. I admired all this and was ready to love Skalon, but at the same time I was irritated by the clumsiness of his manners, as well as by the typically Russian limitations of his outlook, his incapacity to understand nuances or 'pastel shades', and his refusal to see any beauty or truth in them. Also what prevented us from coming really close to one another was that in spite of his erudition about literature, especially Russian, he was completely uninterested in the plastic arts. He totally lacked a musical sense, his judgement of pictures and sculpture was conditioned by the degree of their social significance and concerned only with the subject matter, while architecture as an art did not exist for him at all.

It is also true to say that his pride was easily hurt. If he noticed any lack of respect for his person, he resented it and sulked. No wonder our friendship lasted only five or six years; in our third year at the University a coolness grew up between us, that augured an eventual break. Often he failed to make an appearance at our discussions and after finishing the University he disappeared from our horizon.

Grisha Kalin was also a typical Russian, but in a different category. He was pure proletarian by origin. His father worked as a porter in a house not far from our school and lived with his wife and children in a stuffy, dark porter's-lodge. But the wheel of fortune turned and a spectacular metamorphosis took place. The porter won 100,000 roubles in a lottery (about £10,000) and was transformed from a servant into a gentleman.

I do not wish to suggest that Grisha Kalin was disfigured by any mark of low origin but rather the contrary. Nothing in his appearance, his manner or his mind showed that Grisha belonged to the class of *nouveau riche*. He was a handsome, well-built youth, with a long, thin nose, which gave him a look of Gogol, myopic half-closed eyes, and a well-shaped mouth under a budding moustache. Unlike Skalon, Kalin had easy movements and even a sort of grace. This was a gift of nature, but he developed the suppleness of his body by doing exercises for which he had a passion; he even thought for a time of making a career as an acrobat.

We liked Kalin because he was extremely witty and had on his own studied Russian literature as well as foreign works in translation. He had an exceptional memory and knew a lot of poetry by heart; when he admired a literary work, he would learn all he could about the life of the author. He was all the more attracted to literature because of his own literary ambitions. His early writings enchanted us by their dazzling humour and original style, and I foretold a brilliant future for him and was convinced that the time would come when I would be proud to have been friends with such a remarkable person. But my prophecy was not to come true. In his third year at the University, when he was reading for the Bar, Kalin married a pretty but trivial young girl and from that moment sank into the swamp of a petty-bourgeois way of life.

My friendship with Kostia Somov, like my friendship with Valia Nouvel, lasted until his death. At one time, my relations with Kostia were very close, but I did not at once make friends with him and certainly not in our school-days. This quiet, restrained boy, with irregular features, did not interest me at all during the three years we spent together in the same classroom. His slightly upturned nose, his unkempt hair (better than mine, however), his brown, rather feminine eyes, his pouting lips, and even his ever-lasting brown jacket and black bow tie, I considered to be altogether too childish though lacking the charm of genuine youth. I was certain that Kostia was about two years younger than I was and was amazed to learn that he was, in fact, a few months older. His behaviour and bearing were excessively youthful, especially his way of demonstrating his liking for Dima Filosofov, always whispering and giggling even when he was 18 and Dima 16. This 'crush' between him and Dima had nothing tender or moving about it, but I was far from seeing in these effusions any-thing unseemly, although the other boys did. I certainly never suspected that Kostia Somov would become a famous painter and that his glory would overshadow the dreams I had for myself, and at that time I did not think much of the drawings with which he covered his school-books: they repelled me by their uniformity. He drew nothing but women's profiles. Kostia, was in fact, trying to reproduce the features of a French actress of great beauty and talent, Jeanne Brindeau, to whom he had lost his heart, but there was not a spark of the phantasy and sharp power of observa-tion which later became the essence of his talent. Kostia and I might have linked up through our mutual passion for the theatre, but at school we never exhanged views on this subject. He was shy and avoided voicing his opinions or only dropped a few commonplaces; if I insisted, he with-drew into his shell and sulked.

Then, without letting anyone know, Kostia left school. It must be admitted that he had made even less progress than the rest of us. Some of the subjects he could not grasp at all; others he grasped only with incredible effort. Besides, he was convinced that he was a singular failure in every way. When we heard that Kostia Somov would not be with us in the seventh form after the holidays of 1888, we were not surprised, but there was no limit to my amazement when I learnt that he had left school in order to enter the Academy of Arts.

Perhaps the beginning of real friendship between Kostia and me at the end of our schooldays was partly due to the cessation of his gushing fits over Dima Filosofov, which had always irritated me so much. They ended because Dima stopped coming to school; he was often sick and looked very ill. His parents attributed this to overwork and he was sent abroad, I believe to the Riviera; he was absent from Petersburg for several months, missed a whole year in school and therefore could not keep pace with us. I was not sorry that he was not in our class any longer, for I still feared his malice, his offensive and penetrating sarcasm. The other friends whom he was wont to ridicule also breathed more freely. But a year later, because Valia and I had stayed in the same form for two years running without sitting for an examination, Dima was with us again, having caught up with us. Our little circle had grown in strength, and the question now arose as to whether to include him in it. The majority was against it on account of his haughtiness, but as for me, I was provoked by the challenge and decided to curb his pride. He captivated me by his intelligence and his very aristocratic manner, and I first persuaded Valia and then the others that we needed Dima.

A few weeks later I began to meet Dima even outside school. I brought him home with me, and a few days later he took me to his home, in a street where Valia also lived. These visits grew more frequent and soon I became a part of the Filosofov family, by whom I was warmly welcomed. It soon became clear that Dima's haughty manner was not a result of his background; that he was, indeed, an exception

in his *milieu*. After a while my influence on him also began
to show, and he became much softer and more easy-going
than before. He had obviously become attached to me, and
to Valia; there was even some sentimentality in his attitude
to us. His jokes were just as penetrating, but directed at
others, not at us. I also influenced him in matters of art,
in which until now he had shown no interest. He began to
buy books on art, and, as he was very gifted, with a search-
ing intelligence and, full of reverence for culture, he soon
became familiar with this new sphere. During those
formatory years he looked at everything through my eyes
and agreed with me on all points. In fact, he became my
faithful pupil in all matters concerning the visual arts. He
never argued with me – which could not be said for Valia,
who always tried to hold independent, individual views. He
protested because he could not exist without protesting,
but I needed but little effort to subdue these attempts at
revolt.

To me the Filosofovs' way of life was wonderfully
colourful: they were landed gentry, who up to 1861 had
owned serfs, and life at Bogdanovskoe, their estate, figured
in all their conversations and was described as paradise.
Therein lay the deep dissimilarity between their house and
ours, of which I was then not perhaps quite conscious. We
Benois were purely urban people; my parents did not own a
morsel of land apart from the ground under our house.
The landowners' style of the Filosofovs' life gave it a
special quality. In spite of their ancient origin (their family
went back to Vladimir the Saint and the Baptism of Russia),
and though many of their ancestors had ranked high with
the Princes and the Tsars of the past, they could not be
considered aristocrats of the Court circle. But they were not
middle-class either. It was the class to which the founders
of Russian culture of the eighteenth and nineteenth centuries with all their charm and splendour belonged; the

class that produced the heroes and heroines of novels by Pushkin and Lermontov, Turgenev and Tolstoy, as well as the authors themselves; the class that had established a peaceful, dignified and distinguished way of life, apparently for all time. It had established the very tempo of Russian life, with its sense of duty and system of relationships between members of a family clan. The subtleties of Russian mentality, the establishment of a typically Russian moral sense had all been developed in that class. During my visits to the Filosofovs I acquired a great respect for these qualities, which I had previously known only through books and the imagination of poets. Externally their life did not differ much from ours, but we lived in different worlds all the same. To know their world required no research, and gradually in their house I came to realise its essence and through this knowledge to understand and love the way of Russian life. It seems to me that the chief reason why I became friends with Dima, and through him later with Diaghilev, his cousin, lay in this atmosphere through which I discovered the 'Russian soul'.

I finished my education at the May School in the spring of 1890. Normally I ought to have left school the year before, but Valia and I had been so slack in our lessons, both having been engrossed by other interests and experiences, that in spite of the efforts of our tutors we stayed at the bottom of our class. Long before Easter it was rumoured that we would not be allowed to sit for our finals, and I was not surprised when one day I saw the Director come into our hall. When Mamma went to meet him he told her the reason for his visit. 'It's the Feast of the Annunciation today, but, alas, I have nothing good to announce to you, dear lady. Your son cannot sit for his finals this year; his work has been too unsatisfactory.' My parents were upset by this news, especially Papa, to whom it was an unpleasant surprise (in recent years he had somehow lost sight of me), but Valia and I welcomed the news with joy. However, the horror of examinations returned a year later, in the spring of 1890. In the previous two months we had made a super-human effort to end our preliminary education without disgrace to ourselves and our school. The classical languages and other subjects did not give us too much anxiety, but we were appalling mathematicians and had to resort to the help of a tutor who had in our family the reputation of a magician in preparing the most backward pupils.

At last the formidable days of the finals approached. As luck would have it, a few days before a rumour circulated that a particularly fierce official of the Ministry of Education would be present at them, in order to ascertain whether our private school was following the latest rules issued by the Ministry. This rumour frightened and demoralised us considerably, but after the first examinations we realised that the gentleman with the star on his breast was far from being a serious threat to us, and we soon discovered the explanation of his leniency.

For the last two or three years there had been a boy in our class whom, with some justice, we considered an idiot. How he had managed to reach the last form was a mystery, but the teachers seemed to shut their eyes to his deficiencies and pulled him along. Even the proud, independent Malchin never asked him questions at lessons. This privileged position was explained by the fact that Mitia Kulomsin was the son of one of the most important figures of the Russian Empire – the Chairman of the Council of Ministers – and this high-ranking parent, though he could have had no illusions as to the further career of his son, still wished him to have a degree of sorts. With a school certificate the young man would not go to a university but would be appointed somewhere in the provinces and there end his days like any other Russian citizen not endowed with brains but favoured with good connections.

It was because of this poor boy that the teaching staff at our school were warned that the examinations were not to be too severe and that some leniency should be shown throughout. The formidable official from the Ministry was there to see that the warning was carried out. So, owing to Mitia, our finals passed without the usual anxiety and nobody failed. We three, Valia, Dima and I, would have passed even under more difficult conditions, but probably not so brilliantly and with much greater torment. It is sad to think that all this knowledge acquired with such trouble was forgotten almost at once, and that two months afterwards we would certainly have failed in the same examinations.

The end of school was celebrated at home according to all the traditional rules – that is, with a midnight banquet, a great amount of food and especially drink, beginning with the obligatory punch. But I cannot say that this orgy left a pleasant memory behind it. True, we tried to show our delight in various boisterous ways, by shouting *Gaudeamus Igitur* at the top of our voices, embracing and swearing eternal friendship. But it was all somewhat artificial, like a stage scene in which we were playing parts, and silly, unsuitable parts into the bargain. The celebrations ended sadly. Dima and I both felt sick; Dima vomited all he had drunk and eaten out of the window on our front stairs into the courtyard; and Valia, staggering on his feet, dragged me almost unconscious into my room and laid me moaning and groaning on the bed. In his drunken zeal he pulled the window-curtain so violently (it was morning by then) that the heavy wooden cornice fell down with a clatter, almost burying him. Mamma came running when she heard the noise, and after her Papa and the servants. In great pain I tossed on the bed, imploring help. Pails were brought and bowls and compresses; a smell of vinegar permeated the room as well as the smell of strong coffee.

Between fits of vomiting I could not help laughing to see the drunken Valia fulfilling what he regarded as his duty as a friend. Only when, totally emptied, I had fallen asleep, did my faithful friend go home – where no doubt the same scene was repeated, to the horror of his majestic mother.

My kind parents, not content with having offered me this banquet, now wished to reward me more suitably for the satisfactory end to my school years, and by supplying me with sufficient money enabled me to fulfil my dream of going abroad. In this way I was able to see all those things I had previously known only through reproductions and photographs – the great Gothic and Romanesque cathedrals, mysterious castles, fairylike residences in rococo style, beautifully trimmed gardens, and the old towns full of romantic charm. It was, though not entirely deserved, a very pleasant reward.

THE END

INDEX

Also in The Lively Arts series

A Mingled Chime

SIR THOMAS BEECHAM

This vivid, eccentric, and quirky memoir of his early life has all the characteristics of brilliance and passion that brought Sir Thomas Beecham to the forefront of British orchestral and opera conductors. His prolific output of recordings has ensured his reputation as conductor for posterity; this witty autobiography performs the same office for the man himself.

'The big tenor bell in *A Mingled Chime* is the art of music and it is rung by the artist who of all British executant musicians has established his claim internationally to the title of genius, perhaps the first Englishman to be ranked among the great conductors of the world. The smaller bells are education (public school, university, conservatoire), politics, business, literature and painting, rung by a man of the world, a connoisseur and a wit . . . A mingled chime indeed, containing a detailed and sober account of years of effort to give the British public the best opera and orchestral music . . . containing penetrating musical criticism and equally just criticism of men, shrewd and without malice. Like Papageno with his chime of magic bells he sets us dancing to his tune.' **Times Literary Supplement**

'It would be useless to attempt a summary of the good stories that Beecham relates.' **Listener**

'The author's innumerable anecdotes are told with characteristic wit. His comments on famous composers and performers are fascinating, often provocative, but always shrewd and worthy of being closely pondered. The whole book is of extraordinary interest.' **Manchester Guardian**

'What he has given us in the way of autobiography whets our appetite for more. He writes quite as well as he speaks, and we all know what that means . . . the story of his own myriad musical activities is told without the least exaggeration.' **Sunday Times**

Also in *The Lively Arts* series

Liszt

SIR SACHEVERELL SITWELL

Sacheverell Sitwell, who celebrated his 90th birthday in November 1987, is the modern writer most in tune with the Romantic age – as his many books on its art, its architecture and ballet have shown. His study of Liszt is the most sympathetic and engaging to have appeared this century, Sitwell making this dazzling and protean musician a living figure. Over the last three decades, the reputation and the repertoire of Liszt have been greatly enlarged through the interpretations of such pianists as Arrau, Brendel and Bolet, and conductors like Haitink. Liszt led a life that was in keeping with his fiery and tumultuous talent, and no one has been so adept as Sitwell in making coherent the conflicting strains of his temperament.

'Mr Sitwell's ability to recreate scenes from myth or history, his imaginative skill in restating the themes of music and painting in literary terms, his facility with the devices of nostalgia, are all formidable. His senses range widely, his knowledge and memory of all the arts are remarkable.'   **The Times**

'He is not a writer of any particular age or fashion or school. He is peculiarly and refreshingly alone.'

Pamela Hansford-Johnson

'There is no doubt that subsequent research, especially amongst Hungarian archives, will amend some of the facts of Liszt's life. But this biography will never be wholly superseded, for Sitwell brings to it so much insight, affection, and intuitive understanding of this chameleon man.'

Dame Myra Hess

'Liszt and I could not be more different men. But he was my greatest Hungarian forbear, and my mentor at the piano from childhood onwards. This book summarizes for me what Liszt meant to his own generation, and why we neglect him at our peril. He made the piano that I use the expressive instrument of the soul.'   **Bela Bartok**

A Life in the Theatre

TYRONE GUTHRIE

Tyrone Guthrie was one of the first British theatre directors to be as prominent as the actors in his plays – and they included Olivier, Gielgud, Richardson, Redgrave and Edith Evans. This autobiography, irreverent and opinionated, is justifiably considered the wittiest and most candid recollection of theatrical life in this country ever published by an insider.

'Tyrone Guthrie's book is a stimulating and delightful autobiography, full of the characteristic energy and brilliance of the author.'　**Sir John Gielgud**

'The most exciting and stimulating person in the theatre today, Guthrie's influence has extended from the British Isles to Australia, from Israel to Finland, from Canada to Texas. He is not only a great man of the theatre – an unpredictable and sometimes wayward genius and adventurer – but a great man in himself. His autobiography gives us a handsome slice of the man and his work. The omissions in it are typical of the man – his innumerable acts of kindness to young and old, his generosity, and the fact that so many of us owe him, largely, our careers.'　**Sir Alec Guinness**

'One of the most important books on the Theatre that I have read for many a year. It is informative, witty and unpretentious, and I am sure it will be as fascinating and entertaining for the great public as it is for those of us who belong to the Theatre.'　**Sir Noël Coward**

'Tyrone Guthrie is famous for his light touch when he handles a production in the theatre. Now he has produced a book of memoirs: coming from such authority they are of necessity interesting; they are also light, and easy to read.'　**Sir Ralph Richardson**

'Dr Guthrie's book is hilarious, engrossing, shrewd, ironic, informative, disputatious and inspiring – a perfect mirror, in fact, of the man himself.'　**New York Times**